Dilemmas of Modernity

Dilemmas of Modernity

Bolivian Encounters with Law and Liberalism

Mark Goodale

Stanford University Press
Stanford, California

Stanford University Press
Stanford, California

© 2009 by the Board of Trustees of the Leland Stanford Junior University. All rights reserved.

Printed in the United States of America on acid-free, archival-quality paper

Library of Congress Cataloging-in-Publication Data

Goodale, Mark.
  Dilemmas of modernity : Bolivian encounters with law and liberalism / Mark Goodale.
    p. cm.
  Includes bibliographical references and index.
    ISBN 978-0-8047-5981-6 (cloth : alk. paper)—ISBN 978-0-8047-5982-3 (pbk. : alk. paper)
    1. Sociological jurisprudence—Bolivia.   2. Law and the social sciences—Bolivia.
3. Indigenous peoples—Civil rights—Bolivia.   4. Liberalism—Bolivia.   5. Human
rights—Bolivia.   6. Social change—Bolivia.   I. Title.

KHC315.G66 2009
340'.1150984—dc22   2008029539

Typeset by Westchester Book Group in 10/14 Minion

For Javier and Freddy

Contents

List of Tables and Figures

Tables

Figures

Acknowledgments

THIS BOOK IS THE PRODUCT of over ten years of my own encounters of different kinds with Bolivia: ethnographic research, teaching, public lectures, critical reflection, worrying for friends, and of course, much writing. My professional and personal debts of gratitude that have accrued during this time run long and deep and to acknowledge them all with the kind of detail they deserve would really require a small book itself. Therefore, I must confine myself here to lists of names, places, and institutions and hope that the people I forget to mention will forgive the omission. In any case, my work in Bolivia would never have been possible without those small acts of kindness whose importance and meaning are simply impossible to render in this way; the kinds of acknowledgments that are appropriate to these have already been made.

In Alonso de Ibañez, the following individuals have been especially important to me over the years: the former *corregidor auxiliar* of Molino T'ikanoma, the former *jilanqu* of minor Ayllu Jilawi Cuerpo (Kachari), Bernardino Zeballos, Jaime Cueto, Liborio Rojas, Javier Rojas, Freddy Castillo, and, above all, Lucio Montesinos, whose life and work have been such an intellectual and personal inspiration.

Beyond the norte de Potosí, I must mention the following friends and colleagues, who have bestowed different kinds of support over the years: Gabriel Martinez, Antero Klemola, Ing. Nestor Infantes, Wilberth Tejerina, Gerard and Janette Hazeu, Mike and Aida West, Claudio and Carolyn Hopfenblatt, Roberto LaSerna, Cira Fernández, Cesar Ayaviri, Gilga Basaure García, Pamela Calla, Claudina Roja, Enrique Fugon and Edwin Armendaris (former country directors of the Organization of American States [OAS] in Bolivia), Marcelo

Fernández Osco, Xavier Albó, Ricardo Calla, Rossana Barragán, Claudia Gutiérrez Decormis, Jeanette Alfaro, Gabriela Justiniano, Santos Callejas, and Jeaneth Calatayud.

In Madison, Wisconsin, where the journey began, it is my great pleasure to acknowledge the following friends and former professors: Jane Larson, Beth Mertz, Boaventura de Sousa Santos, Sharon Hutchinson, Karl Zimmerer, Ronald Radano, Lydia Zepeda, Carmen Chuquin, Frank and Chris Hutchins, Mike and Lindsay Batek, Per Kåre Sky, Steve Wernke, Kitty McClellan and John Hitchcock, and my doctoral advisor, Frank Salomon (now the John V. Murra professor). I came to the University of Wisconsin in order to study with Frank Salomon and he was an outstanding guide and role model as I made my way through the thickets of Andean studies, and a good friend.

My thinking about both the ethnographic and theoretical problems of this book has taken shape through conversations (and some disagreements) with far too many people to be able to acknowledge here, but this is not an excuse for failing to at least try and account for the fact that others have had an influence. Key among these would be the following: Ricardo Godoy, Jean Jackson, Linda Seligmann, Joanne Rappaport, Tristan Platt, Olivia Harris, Herbert Klein, Sally Engle Merry, Jane Collier, June Starr, Ben Orlove, Elayne Zorn, Laura Nader, Kamari Maxine Clarke, Rachel Sieder, Pilar Domingo, John-Andrew McNeish, Daniel Goldstein, Sara Cobb, Kevin Avruch, Nancy Postero, Shannon Speed, Richard A. Wilson, Kay Warren, Jane Cowan, and Mauricio García Villegas.

My research and writing over the years would not have been possible without the generous financial support of the following institutions and fellowships: the National Science Foundation, the Organization of American States, the Fulbright Commission, the Tinker-Nave Foundation, the HEA Title VI Foreign Language and Area Studies Fellowship, the Irmgard Coninx Foundation, and the Van Calker Fellowship. I also have received several summer research fellowships from Emory University and George Mason University and I appreciate the encouragement and time I have been provided by these two institutions, including a sabbatical during which I wrote the middle chapters of the book. My graduate research assistant, Adriana Salcedo, provided superb editorial assistance during the preparation of the manuscript.

Different parts of this book took shape through stimulating exchanges with faculty and students during invited lectures and presentations at a number of institutions, including the following: Brandeis University (The Heller School for

Social Policy), Georgia Institute of Technology (Ivan Allen College of Liberal Arts), Max Planck Institute for Social Anthropology, University of Edinburgh (Department of Social Anthropology and Faculty of Law), University of St. Andrews (Department of Anthropology and the Centre for Indigenous Amerindian Studies), University of Oslo (Department of Social Anthropology), University of Bergen (Department of Social Anthropology), University College London (Department of Anthropology), London School of Economics (Department of Anthropology), Stockholm University (Department of Social Anthropology), University of Zurich (Institute of Social Anthropology), University of Amsterdam (Institute for Metropolitan and International Development Studies), University of Erfurt (Max Weber Center for Advanced Cultural and Social Studies), and Harvard University (Department of Anthropology).

My editor at Stanford University Press, Kate Wahl, showed tremendous enthusiasm for this project from the beginning. In the world of university publishing, she is in a league of her own. Her editorial assistant, Joa Suorez, provided prompt and expert advice on the nuts and bolts of the submission process, for which I am grateful.

Finally, like many scholars who find themselves torn between the monastic imperatives of the writer's life and the blissful obligations of being-in-the-world, I must acknowledge the patience, support, and love of my family—Romana, Dara, and Isaiah, *minunile mele*.

Dilemmas of Modernity

1 Modern Dilemmas

Prologue

Perhaps more than any other nation in Latin America, Bolivia is iconic. In the back alleys of the departmental capital city of Potosí, extreme tourism shops traffic in Bolivia's iconicism: twenty-somethings from Belgium and France and Spain and even Chile, bedecked in the sartorial equivalent of world music, halfway along the gringo trail's passage from Otavalo (now that southern Colombia has become too dangerous for backpackers) to Santiago de Chile (or Buenos Aires), and mildly hopped-up from drinking too many cups of *mate de coca* at over 13,000 feet, are promised the thrill of a literal descent into Hell. For only five dollars apiece, groups of culture tourists are given the chance to experience what is advertised as a journey into the inferno. The five-hour tour through the cooperative mines on Cerro Rico is described visually on rows of tightly packed competing signs, which depict cartloads of unnaturally white-skinned travelers moving slowly down through the sulfurous gases and rocky outcroppings dripping with silica dust, past Baroque devils who menace them with pitchforks. The local tour operators are more than happy to transform local mining cultural practice into what is really a Hieronymus Bosch panorama—as any shopkeeper in Bolivia knows, the European imaginary is prefigured.

And two years before George Roy Hill, the director of *Butch Cassidy and the Sundance Kid*, made the entirely predictable decision to film Bolivia in Mexico, it was no coincidence that the man who had transformed himself into an icon chose Bolivia to begin a new revolutionary movement in Latin America. It did not matter to Che that the actual prospect of the bearded revolutionary's sudden appearance in a remote Bolivian village was an even clearer portent of his death than any ill-begotten alliance between the Bolivian government and the CIA; what mattered most was what Bolivia represented—in this case, class exploitation in the abstract, as Platonic ideal. But Bolivia has always been the site of this multilayered iconicism: gringo backpackers journey to Bolivia to trace the path of the metals that allow them to listen to the panpipes of the folk music ensemble Savia Andina on their Walkmans—they move within the networks of modernity in reverse. Even the gaunt, ghoulish, and bullet-ridden corpse of Che Guevara, lying on a desolate slab in the laundry room of Vallegrande's Our Lady of Malta hospital, does not diminish the discursive power of that moment, when an icon in triplicate—Che the revolutionary lying dead in a classically exploited rural village at the heart of the world system's dependent periphery—unraveled as soon as the mundane, what Michel de Certeau (1988) described as "the practice of everyday life," could no longer be simply theorized.

Bolivia, in other words, must be understood in both the disjunctive and conjunctive. The ways in which "Bolivia" is produced—by the whole range of social actors and institutions (both "native" and "foreign")—create representational contradictions that rise to paradox in certain moments; the constitution of the social, in Bolivia as elsewhere, is untidy. Yet as the December 2005 election of Evo Morales and the subsequent political and legal uncertainty have illustrated in spades, the disjunctiveness of social life in Bolivia cannot be simply explained through reference to any of the orthodox dichotomies that have formed the basis of social scientific accounts of different aspects of economic, social, and political life: local versus national (or national versus transnational); indigenous versus mestizo; rural versus urban; Quechua (or Aymara or Guaraní) versus Spanish; communist (or socialist or syndico-anarchist) versus capitalist (or liberal or neoliberal); altiplano versus *yungas*; pan-Andean versus indigenist-nationalist; campesino versus miner (or proletariat); law versus custom. This is not to say that oppositional social practice—as distinct from critique or analysis—is not a salient feature of Bolivians' lives, but one does not gain by forcing the everyday play of sharp contrasts into a rigid dialectic that necessarily excludes the possibility of more nuanced relationships.

However, if one is to avoid simple models or analytical frameworks in the process of contributing to the production of knowledge about and within Bolivia, this does not mean one should not look for what the art historian Michael Baxandall (1987) called in another context patterns of intention—the historical and cultural forces that persist in structuring the possible ways in which systems of meaning relate to each other, the logics through which *these* particular systems of representation become "Bolivian." In order to make any sense at all out of Bolivia's contested present, or the way in which social analysis or cultural critique within Bolivia must encompass multiple and apparently contradictory registers (historical, cultural, epistemological) at the same time in order to approximate truth (that is, resonance across discrete groups of interlocutors), or, finally, in order to participate in an anthropological or historical or philosophical study of Bolivia that is also ethically positioned, one must move from the dissonance of social practice to the patterns of intention that have made Bolivia a site of enduring cultural and discursive creativity. In this sense it is not sufficient to contribute yet another artificially localized case study of some aspect of social life in Bolivia; to do so would be, in light of the patterns described in this book, an actual political act with limited intellectual or other justification. The major claim to relevance of this book is that it identifies and then renders a set of key historical, legal, and cultural frameworks that are both empirical (that is, constituted through social practice) *and* analytical, to the extent they embody concepts that serve to reflect on social practice and invest it with meaning.

To make this point another way, this book is in part an argument for what is perhaps a uniquely anthropological kind of relevance, one that combines contemporary anthropology's eclectic methodologies—ethnography, history and ethnohistory, cultural critique—with the tentative and even reluctant development of nonuniversal social, cultural, and historical theory. When the director of a nongovernmental organization in Potosí dedicated to legal reform and social justice asked me pointedly "how are *you* relevant?," he was really interrogating both the intellectual and social justification for a kind of social research that makes inquiries without formally embedding them in practical projects for social transformation or sustainable development. Some scholars in Latin America have responded to criticisms of this kind by either pushing epistemological boundaries in order to break down orthodox distinctions between science and political action, or by challenging the notion of epistemology itself in order to legitimate multiply valid—even if incompatible—ways of knowing. This book represents yet another way of responding to my *potosino* interlocutor.

If it is true, as James Clifford argued (1986), that ethnography always leads to the discovery of "partial truths," then it also must be true that some accounts are more partial than others. The recognition of essential fragmentariness is not, ipso facto, an argument for self-consciously restricting one's efforts; the constraints to comprehensive social research are all too real in themselves. Yet even though what follows reflects my best efforts—begun in 1996—to document and reflect on certain key aspects of social life in Bolivia, I should underscore the obvious fact that the result is idiosyncratic and makes no claims to positivist objectivity. In describing a particular aspect of an intellectual history that has shaped the plural Bolivian experience for the last two hundred years, I am only too aware that the choices I have made along the way, the points of analytical emphasis, the tentative conclusions and suggestions for future research and critique, even the general implications for understanding the relationship between hegemonic ideas and social practice (that is, the book's theoretical commitments, such as they are), must find their justification within a set of evaluative criteria that are ambiguous at best.

Almost immediately after returning to Bolivia in 1998 (after a three-month period of preliminary research and language training in 1996), I was troubled by a sense of profound unease. I became very quickly intellectually restless and I struggled to find what I had expected to be firm anthropological bearings. I was committed to an orthodox research project within the legal anthropological tradition—anthropologist picks a "culture" and then studies its legal dimensions—and was perfectly comfortable justifying my work on the basis that I was the "first"; that is, the first anthropologist to conduct an extended ethnographic study of law in Bolivia. However, very soon after returning to "my site," which was the province of Alonso de Ibañez in the north of Potosí Department, I was presented with the following challenge: to develop the tools to gauge local processes in ever-increasing degrees of finely grained detail, and, at the same time, to track what appeared to be outlines of a much larger network of ideas and practices that encompassed Alonso de Ibañez in such a way that the province had become only one small node, one point of articulation. This difficulty was particularly acute for someone trained in the sociocultural anthropological tradition, especially in the wake of the important critiques of epistemological metanarratives and the poverty of anthropological theory that had transformed the discipline—particularly in the United States—over the last twenty years.

All of this meant I was only too conscious of the inadequacy of a research strategy that drew artificial boundaries around either a place or group of people and then adopted the standard synchronic framework that purported to offer a comprehensive portrait of people and place within an abstracted ethnographic present—a kind of chrono-cultural dimension that is loaded with unstated assumptions about nature, cultural change, and cultural difference. I also knew, however, that I could not simply ignore local social practices in order to trace the contours of the broader patterns of intention that became clearer with each passing day, because "tracing" would mean, to a certain extent, conceptualizing, envisioning, and giving shape to this larger network through the complicated act of articulating it, and this would seem to eliminate most of the empirical foundation upon which conventional sociocultural anthropology justifies its activities. Although I had not been prepared for the way these two imperatives seemed to pull in opposite directions, I was certain that I could not merely yield to one and intentionally ignore the other. Therefore, I resolved to reconcile this tension by reconceiving the nature of my research; everything that followed was an attempt to mediate between these two currents by documenting their effects and meanings at what were always two ever-present, but distinct, levels: the empirical and the conceptual. In other words, the reflection on technique and process became inseparable from the pursuit and analysis of substantive research findings.

Locations

Bolivia is divided into nine departments, which are further subdivided into provinces, sections of provinces, and, finally, cantons. Bolivia's nine departments, however, map more than simply square kilometers or land distribution; they express a range of complex social geographies, which can be divided not only into jurisdictional units, but into categories of the Bolivian social imagination. Each department is defined by a set of topographical, historical, ethnic, agricultural, political, and even moral characteristics, so that despite the internal diversity, departments frame identity and provide a reference point for public debates over everything from the sequential ordering of dance troupes during Carnival in Oruro to the post-2005 debates over regional autonomy. Potosí is one of the larger and more historically significant of Bolivia's nine departments. The silver and gold extracted from Cerro Rico, or the Rich Mountain, outside of the department's eponymously named capital, Potosí, financed much of the Spanish colonial enterprise until about the mid-seventeenth century. Bolivians themselves like to emphasize the importance of Potosí to the Spanish empire by asserting that enough silver was pulled out of the mountain to build a solid bridge from Potosí to Madrid.

In the north of the Potosí department, there is a grouping of five provinces that forms a head or extension, and which is known as the *norte de Potosí* (see Figures 1.1 and 1.2). In many ways, the norte de Potosí encapsulates much of

Figure 1.1. Map of Bolivia within its regional context

the departmental identity itself, and *nortepotosinos* are alternatively proud
and ambivalent about this fact. The norte de Potosí is the location of several
large mining operations that figured prominently in early twentieth century
Bolivian history; it is the poorest region in Bolivia's poorest department, according to international development criteria; it is where ritual combats
known as *tinkus* still mark key points in the agro-spiritual yearly cycle; and
more than other regions of Bolivia, it is the place where *ayllus* (roughly
glossed as "indigenous social structures") continue to serve as ordering
principles along with jurisdictional logics derived from other political and
legal institutions. However, more than anything else, the norte de Potosí
symbolizes a particular vision of indigenous Bolivia, in which *punas* (high
and dry Andean ecoregions), inaccessible hamlets, and what is believed to
be a basic struggle for survival, come together in the minds of especially
urban Bolivians to produce a response that is part visceral, part ideological.
At a café in La Paz, a middle-class office worker reacted in horror and awe

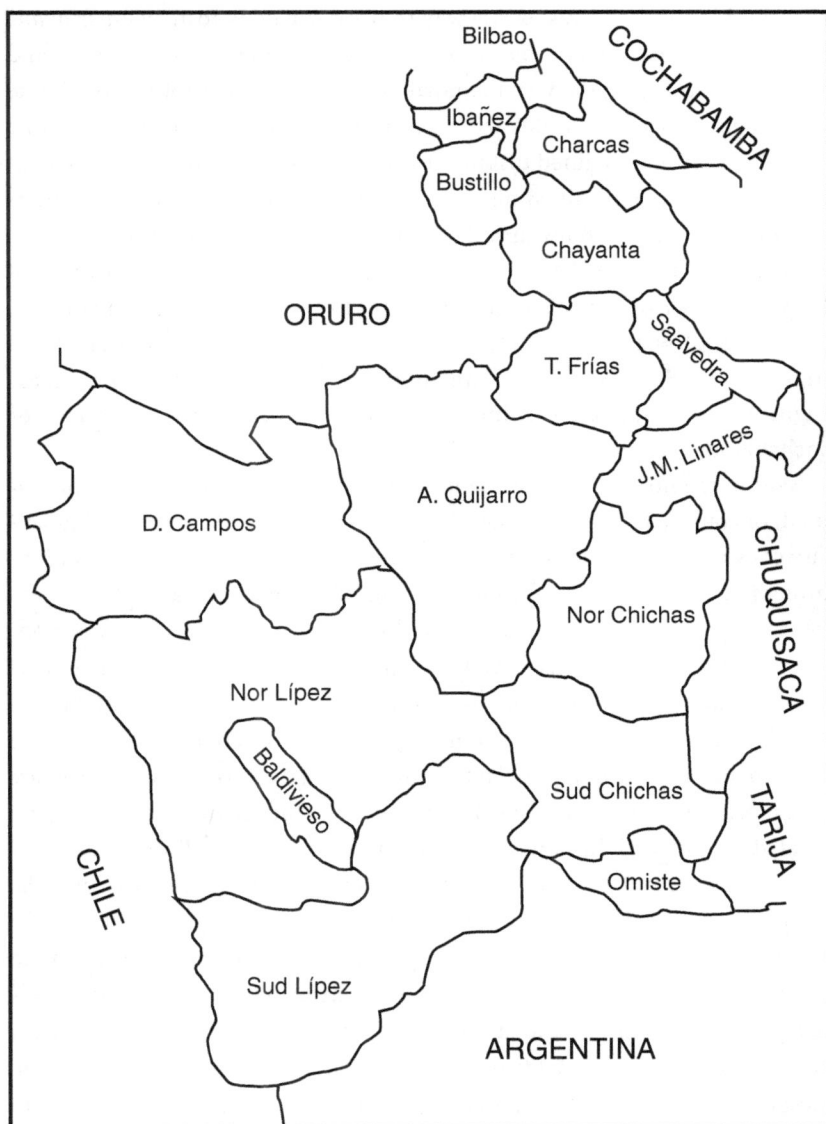

Figure 1.2. Map of Potosí department

when I told him that I was on my way to the norte de Potosí. "*¡Qué frío, qué bárbaro!*" ("How cold, how barbarous!") he said, thereby spontaneously and succinctly expressing the way the norte de Potosí's topography and climate commingle in people's minds with a certain cultural retrogressiveness, one not defined by an imagined distance from some abstract notion of "civilization" but from the imagined historical distance from the trajectory of modern Bolivia. For many Bolivians, the norte de Potosí is barbarous not because young men beat each other to death with rocks in order to mark the onset of the planting season or to herald a bountiful harvest during the time of rain, but because it would seem to lie outside the boundaries of Bolivia's liberal origin myths. Yet as we will see, the norte de Potosí is as essential to these origin myths, or patterns of intention, as any urban barrio of La Paz, or Cochabamba hacienda.

Within the norte de Potosí itself, the problem of identity is more complicated, of course, although the ways in which something like a national imaginary constitutes the norte de Potosí enter into local and regional self-definitions through popular media, local appropriations of national legislation (which expresses a particular image of the norte de Potosí), and the activities of nongovernmental organizations (NGOs), whose presence in the region is in part based on an idealized understanding of the *extremo* norte de Potosí. If "extreme" carries a double meaning in this common reference—far from the departmental capital and far from the categories of modern Bolivia—there are certain basic material and political implications to the region's otherwise complicated remoteness. In Potosí, as in other departments in Bolivia, the allocation of governmental resources tends to follow a concentric principle: the farther a region is from the seat of power (usually the departmental capital), the less likely it will benefit from everything from road repair programs to school construction funds to visits from departmental political officials. Although the work of transnational NGOs over the last twenty years in places like the norte de Potosí has qualified this principle to a certain extent, there is no question that a region's sheer distance from a departmental capital can lead to neglect, isolation, and a kind of social marginalization.

Take, for example, the seemingly simple problem of roads. One does not have to be a geographical determinist to see how the presence or absence of well-maintained, strategically routed, and well-traveled roads becomes a key aspect of local cultural practice and identity. Provincial towns throughout Bolivia that are near roads of this kind are more cosmopolitan, more economically integrated into national and even wider markets, more likely to attract the attention of transnational NGOs (whose presence is marked by fleets of late-model sports utility vehicles), and, especially more recently, more likely to express local or regional versions of national social and political movements. The impact of roads throughout rural Bolivia can be exponential: the better the road, the more well-connected to departmental capitals, the more frequently serviced by flotas and camiones,[1] the more rapidly towns develop broader frames of reference, experience economic integration, and nurture relationships with transnational development actors. Conversely, provincial towns that are not located near good roads recede even farther and faster in the mirror from those that are. If the out-migration of almost everyone from a town can be described as a kind of death, then many towns throughout rural Bolivia are dying, in part because they are not near, nor can they be near, strategically important roads. Where not even fifty years ago the continued existence of provincial towns in Bolivia could be justified because of their location in relation to zones of productive agriculture (where products were moved in and out by horse or burro), today the presence or absence of a good road determines certain basic facts about a town's already fraught existence.

In the norte de Potosí, several provinces are much closer in distance to the departmental capitals of Cochabamba and Oruro. This means that nortepotosinos are much more likely to look to these two urban centers as a source of seasonal labor, locations to send children for school or technical training, places to buy electronic goods or building products, and markets for surplus agriculture. Indeed, many nortepotosinos have never been to the capital of their own department, even if they make regular trips—for the reasons indicated, and others—to the similarly eponymously named capitals of Cochabamba and Oruro. The problem is that these two departments have no responsibility for the norte de Potosí, because it lies within another department's boundaries. The result is that the few major roads that do traverse the norte de Potosí are very poorly maintained, subject to constant erosion, and, during what is usually a heavy rainy season (November to April), often impassable for weeks at a time. These problems are compounded by the fact that interdepartmental roads through the norte de Potosí can typically pass through three different departments (Potosí, Cochabamba, Oruro) and many different provinces, which further diffuses the sense of political and legal responsibility for what everyone agrees is a sine qua non for local development and prestige and any hope for prosperity—a well-maintained interregional road. Individual towns and, even more, the hundreds of small hamlets that line the routes of major roads, all obviously have a stake in ensuring that their access to the wider world is preserved. However, except for the portions of roads that run directly through towns and hamlets—which *are* usually very well maintained, often as part of *ayni,* or collective labor obligations—the vast majority of road-space in the norte de Potosí exists in high and remote places far from even the sparsest forms of habitation.[2]

Alonso de Ibañez is the northwesternmost province in the norte de Potosí. Its capital, Sacaca, sits at 3,615 meters in a valley that is surrounded by hills (see Figure 1.3). Sacaca is connected by flota and camión to Oruro, which is about six hours to the west depending on the season. Sacaca also is connected to Cochabamba, which lies to the north, by less-regular bus travel; the trip takes about eight hours, again depending on the time of year. As late as the 1960s, according to some older people in Sacaca, those who had horses still rode them to Oruro for supplies and to conduct business, a round trip that took three days. Alonso de Ibañez is approximately 2,170 square kilometers (Bolivia-INE 2001) and most of the province lies between 3,000 and 4,000 meters, which would place most of it between the high or upper puna and low or lower puna.[3] There are also some lower intermountain regions of the province, where corn, peaches, prickly pear, and lower elevation crops can be grown (Figure 1.4). Other major crops grown throughout the province are potatoes, quinoa (Figure 1.5), wheat, peas, scallions, lettuce, beans, barley, *tawri,* sweet potatoes (*camote*), and oca, but potatoes are by far the most important crop. Nearly every patch of land in the province that is not almost vertical is either under seed or lying fallow. As in many other parts of the Andes, potatoes are used to make *ch'uño,* a freeze-dried version of the crop, which is eaten at all times of the year and not just in periods of relative scarcity.[4]

Somewhat surprisingly, although in both Sacaca and the province's hamlets most people live through a combination of agriculture and pastoralism, the use of llamas and other camelids is not common. There are llamas in some of the hamlets to the west and southwest of the capital, but llamas have increasingly been replaced by burros, goats, sheep, and pigs. In every part of the province, people raise guinea pigs (*qoy*), which are eaten on special occasions and are considered a great delicacy in the same way they are in other parts of the Andes. Although there are chronic health problems in the province, especially in the hamlets, people do not starve. The soil in Alonso de Ibañez is generally poor compared with soils in the Cochabamba Valley, for example, with the result

Figure 1.3. Sacaca, Alonso de Ibañez

Figure 1.4. Abundant cornfield, Vitora, Canton Ovejería

Figure 1.5. Quinoa field in full bloom, between Churata and Llapa-Llapa, Canton Wila Wila

that fields take a long time to recover through fallowing (sometimes three to four years). Farmers are under a constant pressure to plant in plots that might not be quite ready, because of the increasing impact on land through micro-division and an ongoing need to have crops for sale in order to access the cash economy. In addition, because of the steeply graded topography, the soil in Alonso de Ibañez is severely eroded (see Figure 1.6). Not only does this fact add to the challenges of finding suitable land to grow crops, but it also increases the chances of flooding and other related damage during the rainy season.

The population of Alonso de Ibañez is about 25,000. The town of Sacaca, which is both the provincial capital and capital of the province's first section, has a population of 1,500; Caripuyo, the capital of the province's second section, has a population of about 400. This means that the combined population of the two towns in Alonso de Ibañez represents only about 8 percent of the province's total population. Outside of Sacaca and Caripuyo, there are about

Figure 1.6. Eroded fields above Waraya, Canton Sillu Sillu

two hundred hamlets spread throughout the province. According to national census figures (INE, 2001), the average size of hamlets provincewide is 180 people, although people in the province estimate the size of their hamlets by numbers of families, not people. The hamlets are referred to locally as "estancias," "*ranchus*" (a Quechua or Aymara variation of the Spanish "ranchos"), or "*comunidades*." Almost everyone in the province, including people outside the capital in both sections and in the capital itself, speaks Quechua at some level. Many of the hamlets in the second section are Aymara first-language hamlets. In these hamlets, Spanish will often be more popular as a second language than Quechua among the men, with Quechua serving as the more common second language for women because it is the language of regional markets. With few exceptions, all residents of the town of Sacaca itself are bilingual Spanish-Quechua speakers, with a few townspeople speaking Aymara as well. In general, Aymara is on the decline in Alonso de Ibáñez in the same way as it is throughout the norte de Potosí.[5]

Finally, there is the subject of ethnicity in the norte de Potosí, which is a difficult one for several reasons. First, as we will see throughout this book, the constitution of identity takes place within a historical context in which categories of belonging have emerged during different periods in response to different political and social imperatives. The result is that identity in the norte de

Potosí, as elsewhere in Bolivia, can be understood through the image of shifting layers or strata, which coexist uneasily and indefinitely. In other words, there really is no neat and tidy analytical model for describing identity in the norte de Potosí; these layers are not nested hierarchically. Further, some layers of identity are not permanently associated with what can be called "classes" in any meaningful sense, especially if by classes we mean to analyze identity in terms of power or differential access to resources. Although layers of identity are partly shaped through legal categories, partly through rotation through a series of political offices, partly through the accepted public performance of ritual obligations, and so on, identity is not simply *derived* from cultural practice. Moreover, the idea or discourse of "identity" itself has become part of the process of identity formation in Bolivia over the last twenty years, especially during the apogee of multiculturalism during the early to mid-1990s, when slogans like *identidad con dignidad* (identity with dignity) became a popular rallying cry for social and political movements organized around different forms of collective belonging.[6] This way of employing "identity" converts the idea of a "dignified identity" into a social category that is abstracted from what might be called "actual identity." As a consequence, identities in the norte de Potosí, as elsewhere in Bolivia, have become bifurcated: on one side, is that shifting, multilayered identity that is the product of particular historical and cultural contexts, while on the other side, a form of identity has emerged in Bolivia that is highly formalized—identity-in-itself.

If we broaden the question of ethnicity in the norte de Potosí to include this more complex understanding of identity, then several points can be usefully made about how people understand themselves—and are understood by others. As elsewhere, the problem of self-definition is relative to context, so that people in Alonso de Ibáñez talk about themselves in different ways depending on where they are and who they are with. However, without ordering them in any formal way, the following categories or layers of identity are present in Alonso de Ibáñez and play a role in shaping the way people in the province encounter broader patterns of intention: *runa* (Quechua for "man" or "the people"); *q'ara* (literally, "naked" or "unpeeled," used to denote non-*runa*, typically those from outside the region, or imagined city dwellers); campesino ("peasant," a term that was adopted in Bolivia in the early twentieth century to replace "Indian"); *sacaqueño* (those from the provincial capital itself); *ayllu* (there are many different ayllus in Alonso de Ibáñez, and each contributes its own layer of identity); hamlet or town; *sindicato* campesino (or "rural peasant union"); region (people from the higher puna regions think of themselves—and are described by others—somewhat differently than those from valley regions, where different crops can be grown); the order of first, second, and perhaps third languages (e.g., Quechua → Spanish or Aymara → Quechua → Spanish); degree of literacy; gender; political party affiliation; and age (which, for men at least, implies different histories of participation in the range of politico-legal authority positions). And these are simply the way categories of identity would be understood within the norte de Potosí itself; if a person from Alonso de Ibañez found himself stationed in one of the army's Amazonian brigades, or working in the coca fields of the Chapare, these layers of identity would be configured in different ways, and other layers would be added and given more prominence.

Dilemmas of Modernity in Bolivia

In late 1999, I spent an afternoon discussing *derechos humanos* (human rights) and *desarrollo sostenible* (sustainable development) with a local official in the village of Wila Wila. Our encounter was only one in a long series of meetings he conducted with outside experts, who in many parts of rural Bolivia are referred to generally—and revealingly—through the Spanish as either *ingenieros* (engineers) or *técnicos* (technicians), signifiers that show how modern subjectivity is understood throughout Bolivia exactly as it was intended to be—at the service of instrumental rationality. We discussed the work that legal and infrastructure NGOs were doing in the province, what "human rights" might mean for Bolivia's future, and the ways in which life had changed for people in his village over the last twenty years. It became immediately apparent that he and I had a very similar understanding of what "development," "progress," and "human rights" were intended to mean. Despite what I assumed would be an encounter that demonstrated the essentially ambiguous content of modernity's key signifiers, what this—and others—showed was that the fixedness of intended meaning is a primary way in which modernity's instrumentalities are expressed in practice, something the social researcher is hard pressed to countervail by simply envisioning theoretically possible alternatives. However, even though the Wila Wila official and I clearly shared an understanding about the intended meanings of these keywords, and, more important, the processes they evoked, we diverged sharply over how to value or judge these meanings. While I had arrived to the conversation, as I had to Bolivia, imbued with the compelling Escobarian narrative that sited the discourses of "development" and "human rights" and "progress" within the dark history of economic, political, and legal exploitation that characterized the "making and unmaking of the Third World," my campesino cosubject valued development and progress quite differently, indeed nearly oppositely. For him, the coming of the era of sustainable development and human rights meant potable water, solar showers, genetically modified potato seeds, the ability to finally grow an agricultural product marketable outside the area (eucalyptus), and, more than anything else, a spiritual system that seemed to justify development and the triumph of rights—evangelical Protestantism. These were not markers of a *hegemonic* pattern of intention, one that seduced Bolivia with material and spiritual good works at the same time it further incorporated it into an essentially exploitative transnational mode of production; they were, rather, markers of a worldview and philosophy of living that had finally, against all odds, reached the village of Wila Wila, and none too soon.

This experience revealed the first key dilemma at the heart of my project, one also at the center of what Habermas (1996) describes as the "unfinished project of modernity": how to mediate the empirical and conceptual gap between the critiques of modernity and its discontents on the one hand, and, on the other, what is, as in the case of my Wila Wila interlocutor, a positivist and essentially optimistic engagement with the project of modernity by a range of social actors and institutions. This dilemma is what linguists would call the problem of polyvalence: a discursive disjuncture in which parties share a basic set of understandings about a text's intended meaning, but disagree over how to judge or value this meaning (see, e.g., Davos 2003). As I said, this dilemma is both empirical and conceptual. It is empirical in that anthropologists and other critically oriented traditional intellectuals, whose professional work involves close and extended participation in the local practice of everyday life, run the risk of being rendered irrelevant—or worse, threatening—when this basic disagreement over the value of modernity becomes publicly apparent. In Bolivia, the problem of polyvalence has become even sharper over the last twenty years in light of the massive influx of NGOs, which are oriented in the same way as their local "clients," and whose representatives travel throughout rural Bolivia not, like anthropologists do, merely (in most cases) to learn from or understand, but bearing the fruits of modernity's triumphs in the wake of a convoy of sports utility vehicles. This dilemma is also conceptual. If anthropologists and other critical social researchers have become the primary interpreters of modernity and its vernaculars, how is one to theorize the relationship between the multiple meanings of modernity and its *values*, a relationship that is itself plural? Is it enough to simply acknowledge the social fact of polyvalence or must any broader account intended for cross-cultural application simply abandon the pretense of generality? This kind of retreat from efforts to definitively conceptualize "modernity" is what John D. Kelly (2002) described as "getting out of the modernist sublime."

On March 25, 1999, the Bolivian National Congress passed Law No. 1970, which had the effect of republishing the Code of Criminal Procedure with amendments. Among the several changes was one that received very little attention at the time in either the popular press or among the legal and academic communities. This was new Article 28, which was entitled Community Justice. This article, which appears in Title 2, Chapter 2, reads in part:

> a criminal action will be concluded when the crime or offense is committed within an indigenous or peasant community by one of its members against another, and its natural authorities will have resolved the conflict in conformity with their Indigenous Customary Law, whenever said resolution is not contrary to the fundamental rights and personal guarantees established by the Constitution.

From a matter of statutory interpretation, there are several critical aspects to Article 28. This provision on "community justice," despite its unheralded eventual appearance, had been the subject of intense controversy within the Bolivian Congress ever since the possibility of adding an "indigenous rights" provision to Bolivian law had been raised during the presidency of Gonzales Sánchez de Lozada during the mid-1990s. The most common line of critique was anchored in a thinly veiled racist discourse that contrasted the supposed "savagery" of "Indian law" with the nobility of Bolivia's constitution. Critics pointed to the rise in incidents of *linchamientos* (lynchings) in the periurban barrios of Cochabamba,[7] and in the smaller provincial towns of La Paz Department, as a harbinger of how the Bolivian nation-state would become stalled in its two hundred-year-old march toward civilization if it were to "dilute" the core universalist principles that define republican Bolivia by recognizing any normative system that was customary, particularistic, or rooted in Andean traditions; in other words, any "law" that was an expression of an earlier stage in cultural and political evolution.

So it is striking that the content of Article 28, which on its face has the appearance of introducing a principle of law that runs counter to the entire edifice of Bolivia's modern jurisprudence, was not inserted into Title 1 of the Code, which is the section reserved for statements of basic "constitutional guarantees" in the area of criminal procedure. Rather, it was added incongruously to a list that describes a series of relatively mundane procedural requirements for pursuing a criminal case, sandwiched in between an article that enumerates circumstances that cause a criminal case to be automatically "extinguished" (Article 27, *Motivos de extinción*) and one that is a statute of limitations (Article 29, *Prescripción de la acción*). In this way, the language of Article 28 reveals an internal contradiction, which is also the legal expression of another dilemma of modernity in Bolivia. By qualifying the legitimacy of "Indigenous Customary Law" in such a way that the individual human rights provisions of the Bolivian constitution serve as a trump on the free exercise of community norms and practices, this abstract and putative "indigenous law" is rendered impotent.[8] If customary law means anything as a normative framework, it is that it is historically contingent, relative to place and time, essentially dynamic, and expressive of the cultural imperatives of whatever community or village or ethnic group in which it is expressed through sociolegal practice. It reflects a legal epistemology, in other words, that is diametrically opposed to the one that forms the basis of Bolivian state law, which can be understood as *hyperuniversalist*: It begins with a mix of Spanish, Roman, and Canonical jurisprudential principles—each of which embodies natural law after its own historical fashion—and adds to it principles drawn from the secularized natural rights traditions that were most immediately relevant at the emergence of Bolivian nationhood in the early nineteenth century—the U.S. and French. This internal contradiction within Article 28 reflects a broader dilemma that affects subaltern populations in Bolivia in particular ways.

While Marxist and neo-Marxist approaches to endemic social problems, like land distribution, corruption within relations of production, and the monopolization of control over scarce resources, lost legitimacy in Bolivia after the reemergence of civilian government in the 1980s, the adoption of liberal rights frameworks by peasants and the urban marginalized did not lead to the anticipated transformation of Bolivian society. This is because the means through which rights came to be the preeminent discourse for subaltern resistance—that is, collective rights—rested on a paradox: the codification of the particular *through* the universal. But even if self-defined indigenous organizations or peasant movements in need of a unifying normative framework within which social problems could finally be resolved were, at times, able to

advance their interests within the discourse of indigenous rights, it was not because this discourse embodies a philosophically potent alternative to legal
modernity. Rather, formal symbols of social change, such as Articles 171 and 28,
were expressions of a strategy that was in large part directed by national elites
based on short-term political expediency. By embracing a rights framework
within which long-term social problems were recontextualized, indigenous
and peasant groups in Bolivia inadvertently reexposed themselves to the entire
range of liberal stratagems that have been used since the early nineteenth century to forge categories of modern subjectivity through the law. At the same
time in 1991 that a massive coalition of indigenous and campesino organizations was marching from Trinidad in the Beni to La Paz under the banner of
"human rights for all Bolivians," the gathered multitudes were also, with each
passing kilometer, (re-)constituting themselves as rights-bearing modern subjects in the way liberal Bolivia had always envisioned.[9] The march was, in part,
a metaphor for getting *into*, not out of, modernity.[10] The poor and marginalized Bolivians who eagerly take up the banner of human rights have ironically *less* discursive space now to complain about the deprivation and increased alienation that result when a nation's citizens redefine social relations in
terms of contract rights, private property, and the liberal pursuit of enlightened
self-interest.[11] What the categories of the modern give with one hand, they take
away with the other.

Finally, there is the dilemma of interpreting *modernidad* in Bolivia. Who
has a legitimate claim to authority in reflecting on the dominant patterns of intention that have hovered over social life in Bolivia for the last two hundred
years? Do traditional intellectuals like anthropologists have a social role to play
in using ethnographic techniques to "access[] 'local' modernities," as Debra
Spitulnik argued (2002)? Should the professional social researcher's—or
theorist's—gaze be privileged over those whose work does not entail the articulation of rules of analysis, those "principles of visual economy" that structure
the sustained observation of everyday life (Poole 1997)?

In her compelling study of the way in which the relationship between race
and vision was transformed in the Andean world under the constraints of
modernity, Deborah Poole develops a three-part analysis: the first studies the
way individuals are related to the technologies that capture their images; the
second focuses on the technology itself; and the third studies the wider systems
of representation within which "graphic images are appraised, interpreted, and
assigned historical, scientific, and aesthetic worth (1997: 10). Yet as she suggests,

this is a prescription for the study of modernity more generally. Since the technologies of knowledge production have become inextricably embedded in the systems of (scientific) representation that reinforce modernity in its academic, bureaucratic, and governmental expressions, any critique of modernity should be compelled to make the organization of knowledge itself subject to critical scrutiny. And if the production of knowledge—and the "cultural and discursive systems" that legitimate some producers and not others—is reduced to simply one object of inquiry among others, how does the professional interpreter create a space for analysis that has any claim to authority? Can a claim to authority be envisioned that is not irremediably subject to the same critique of hegemony that forms the foundation for the critique of modernity itself?

Poole's response is to admit that she remains "skeptical about [her] ability to answer . . . questions concerning Cusqueños modernities, selves, resistances, and identities" through the application of the techniques of her discipline. As she explains, "[e]ven after my excursion into the historical archives, I retain a residual unease about speaking for these mute Andean subjects. What I do hope to convey by looking at these peoples' images is an idea of the power that both visual ideologies and visual technologies have to sediment and materialize the abstract and frequently contradictory discourses of racial, ethnic, and class identity that crisscross *our own lives* as they do those of the photographs' Andean subjects" (1997: 214; emphasis added). This is anthropology as cultural critique, the study of modernity in the vernacular as a way of better understanding the producers of ideologies and technologies and their role in constituting modern subjectivities, whether in Peru or elsewhere.

Still, the problems of interpreting modernity are made more complicated when the researcher is not simply engaging with historically "mute Andean subjects," but with social actors who have become theorists of modernity in their own right: farmers, union activists, school teachers, engineers, local politicians, lawyers, religious officials, and others, who have internalized the modernist sublime and strive to conceptualize it. I first became aware of this dilemma through my relationship with Lucio Montesinos, who has been since the late-1990s one of my closest and most important interlocutors. He is the only titled lawyer in his corner of Bolivia's Potosí Department. He received formal training in international human rights law in Oruro, Cochabamba, and La Paz over the course of a year in the mid-1990s in preparation for his work with an innovative legal services center that was authorized by the same set of liberal legal reforms that led to new Articles 171 and 28. As he described this experience himself, the series of lectures he was required to attend on the history of the Universal Declaration of Human Rights (UDHR), the training that located the workings of the legal service center in relation to a "global movement for rights and human dignity," and the lessons he drew from his own ethical practice in the province, all had the effect of transforming him into "a man of knowledge," someone with a detailed and accurate understanding of the intellectual history that made these processes possible; in effect, Montesinos had become a social theorist. Yet despite Don Lucio's obvious uniqueness in his time and place, it is not at all surprising that I should find myself in a "remote" provincial town, in a part of Bolivia that is derided by urban intellectuals as "cold" and "poor" and "dirty," having a conversation about the civilizing effects of human rights and their latent power to lift peasants out of a centuries old cycle of indignity and oppression, which has endured, according to Lucio, not because of economic or other structural forms of inequality, but because peasants in Bolivia have been ignorant of their true moral worth and basic equality *as humans*.

It is not surprising because this is precisely how modern subjectivities emerge. The systems of representation, the structures of meaning that are understood both historically and vernacularly as "modernity," are not imposed, they are not colonial; they are self-imposed, they are "imperial" (here I fully agree with Hardt and Negri 2000). What makes this act of disciplinarity also a problem of interpretation is the fact that it is not at all implicit or subtle; on the contrary, the modern subject is by definition all too self-aware of the intellectual, economic, and political movements in which he is now embedded. Indeed, one inhabits the modern as much by theorizing its meanings as by enacting them in the routine of social practice. To document and then understand this demands much more than simple epistemological openness or a willingness to let go of the easy comfort of professionalization. What is needed is a new understanding of social theory itself, one in which "social" is not a mere qualifier that identifies a subclass of theory *about* the social, but one that refers, rather, to theory pursued *by* the social, that is, by ordinary social actors in the course of locating themselves in relation to contemporary movements of ideas and practices.

Encountering Liberalism

If "modernity" is the broadest pattern of intention through which social life in Bolivia can and, I would argue, must be understood, then "liberalism" describes a set of instrumentalities that mediate between modernity and its vernacular expressions. There are two types of instrumentalities that must be distinguished in order to understand what I mean. First, there are the actual institutional, political, or other means through which the discourses of modernity are constituted, resisted, and appropriated in social practice; a description of these within one part of rural Bolivia will form the largest part of this book. But there is also an intermediating conceptual level that serves to locate Bolivia's modern trajectory in time and place, one whose purpose is to historicize it. When I say that liberalism describes a set of instrumentalities, I am referring to this level beyond the vernacular. If it is true that Bolivia was born, to adopt one of Malagón Barceló's aphorisms, "beneath the sign of liberalism," then one must also come to terms with a consequential dialectic, with a struggle that has shaped the emergence of postcolonial Bolivia: that between liberalism and its counterliberal antitheses. By focusing on everyday encounters with a particular set of intermediating concepts—the triumph of liberty and the individual, natural and then human rights, the apotheosis of private property through the capitalist mode of production, the fight for government by consent—one also identifies those consequential ideas that link the mundane to the world-historical, the local to the global. When I examine, for example, the gendered nature of law in Bolivia, the way changing narratives of gender overlap with similarly changing narratives of rights, violence, and the possibilities for empowerment within the law, it is not enough to simply relate the findings from an ethnography of a local court of first instance, a *juzgado de instrucción*, in the north of Potosí Department. I also must read its practices as a local articulation of a broader narrative, one in which the liberal rights of the individual man or (much later) woman, which underlie Bolivian (and, later, transnational) law, come into conflict with a local and alternative framework within which gender relations are constituted quite differently.

Lives in the Law

There is still one analytical step remaining at this point: a description of the relationship between law and liberalism in Bolivia. This is the point at which the analytical framework I develop must find its meaning within the different ethnographic, ethnohistorical, and critical narratives that form the book's substance; it is also here that the study becomes much more idiosyncratic. I think a range of recent research and analysis about various aspects of society and history in Bolivia demonstrates the importance of liberalism (and its antitheses) as a dominant pattern of intention in postcolonial Bolivia, even if the manner of describing this intellectual history takes different shapes depending on the topic, respective disciplinary tradition, and style of analysis. This can be seen in recent studies that address various time frames within this intellectual history: Daniel Goldstein's analysis of the way periurban Bolivians in the 1990s used performative violence to "become visible" in "neoliberal Bolivia"; José Miguel Gordillo's (1990) study of "modernity, politics, and identity" from the time of the National Revolution of 1952 to the military coup of General Barrientos in 1964; Laura Gotkowitz's (1997) description of the production of the liberal Bolivian subject through the intersections of race, gender, and citizenship from the end of the nineteenth century up to the National Revolution; and, finally, the growing body of work on nineteenth century Bolivia proper, which has made the emergence of liberal Bolivia—and reactions to it—a major topic within interdisciplinary Bolivian studies (see, e.g., Barragán 1999; Barragán, Cajías, and Qayum 1997; Langer 1988, 1989; Larson 2004; Platt 1982, 1984, 1987a; see also Larson's more recent bibliographic review essay on the historiography of nineteenth century Bolivia [2004: 282–89]).[12]

Despite these congruences, one of my arguments here is that liberalism cannot be used simply as a description of a historical moment in Bolivia, even if we understand this usage "metahistorically" (White 1973); that is, as a rhetorical act that reveals an "elective affinity between the act of prefiguration of the historical field and the explanatory strategies" (p. 427) that are used not only by the historian, but also by the social actors whose lives the historian recounts. Rather, I understand liberalism as the conceptual means within which "Bolivian lives" (Valderrama Fernández and Escalante Gutiérrez 1996) across the range are inserted into an emergent modernity; it is also functional as one side of the liberal-counterliberal social dialectic, whose felt impact has waxed and waned from the nineteenth century to the present.

Even though this collective body of work examines a number of different categories of instrumentalities through which liberalism serves to historicize Bolivia's modern trajectory (politics, race, ethnicity, gender, economic), one crucial instrumentality has been largely ignored by social scientists, historians, social theorists, and other traditional intellectuals: law. This is not to say that law and legal categories do not figure in studies of nineteenth century tribute categories (Platt 1982), in reinterpretations of lynching and the emergence of performative violence in contemporary Cochabamba (Goldstein 2004), in critiques of the "absurd coca war" (Albó and Barrios 1993), or in analyses of gender (Arnold 1997a), among others. In each, however, law is treated peripherally or illustratively, as one institutional or social sphere in which a broader topic or set of themes find expression. This is one of the deeper mysteries of Bolivian studies (both within and outside Bolivia), which is made all the more surprising since "law," understood in all of its normative, discursive, institutional, and cultural complexity, has been a key organizing principle in Bolivia, a fact that could also be demonstrated by reaching beyond the scope of the current study, into the colonial period, when everything from parochial jurisdictions, to the creation of a hierarchy of colonial subjects, to the organization of the Potosí *mita* (the annual forced labor migration), was organized within and through law.[13] In other words, law in Bolivia has both embodied and constituted a whole range of other social categories; for example, gender relations, relations of production, religious practice, and even social identity itself. Yet could the reverse be claimed?

In their book *Lives in the Law*, Austin Sarat, Lawrence Douglas, and Martha Merrill Umphrey argue that "[l]aw comes alive in and through the lives of persons, groups, and nations. Law takes shape through the process by which it molds biography and identity. Similarly, lives are formed and given meaning in and against the law, for law shapes choices, imposes constraints, provides opportunities, and serves both as an overt reference point and as an imaginary/symbolic presence" (2002: 1). This is as true in Bolivia as it is in the United States—perhaps even more so. In the United States, the relative strength of state institutions has meant that law's jurisprudential dimension has been arguably more consequential—and, in this sense, closed to the imperatives of biography and identity—than its social or cultural expressions. This means that law both does, and does not, "come alive through the lives of persons," except, again, in the lives of judges and lawyers and perhaps claimants. Although the legal consciousness movement within contemporary law and society studies in the United States has richly documented the importance of law in shaping other social categories (see, e.g., Ewick and Silbey 1998; Garth and Sarat 1998; Merry 1990), the actual hegemony in social practice of formal legal institutions in the United States has, somewhat paradoxically, limited law's elasticity and potential to serve as a first order means through which the nonlegal can be constituted and contested.

In Bolivia the opposite is true. Despite a formal jurisprudential hegemony, state legal institutions are in practice weak in Bolivia, particularly outside of the few major cities, which has had the effect, among other things, of enabling law to develop primarily as a cultural and discursive system of representation, one which is imbricated with social lives and identities in such a way that "law" embodies both the normative (systems of rules enforceable, and enforced by, locally legitimate authorities) *and* the nonnormative, in the sense that law, in addition to acting *as law*, also constitutes other key social categories. The elasticity of law in Bolivia has been its most defining characteristic, which becomes all the more important in light of the fact that law is officially prefigured and thus formally closed to all nonlegal cultural, political, and economic imperatives. As in other Latin American counties in which legal systems also combine several hyperuniversalist legal epistemologies, Bolivian law-in-the-books is the only theoretically possible expression of law; it is the codification of *the* law, whose ultimate transcendence is reestablished every time it is invoked synonymously as "the word," *la palabra*, as when a judge asks his clerk to retrieve a codebook to determine "what the word says."[14] The empirical chasm between jurisprudential law and law in—and as—social practice in Bolivia is one important reason "law," and not some other possible first order organizing principle, "shapes choices, imposes constraints, provides opportunities, and serves both as an overt reference point and as an imaginary/symbolic presence."

The Ethnography of Grandeur

In his study of "myths and meanings" on the Zambian Copperbelt, James Ferguson argues that the critical ethnography of local understandings of "modernity" in classic dependencies like Zambia is also, more generally, an "ethnography of decline," the account—and accounting—of crushed expectations, declining living standards, and the psychological trauma that inevitably results when the discursive formations of modernity are proved to be mere ideology at the service of global capital. As he explains:

> The way of life I observed on the Copperbelt was not only a depressing one, it was also one that I experienced as difficult to grasp. . . . With their jobs disappearing, their real incomes being cut in half and then cut in half again, their future plans and expectations being shattered, Copperbelt residents in the late 1980s did not inhabit a stable and well known social order. They did not know what was happening to them and did not understand why it was happening. Neither did I. . . . When I tried to get from them an insider's view of their social world, what I found resembled less a stable, systemic order of knowledge than a tangle of confusion, chaos, and fear. (1999: 18–19)

Ferguson draws both theoretical and methodological lessons from the engagement with this disorienting social chaos. On the one hand, like I do here,
Ferguson adopts a nonlinear and nonteleological social theoretical framework
in order to critique the related discourses of linear historical evolution and economic and social progress. This is an important move, particularly in light of
the fact that even formally critical approaches to processes of social and economic transformation within an increasingly hegemonic global mode of production "have all depended, in different ways, on an underlying metanarrative
of modernization" (1999: 20). The most obvious example of this is the entire
range of counterliberalisms, which offer radically different visions for social
and economic ordering that are nevertheless as fully dependent on modernity's
metanarratives as the liberal visions they oppose. But the critical stance Ferguson adopts is radical for another reason: it is decontextualizing at the same
time it contextualizes, or locates, the experience of modernity on the Zambian
Copperbelt as the reflection of a contested narrative of representation. That is
to say, Ferguson is forced to question the very legitimacy of the techniques of
engagement—primarily ethnography—that are the means through which he
establishes what is ultimately a nonmodern account of Zambian "expectations
of modernity." In other words, and this echoes the dilemmas I describe earlier,
Ferguson's study is as much a critique of modern social scientific epistemology
as it is a critique of the broader political and economic patterns that encompass
contemporary Zambia. Although a recognition of this dilemma has troubled
many anthropologists at least since the mid-1980s, Ferguson's book is, among
other things, evidence for how unsettling this problem is in practice for traditional intellectuals. One admires Ferguson as much for his honesty as his insight; it is an ambivalent epistemological context indeed that requires one to
acknowledge "the sense of not being entitled to speak authoritatively about an
ethnographically known place" (p. 20).

Ferguson's response to the methodological horn of this dilemma is to pursue what becomes in his account the ethnography that dare not speak its name;
he employs techniques that are, at most, *ethnographic*, but not as a means to the
traditional end—an ethnography expressed through a monograph. Rather, he
reconceptualizes himself as a coequal modern subject and resident of the Copperbelt, just one more confused narrator struggling to "hazard various ideas
about the larger configurations" that can only, at best, provide rough structures
of meaning within which social actors attempt to "get[] around the whole terrain . . . that continues to be haunted by ideas of modernity that are harder and

harder to make sense of in relation to the actually existing present" (p. 21). The ethnography of decline is one response, in other words, and not a solution, to the types of theoretical and phenomenological problems that I have described more generally as the dilemmas of modernity. It is no doubt true that a formal unraveling of what Giddens (1984) described as the double hermeneutic of social research on modernity, research that also is constituted and legitimated by social actors through modernity's key discursive formations, must form a kind of parallel narrative that shadows the ethnographic, scientific, or objective one. The elevation of polyphony within this emergent anthropological epistemology is a move that does create new spaces for critical reflection, even if some of the innovation here is literary-aesthetic; as Ferguson remarks parenthetically, "polyphony makes a better read" (1999: 23).

But as it turned out, the Fergusonian account of modernity was necessary but not sufficient for my own project. When I returned to Bolivia in 1998, I was fully prepared to pursue something like an ethnography of decline, particularly since I was, like many anthropologists trained more broadly in Latin American studies, fully committed to employing a neomaterialist approach in order to expose the gap within Bolivia between the discourse of (in my case legal) development and the reality of economic immiseration. This gap was pronounced. Despite a move to tether "development" to liberal trade, land, and legal policies beginning in the late 1980s with the Paz Estenssoro government, and continuing through the "neoliberal" regimes of Sánchez de Lozada (1993–97) and the center-right government of Hugo Banzer Suárez (1998–2001)—the former military dictator who had reinvented himself as a liberal dedicated to economic privatization and the growth of civilian institutions—by the late 1990s, Bolivia was in the midst of a steady decline, as indicated by a drop in real wages, a rise in unemployment, an increase in levels of political violence, the emergence of vigilantism and extrajudicial killings and attempted killings, an increase in foreign (mostly U.S.) interference in internal affairs, and in the country's enduringly dubious distinction as the second poorest county in Latin America (after Haiti).[15] And there is no question that the different periods of my research that followed over the years, which stretched right up to the eve of Evo Morales's election in December 2005, could have been framed in such a way that the distance between the discursive and material realities became the object of study and critique.

Yet to do this would have been to impose an analytical framework on a set of processes that, while similar—from a certain historical perspective—to the one described by Ferguson, nevertheless demanded to be interpreted in a distinctly different way. The study of legal and political discourse and its instrumentalities did not result in an ethnography of decline, despite the actual evidence of decline as measured by the statistical categories of scientific bureaucracy. Rather, it is better characterized as an ethnography of grandeur, the close engagement with the whole set of liberalism's universal categories, which compel actors to internalize not something as undifferentiated as "hope," but a deep and rationalized belief in the absolute certainty of a tight bundle of existential, political, economic, legal, and moral truths.

To understand ethnography—or, in Ferguson's more epistemologically modest framing, the merely ethnographic—in this way is, among other things, to shift the focus away from people's experiences of deprivation and economic exploitation, the material conditions of the working and subaltern classes, whether in Kitwe or in the norte de Potosí. This is a difficult move, especially in light of what appear as unarticulated, but nevertheless sharp, ethical imperatives that accompany a social research project that unfolds through the lives of people who find meaning and dignity at modernity's ragged edges. But I would argue that when a local legal intellectual in the norte de Potosí, who is also a subsistence farmer and pastoralist living precariously at 3,800 meters, with a yearly income of less than U.S. $200, expounds at length on the benefits to Bolivia in general, and to him and his family in particular, of *los derechos humanos universales*, I have a corresponding duty not to report this ethnographic testimony as a form of false consciousness, as proof that peasants and workers in Bolivia have a mistaken understanding of their role in history. In other words, to contextualize my interlocutor's self-consciously reasoned belief in the transformative power of liberalism, to locate it in relation to any number of poststructuralist or political economic analytical models, to interpret it in light of what I know to be objectively true when social and economic life in Bolivia is gauged comparatively, would be to deny him agency, to convert a necessarily engaged ethnography into just another enlightened paternalism.

If the foregoing describes the different contexts and central arguments within which the materials (taken as a whole) that follow must be located, the rest of the book is, in a sense, a series of corollary arguments anchored in what are at places quite detailed descriptions of Bolivian encounters with law and liberalism in the norte de Potosí. But before the descriptive lens is narrowed, Chapter 2 develops a set of historical and theoretical frameworks for understanding law in Bolivia beyond what can be accomplished in an introduction. Chapter 3 then examines the ways in which Bolivians appropriate transnational legal discourses in the process of producing a kind of vernacular normativity that shapes, and is shaped by, the dominant patterns of intention in postcolonial Bolivia. Chapter 4 explores the ways in which gender becomes another key social category in Bolivia through which the points of tension created by the engagement with liberal legality are brought into sharp contrast; indeed, the study of the emergence of new narratives of gender, and gendered narratives, within the law provides one of the best ethnographic windows into the way relations are power are being reordered in contemporary Bolivia. In Chapter 5, I examine the experience of becoming liberal in Bolivia through another key mode: the recent relocation of Bolivia, and Bolivians, within a dominant transnational ethical regime—universal human rights—after yet one more in a long line of interliberal periods. Chapter 6 moves beyond the boundaries of law to examine what I describe earlier as the problem of internal contradiction: the dilemma that emerges, especially for the poor and marginalized in Bolivia, from the fact that liberalism's more materially benign dimensions—universal human rights, for example—are necessarily bundled with a particular conception of the individual and his relationship with the fruits of his labor, a conception that, when expressed in practice, has the effect of diminishing liberalism's moral promises.

The bulk of the sustained ethnographic attentiveness that forms this book's foundation was completed in August of 2005. In the meantime, Bolivia has entered yet another period in which the project of modernity through liberalism has been called into question. I discuss these developments in the Conclusion, which reflects in part the period of my research conducted on the eve of what is often described as an epochal rupture: the election of Evo Morales, the creation of a Constituent Assembly, and the chaotic sharpening of regional and ideological dynamics within Bolivia. As will become clear, however, well before the concluding chapter, I am skeptical of this millenarian way of interpreting contemporary developments in Bolivia, as ambiguous and fraught with peril as they must remain for those who would characterize them.

2 Paris in the Andes

Law and the Modern Subject

THE FORMAL MOMENT WHEN BOLIVIA EMERGED from nothing—as an idea, a geopoliti-
cal space, and, eventually, a legal and political community in a permanent state
of contested becoming—can be measured fairly precisely: August 6, 1825, when
the regions of the old *Audiencia de Charcas* (an administrative division of the
Spanish colonial empire) were pulled together by a group of heroic and out-
sized Enlightenment soldier-philosophers and declared formally independent
from both the Spanish empire and the larger and more consequential polities
to the north (Peru) and south (Argentina and Chile). Just as the history of the
large and diverse native populations of the New World cannot be separated
from the discursive frameworks that, in a very real and important sense, constituted them (Todorov 1999), so too with Bolivia. Like other Latin American
nation-states, Bolivia must be understood first and foremost as an idea that is
embodied by a set of basic assumptions about human nature, the operation of
natural laws in the social world, the proper ends of life, and the relationship
between the individual and community (see especially Larson 2004 and Mignolo
2005).[1] To understand Bolivia in this way is not to deny or ignore what might
be described as the actually existing cultural and moral diversity within the
ideological space demarcated by "Bolivia." But it is to acknowledge that it was
born from a particular ideological and moral vision, one that has shaped social
and political life ever since, even if at times this vision has been obscured, rejected, or contradicted. By understanding Bolivia in this way, two important
distinctions should be drawn. If Bolivia must be understood as the embodiment of a set of basic assumptions, it is also true that (1) the idea of Bolivia is
just that, an idea, one that was not inevitable or permanent or prior to other

possibilities; and (2) the creation of Bolivia as an expression of a particular moral and ideological vision was an essentially political move, one that reflected—and, to the extent that the idea of Bolivia remains contested, continues to reflect—the assertion of will by groups of social actors whose interests were served by the emergence of *this* Bolivia.

Yet even if the idea of Bolivia brings together a contested and diffuse constellation of meanings and social practices, we must nevertheless develop the tools to see the reflections of this broader process in the most local of events, and be able to track the impact of these local reflections on the broader process. A basic argument of this chapter, and the book as a whole, is that "law" is a preeminent category through which the idea of Bolivia continues to be shaped. I enclose law in quotes in order to signal that the meanings of law in modern Bolivia have remained fluid, even as particular legal forms have been strategically reified during certain periods by various social groups or individuals as a way to harness legal discourse and deploy it in the service of a range of different purposes. This chapter establishes a framework through which the constitution of Bolivia through law can be understood, both analytically and through reference to certain key moments in this intellectual-historical process. Malagón Barceló's aphorism (1961: 4) that "America was born beneath the juridical sign" is as true for Bolivia as it is for other countries in Latin America, and several ways will be proposed in which the essential role of law and legal processes in framing structures of meaning can be understood as the book moves through its different ethnographic and ethnohistorical narratives.

The Problem of Law as an Object of Study

When I first began my research in Bolivia in 1996, I did so without much guidance from the literature. Even more so than in other areas of Latin America, there was—and still is—a dearth of studies of and about law. By "studies" I mean accounts of research that combine a sustained empirical engagement with law-in-action with critical or analytical reflection. By contrast, the literature is replete with legal histories (e.g., Vaca Díez 1998), works of jurisprudence (e.g., Guzmán Santiesteban and Muñoz Crespo 2002), studies of the relationship between legal and other state institutions (e.g., Valencia Vega 1984), even biographies of modern Bolivia's lawgivers and historically important *jurisconsultos* (e.g., Gómez de Aranda 1978). Despite the obvious differences within this body of work, the Bolivian legal studies literature has three things in common, three main characteristics that made it an incomplete guide in light of the sorts of questions I was interested in pursuing. First, law is understood in such a way that its meanings are fixed, even if they remain to be discovered through the techniques of analytical jurisprudence. Law, in this sense, is not connotative, but denotative: by referring to law, one indicates a finite set of universal normative principles that are, to greater or lesser degrees of accuracy, codified through the positive law of the legitimate sovereign; in this case, the Bolivian state. The only method for correctly discovering the form that universal normative principles *must* take through the positive law is deduction: from the set of normative first principles, demonstrated or not, intuited or discerned in the Platonic ether through the application of reason, a list of laws can be logically derived. Law, in other words, is taken to mean this jurisprudential process, and the ontological assumptions that prefigure it.[2]

This jurisprudential understanding of law denies even the possibility of social scientific attempts to either describe the nature of law, or to give an account of what law does in practice. And because law is defined in a necessary relation to the state and its agents—those legislators, law professors, and barristers whose highly trained legal minds are brought together to refine the expression of the law by refining and correcting the deductions from first principles that reveal it—the law's reach is coextensive with the reach of the state and its representatives. This means that the entire expanse of rural Bolivia, or so I believed, would be "outside the law" (Harris 1996). This also implied that only an empirical study of *normativity* was possible, because obviously rural Bolivians lived their lives within systems of rules of some kind, but not of law, whose presence, like the presence of the state itself, was—on this view—at best symbolic, the isolated *juzgado de instrucción* or police official stranded in a sea of legal and political alterity.

Second, if Bolivian legal studies present a rigid definition of what law is, they also reflect a carefully circumscribed view of the spaces where law is done: courtrooms, conclaves of influential urban bar associations, law faculty seminars, the chambers of congress, and, above all, the writings and analyses of those individuals whose task it is to deduce the law. The spaces of the legal imagination in Bolivia are closely linked with a set of parallel discourses that similarly divide the Bolivian nation into zones that reflect both ethnic and class imperatives. The geography of law in Bolivia also is mirrored in what is a stark ideological urban/rural dichotomy through which *el campo*, the countryside, is contrasted with the city: While the city is the site of all of the civilizing influences of church and state (including the law), the campo lies outside the walls and is governed by a mélange of *costumbres*, or customs. These customs operate to keep in check a population whose natural passions and vices would otherwise lead to violence and chaos, but whose status as norms locates them in the category of *non*-law, and, depending on the norm in question—especially those prescribing corporal and even capital punishment for certain transgressions—even *ill*-law, a category against which the law (of the city) must maintain constant vigilance. Another way to make this point is to say that the dominant imaginary in Bolivia construes law as concentric. The first circle represents law in its purest theoretical and practical expressions. With each wider circle, the law becomes more and more diluted until finally the universe of normativity becomes nonlegal; then, at the outer edges, normativity expands so far outside the core of legality that it must be defined in opposition to law, as *illegal* normativity.

Finally, just as Bolivian legal studies offer a narrow view of what sets of ideas or practices should be considered as law, and a correspondingly restricted understanding of the social spaces within which these legal ideas and practices are to be found, so too does the literature present an orthodox view of *who* can be considered legal actors. Apart from the range of social agents who find themselves subject to the law for various reasons, or who find occasion to appropriate state law at one time or another, true legal actors are those individuals who live their lives within the law and whose activities shape it and reinforce its dominance. Private lawyers, judges, *fiscales públicos*, or public prosecutors, legislators, legal scholars, and, to a lesser extent, legal journalists, who specialize in reporting on, and describing the social significance of, new and important legislation, form the main body of legal actors, according to the doctrinal, or jurisprudential, view.

However, as this book shows, each of these major assumptions about law in Bolivia—the what, where, and who of law—turned out to be empirically mistaken. Even if we grant, for purposes of argument, the narrow definitions of law expressed within mainstream Bolivian legal studies, one nevertheless encounters law, legal spaces, and legal actors in places like the norte de Potosí, that traditional zone of exclusion and alterity that is the antithesis of everything urban Bolivians have been taught to believe about their modernity. Moreover, an interesting set of problems is created by this empirical gap between orthodox legal understandings and the reality of everyday lived experience, in which law's range in Bolivia cannot be mapped concentrically, but must be envisioned as a network of legality, what Boaventura de Sousa Santos (1995) has called "interlegality." This is not simply, or even most importantly, a theoretical problem, but is rather a social one in which the dominant legal imaginary in Bolivia works to obscure the actual unfolding of law.

Law in Bolivia is—from both an analytical and discursive angle—much more than the jurisprudence of legal scholars and the rules of the constitutional court; given this, the spaces where law is done are broadly diffused and, while they obviously include courts, law offices, and the like, also include other spaces, like the meeting rooms of rural political leaders, or the offices of transnational human rights NGOs, which serve as places where law is encountered and shaped; and, finally, the category of legal actors must be enlarged to include all the different people who move in and out of the boundaries of this more expansive vision of law. In doing so, for example, a range of peasant intellectuals—among others—must be understood as "learned in the law," because the understanding of law adopted here decouples it from its traditional institutional associations. As will be seen, an individual's deep engagement with law can have different rationales and different sources of legitimacy. To say this is not to deny the hegemony of law's traditional locations or regimes of practice, but the perspective developed here, based as it is on a sustained ethnographic engagement with law in its different registers in Bolivia, implies an alternative legal cosmology.

From Legality to Sociolegality and Back Again

My first instinct, once it became clear that law in Bolivia operated at different registers, and in different modalities, than I had been led to originally believe, was to try and capture this expansiveness by moving from a focus on law to a focus on *sociolaw*. A sociolegal framework expresses several analytical and methodological moves. It reflects the view that law as a system of enforceable rules is always ontologically embedded in, and thus inseparable from, a broader set of social categories. So even if law can be isolated for limited political, theoretical, or other purposes, its boundaries essentially commingle with the nonlegal in such a way that law should not be treated as discrete and fixed. The move to sociolegality also has an important methodological implication: If "law" is reconceptualized as "sociolaw," a way of understanding normativity that views law as essentially social and thus constituted *through*—not constitutive *of*—practice, then it can be studied like any other social process. The idea of sociolegality is thus a way of legitimating the empirical study of law *in* society. Finally, the move from legality to sociolegality is a way of emphasizing the influence on law of the wider political-economic structures of power which, from time to time, coopt law, and, at the same time, using the social scientific study of this law-power nexus in order to destabilize it. A sociolegal approach to law thus expresses its own type of normativity in that it reflects, particularly in its legal anthropological variations, an ethical commitment on the part of the researcher to use an expansive and essentially social understanding of law in order to decenter it. This is made possible, in part, because a sociolegal perspective relativizes law, not in a cultural sense, but by treating it as simply one more, admittedly consequential, social category, subject to the usual forms of political and economic influence and inequality.

However, the problem with treating law as sociolaw is that this is first and foremost an analytical procedure with roots in the legal realist movement of the early twentieth century, rather than a description of the empirical experience of law in any one place and time. In other words, a sociolegal framework merely replaces jurisprudential biases with social ones. One assumes that law is just another porous social category, fully dependent on other social processes and institutions, protean, fickle, and impossible to delimit with any sense of certainty. It is important to underscore how much sociolegality, as an analytical framework, exists in an almost dialectical relationship with the orthodox jurisprudential approach to law: All of the assumptions about law from the jurisprudential perspective are simply inverted. In doing so, however, sociolegal studies commit the same error as jurisprudence—the meanings of law/sociolaw are fixed in advance—even as they drop the two aspects of jurisprudence that have made it such a dominant orientation: its analytical rigor and willingness to define law in such narrow terms that its categories can be easily articulated and classified. The sociolegal approach very easily can become a social scientific nightmare, in that law is described so broadly, and with so little attention to theoretical coherence, that it becomes coextensive with society itself. There are two basic problems with this. As a matter of analysis, one cannot have it both ways: law must either exist in different ways in different places as a distinct and articulable social category, or not. It is simply not sufficient to isolate law but then go on to treat it as if it were essentially indeterminate. Indeterminacy is not the same thing as complexity. If law does indeed describe a more complicated normative universe than the one assumed by jurisprudence, this does not mean that with different and more flexible methodological tools, or guided by a different epistemological framework, one cannot (or should not) determine what law is and does in particular places or within particular historical trajectories.

Even more problematic is the fact that a sociolegal approach to law, despite its supposed social scientific and thus empirical commitments, cannot do justice to the actual meanings of law for a whole range of social actors. By assuming that law is so diffuse that its boundaries are essentially those of society itself, sociolegal studies are unable to account for the ways in which law's supposed categorical rigidity, rhetorical preeminence, and normative sovereignty, are all characteristics of law that many social actors themselves depend on, strategically appropriate, and, above all, reproduce. It is an act of ethnographic sleight-of-hand, not to mention theoretical implausibility, to describe at great lengths the ways in which the formality and boundedness of law are key social markers, but then go on to explain away the local commitment to formality and boundedness as products of a kind of false consciousness and thus not dimensions of what law is in the particular social context in which these markers are found. To make this point another way: Law can be both more *and* less determinate than the jurisprudential approach assumes.

The analytical alternative to both the jurisprudential—which dominates Bolivian legal studies—and the sociolegal, which is the paradigm for most social scientists interested in law, is one that manages to contextualize law at the same time it takes law's philosophical self-assertions seriously, which operate in society even though they are supposed to be isolated from it. So when the Bolivian congress promulgates a new law that is justified on the basis of its jurisprudential or deductive truth, or when the idea of human rights is introduced to rural Bolivians as the expression of a timeless universal morality, the philosophical or conceptual dimensions of this law acting in society cannot be understood either through redefinition or by assuming that they are other than what they purport to be. This is because claims for universality, in the case of human rights, or assertions of jurisprudential correctness, in the case of notable Bolivian legal reforms over the last twenty years, are examples of the social life of legal ideas, not evidence of legal ideas *as* social life (or sociolegality), which is, as I have argued, a theoretically dubious inversion meant to capture the complicated ways in which legal ideas are expressed in social practice. If there is a major assumption of the alternative developed here, and one that guides this analysis of law throughout this book, it is that the contours of law have both theoretical *and* social dimensions, each of which can and must figure into any attempt to understand the power and meanings of law as both a distinct category of lived experience, and as a means through which broader historical patterns of intention are instantiated.

The move from sociolegality "back" to legality reflects not only what might be argued is a more methodologically sound approach to what was understood by the legal realists as the gap between law-in-the-books and law-in-action, an advance (if it is one) that is ironic given the fact that the sociolegal response was justified, in part, because of its greater ability to distinguish between the reality and rhetoric of law. (That is to say, by returning to sharper analytical lines and restoring to legal ideas their conceptual autonomy, we are better able to understand the different ways in which these two dimensions define law, not as a matter of abstract theory, but as the result of what I have described else-where as "ethical theory as social practice" [Goodale 2006a], the ways in which social actors theorize about law and other normativities as a form of social agency.)

As the examination of legality in Bolivia shows, this move also offers much more than a heightened sense of what Hegel would have described as law's complicated empirical actuality (*l'effectivité empirique*). Instead, a willingness to see law in Bolivia and elsewhere for what it purports to be and do imparts to the study of law a stronger sense of ethical commitment, especially when, as here, the encounter with law is also the encounter with subaltern social actors for whom the formal conceptual and institutional dimensions of law are all im-portant. Seen in this light, the sociolegal approach that I move away from here always runs the risk—again, somewhat ironically, given the intentions of many of the its practitioners—of obscuring the fact that what it understands to be the ideological aspects of law's jurisprudential registers are actually key factors that make law a viable means through which socioeconomic or other kinds of in-justices can be addressed by precisely those groups in society who would ap-pear to be furthest from law's reach.

It is useful in this context to recall E. P. Thompson's little-invoked, but ir-resistibly persuasive, analysis of the relationship between ideology and law, which he develops at the end of his social history of England's Black Act of 1723. As he says (Thompson 1975):

> the law . . . may be seen instrumentally as mediating and reinforcing existent class relations and, ideologically, as offering to these a legitimation. But we must press our definitions a little further. For if we say that existent class rela-tions were mediated by the law, this is not the same thing as saying that the law was no more than those relations translated into other terms, which masked or mystified the reality. . . . For class relations were expressed, not in any way one likes, but *through the forms of law*; and the law . . . has its own characteristics, its own independent history and logic of evolution . . . . We reach, then, not a

simple conclusion (law = class power) but a complex and contradictory one. . . .
The rhetoric and the rules of a society are something a great deal more than
sham. In the same moment they may modify, in profound ways, the behaviour
of the powerful, and mystify the powerless. (262–65; emphasis in original)

A sociolegal approach to law too often ignores Thompson's basic point: To
not treat the forms of law seriously, in their own terms, is to miss both the
consequences of law's power, and what would now be described as law's
emancipatory potential for those most in need of law's imperfect and all-too-
easily manipulated logics.

By refocusing on the ideas that are embedded in law-in-the-books, anthropologists, and others interested in understanding legality empirically, quite
often must align themselves more closely with social actors as they struggle to
make sense of law, locate themselves in relation to its demands, and, as I have
suggested, come to harness its potential in their struggles for justice and dignity. Another way of describing the contrast between the framework adopted
here and the sociolegal response to a naïve jurisprudence is to say that I reject
the attempt to *objectify* law, as reflected in either formal jurisprudence (where
law is the objective result of a process of deductive reasoning) or sociolegal
studies, in which law is treated as just another social process. Rather, the approach to law that is employed throughout this book is thoroughly intersubjective; it assumes that the researcher participates with other social actors in the
encounter with law and thus the broader patterns of intention (like liberalism)
that law serves. To see the study of law in this way is to avoid many hoary disputes over epistemology, the political implications of social research, and the
relationship between "subject" and "object." The kind of research that forms
the backdrop for this book shows that encounters with law, which are reflected
through what is a social process of legal interpretation, involve the conceptual
and the empirical in equal parts. Indeed, as will be even clearer in the next section, to "study" law empirically in Bolivia is also to cotheorize its meanings
with other social actors, to contribute to what can be understood as a "vernacular jurisprudence," even if such participation is bracketed along with other
forms of social practice in order to create analytical distance.

Law and Intellectual History, Law as Intellectual History

As the different chapters in this book demonstrate, the law in Bolivia instantiates
at all levels a set of broader frameworks that shape social life and the contested

status of the modern subject. But as I reflected more carefully on the ways in which a particular kind of social research reveals these broader frameworks, it became clear that the study of law in Bolivia, despite efforts to recenter law in relation to other social categories, could not be separated from the study of ideas in history. Put another way: The study of law in Bolivia *is* the study of ideas in history. Law in Bolivia obviously is not static—it evolves, is transformed, takes on different political meanings, serves now this alignment of political-economic interests, now that alignment. Although, as I argued earlier, law in Bolivia shifts according to both its own jurisprudential logics and the social logics that interpenetrate with them, these are never fully contained; they never form a perfectly symmetrical system. Even the most arcane provisions of the Bolivian Code of Civil Procedure, for example, reflect a broader idea, or, even more, constellations of significant ideas that come together to form what I have been describing as patterns of intention. This means that in order to study law in Bolivia it is necessarily to study intellectual history, because the constellation of significant ideas within which law is embedded is itself an artifact of history. This emphasis is important for understanding the basic thrust of this book: If the study of law is the study of intellectual history, and the study of intellectual history is the key to understanding modern subjectivity in Bolivia, then to study law is, in part, to study the constitution of the modern subject in Bolivia. This quasi-syllogism is useful only if law-as-intellectual-history is central or primary compared with other, nonlegal, intellectual histories that also might shine a light on Bolivia's contested modernity. But what does it really mean to say that the study of law is the study of intellectual history? This is not an intellectual history that privileges great thinkers, although when important ideas expressed through law are put into practice, it is usually through the efforts of certain individuals who are compelled by the grandeur of these ideas, by their promise of emancipation, and by the way they represent, as with human rights, a stark contrast to local understandings of gender, the relationship of the individual to the collective, and ideal forms of governance.

Rather, this is an intellectual history that studies the social force of ideas, the way social actors encounter and constitute ideas as part of broader forms of social practice. Again, to use human rights as an example, they embody a set of ideas about the world that are becoming increasingly dominant at certain levels, and an intellectual history of this development locates the appropriation, vernacularization, and politicization of human rights within the broader historical trajectory that contextualizes these "local" encounters.[3] One can say that researchers actually participate in these intellectual histories by narrating them, and the close engagements associated with ethnographic research and analysis mean that by studying law-as-intellectual-history, the researcher often will participate even more directly by cotheorizing with interlocutors who struggle to come to terms with the increasingly complicated transnational legal universes that have emerged over the last fifteen years. The study of law-as-intellectual-history is also, therefore, in part constitutive of particular intellectual histories. This makes this approach to law in society itself normative, a fact that opens up to a range of ethical issues.

The Anthropology of Law as Critical Intellectual History

Before I direct the angle of focus away from the analytical framework within which the study of law in this book should be understood in order to describe the specific historical context that frames legality in Bolivia, I must add one more dimension. If the study of law is necessarily the study of the intellectual histories that come to produce the modern subject, this move—from legal studies as such to legal studies as intellectual history—is not simply an effort to forge a more nuanced critical methodology. Because of its epistemological assumptions, it is all the more important that something other than *verstehen* is foregrounded as the outlines of the wider intellectual history begin to emerge. To produce knowledge about the patterns of intention within which law is constituted and made instrumental, and to narrate the lives of social actors who move within and against the boundaries of law, is necessarily to reshape, even if in imperceptible ways, the local political and legal landscapes whose topographies provide the researcher's data. It is not sufficient to remain silent about this fact, which is yet one more reason why the kind of intellectual history that frames my approach to law in Bolivia can never be dominated by what Ian Hacking refers to, in his review of Colin McGinn's book *Mindsight*, as the "dry business of referring and refuting" (2005: 70), the development of alternative modes of social analysis as a kind of intellectual scrummage. Rather, because the encounter with law in Bolivia also is necessarily the encounter with unequally weighted and contested structures of power, the researcher serves a valuable purpose by maintaining a skeptical distance between law and its stated purposes. This is an orientation that anthropologists of law in particular have found useful over the last fifteen years (see Lazarus-Black and Hirsch 1994; Wilson 2001; Riles 2000), and the ethnographic engagement with law in context does lend itself to this kind of critical interposition (see, e.g., Starr and

Goodale 2002), but other scholars also have embraced skepticism as a methodological framing device (e.g., Kairys 1996; Unger 1986).

In arguing for locating the study of law within an intellectual history that is critical, I am linking it explicitly to other approaches to social research in which criticality is used to qualify social inquiry by making it purposive beyond the narrow confines of the inquiry itself. There is, of course, a way in which a social theorist can assume a kind of permanent skepticism toward theoretical or social scientific paradigms and orthodox frames of reference, but this is not what I mean here. In reconceptualizing the study of law in Bolivia as *critical* intellectual history, it is distinguished by the three basic dimensions that characterize critical social research more generally, according to the political philosopher James Bohman in his essay (2005) on the history of critical theory: it is explanatory, practical, and normative. It is explanatory to the extent to which it identifies how law actually is used to reinforce broader historical patterns of intention in Bolivia that increase political and economic hegemony, and decrease what can neutrally be described as the possibilities for freedom. It is practical to the extent to which the researcher encounters historical patterns of intention mediated by law *alongside* key interlocutors and other social actors, which means that the reconstruction of the relationship between law and these patterns of intention is necessarily collaborative. As would be anticipated by Horkheimer (1982) and other critical theorists, the study of law as critical intellectual history identifies individuals and groups who are in a position—partly as a result of their collaboration, partly through the range of other social circumstances—to change the relationship between law, the force of particular ideas in history, and structures of economic and political domination.

Finally, the study of law as critical intellectual history is normative in that, as Bohman describes of critical theory more broadly, it aims to "provide both clear norms for criticism and achievable practical goals for social transformation" (2005). As we will see, there is a remarkable convergence between the main practical goal for social transformation within critical theory more generally—a movement toward more control by individuals and communities over the conditions of social life—and the specific objectives of individuals and communities in different parts of contemporary Bolivia. It is therefore possible to draw from this historical-theoretical tradition in framing the study of law despite the fact that the patterns of intention that such a critical study reveal are quite different from—though isomorphic with—those against which critical

theory has been historically directed (e.g., industrial capitalism, the culture in-
dustry) in the northern European or American metropoles.

Paris in the Andes

After the founding of the new Bolivian nation in 1825, one of the first and most
important acts by the uneasy alliance of ex-royalist and victorious republican
leaders was to write a new constitution.[4] As in France and the United States
after their revolutionary moments, the Bolivian leaders understood that a new
constitution of laws was both a symbol of the aspirations of the new republic,
and the means through which the modern Bolivian subject would be shaped.
The Bolivian Constitution of 1825 was a classic Enlightenment legal document.
It established the separation of powers between the legislative, executive, and
judiciary, and established a system of representative democracy modeled in
large part on the U.S. Constitution and inspired by both the Declaration of Independence and the French Declaration of the Rights of Man. Although this
first constitution was replaced by the 1826 Boliviarian constitution—which remained in effect until 1831—the essential legal-ideological structure had been
established. Bolivia was to be a nation founded through the rule of enlightened
and rational law; the legitimacy of political power was based in the will of the
citizenry (even though the class of citizens was significantly restricted, as it was
in the United States); the legal framework of the state reflected a compact between citizens and their representatives in government; the judiciary was to be
composed of legal scholars whose role was to measure acts of the other
branches of government against the standards of natural law; the Bolivian citizen was redefined as a legal category based on a framework of interlocking civil
and natural rights; and, finally, the initial constitutional framework in Bolivia
was premised on the belief that the law should both shape the emergence of a
modern and liberal Bolivia, and serve as a bulwark against the illiberal concentration of political power based on force, heredity, or slavery.

What could be described as the disciplinarity of Bolivia's initial legal-
ideological framework is especially important for my purposes. Although the
Bolivarian constitution of 1826–31 was anomalous in certain respects (for example, in the way it created a life presidency), in others, it established the basis
on which law would become the preeminent means through which Bolivian
subjectivities would be constituted, an idea that was reproduced throughout
the country in every provincial town, within every rural juzgado de instrucción.
To take just one example: the *Cámara de Censores*, or Chamber of Censors (an

entity with both Enlightenment and Roman roots), was given the legal responsibility to oversee the moral education of the Bolivian citizen and to nurture
the development of arts, sciences, and public culture (Bol. Cons. of 1826, Ch. 2,
Art. 60).

Bolivia's legal-ideological foundations have been interpreted in several
different ways by subsequent historians, political activists, and legal reformers.
The first has been to treat these Enlightenment and liberal origins as something
like a sham, especially in light of the fact that throughout most of the nineteenth century (and beyond) very few of the founding legal, political, or ethical
ideals were realized in practice in any meaningful way. Until after Bolivia's dis-
astrous involvement in the War of the Pacific (1879–80), and the promulgation
of the reformist 1880 Constitution, the argument goes, social and legal relations
in Bolivia continued more or less uninterrupted from the late-colonial pattern
of exploitation and elite aggrandizement, as symbolized by the emergence of
antiliberal caudillos and the strengthening of hacienda landowning in different parts of the country (see, e.g., Dunkerley 1981; Peralta Ruiz and Irurozqui
Victoriano 2000).

Another perspective on Bolivia's initial legal-ideological framework has
been to see it as relatively successful in terms of its stated objectives, but to view
it from the vantage point of what is understood as a separate, unequal, and
parallel political space: the one occupied by Bolivia's different indigenous ethnic groups, who were formally excluded from the early nineteenth century
state constitutions on the basis of literacy or wealth restrictions. This has been
the approach taken by a generation of influential anthropologists, historians,
and ethnohistorians, who have described the state-Indian relationship through
a number of social compacts with prerepublican origins (see, e.g., Condarco
Morales 1982; Larson 2004; Mendieta Parada 2006; Platt 1982; Rodríguez 1983).
This strand of analysis conceptualizes the legal-ideological reach and power of
the early Bolivian state concentrically: the farther from La Paz or Sucre or perhaps Cochabamba, the sharper the boundaries between what is understood as a
series of liberal city-states and the rest of indigenous Bolivia, which is forced
into relations with the state to greater or lesser degrees depending on the era
and particular set of political and economic circumstances.

Finally, there is what could be understood as the pessimistic approach to
Bolivia's legal-ideological foundations. Here, Bolivian history since 1825 is read
as the tragically incomplete triumph of modernity over tradition and back-
wardness (in the form of rural Bolivia, not its hegemonic urban elites), in

which a republican Bolivia was forged from the fires of revolution and the nation's march toward progress has been obstructed by periods of military dictatorship, economic catastrophe, the place of Bolivia within global capitalist networks, and, especially, the continuing problem of Bolivia's majority indigenous populations (see especially Alcídes Arguedas's social critique *Pueblo enfermo* [1909] and his novel *Raza de bronce* [1919]).[5]

The perspective adopted in this book, which will be explored in detail through the consideration of both specific encounters with law and liberalism, and the movement between these specific encounters and the broader patterns of intention that give them meaning, is, in part, a synthesis of each of these different approaches to Bolivia's postindependence legal history. There is no question that—from a certain instrumentalist perspective—the abject failure to realize Bolivia's early constitutional principles in practice does cast a shadow over the entire historical process, so that it is difficult not to treat early Bolivian constitutional history as a kind of caricature. But to focus on what is somewhat inaccurately described as the gap between theory and practice is to miss what is, I argue, the most salient features of Bolivia's emergence as a nation *through* law. Moreover, the anthropological and ethnohistorical approach, which has been recently picked up and reproduced within current political and social struggles, serves in part as a necessary corrective in that it treats rural and indigenous Bolivia as a source of history, albeit in a form that is often oppositional: to the state, to economic and political elites, and, more recently, to the presence of powerful transnational actors. Nevertheless, the two Bolivias perspective on legal and political history tends to reify what are in fact more fluid relationships (urban/rural, mestizo/Indian, runa/q'ara, etc.). It also tends to underemphasize the difference between what I have described elsewhere as "categories of exclusion" (Goodale 2006b)—many of which are the products of law—and the more important history of social practice in Bolivia through which these formal categories become problematized and challenged. Finally, the pessimistic approach to Bolivia's liberal constitutional origins has the advantage of taking such ideological pretenses seriously; in other words, even if this triumphalism can be easily dismissed as mere justification for what has always been the concentration of power within a shifting group of elites in Bolivia, what cannot be so easily dismissed are the implications of Bolivia's legal-ideological foundations. If the intellectual history of modern Bolivia reveals anything, it is that the legal-ideological principles through which Bolivia was conceived have shaped Bolivia's trajectory since 1825, in all areas of life and in all regions of the country. This book is, in part, an attempt to explain why and how these principles have been so consequential.

Patterns of Intention

So far I have described the emergence of liberal Bolivia in broad terms, but here I want to make several arguments about the importance of Bolivia's legal-ideological foundations as specific as possible. The first is that modern Bolivia was constituted in a very particular way, through a liberal conception of law in which law does much more than merely establish the mechanism for creating and enforcing rules, or for expressing moral aspirations; rather, law is the basic social mechanism through which subjectivity itself is given its fullest meanings. The conception of the person that is forged through liberal legal categories can be fairly easily characterized. First, the individual is *defined by* a set of inherent rights. Although there is some dispute about what was understood to be the ultimate provenance of rights in the post-Enlightenment constitutions of Latin America (Trigo 1958; Vaca Díez 1998), there is no question that the framers of Bolivia's initial liberal legal foundations intended to reimagine the Bolivian citizen as the bearer of natural and inalienable rights, those rights which, as in the late eighteenth century United States and France, were understood to be as self-evident as the basic fact of humanness itself. By inscribing Bolivia within a natural rights framework, those who first envisioned Bolivia made the *individual* the first and last social unit, and *rights*—and not some other normative possibility—were made the legal means through which the individual related to both other individuals and to the state.

Second, the liberal legality at the foundation of modern Bolivia is both self-legitimating and legitimizing: It is a law whose legitimacy is embedded within its logics and procedures, rather than in an external political or moral authority (such as the church), and it is the means through which the political, the economic, and the moral are themselves legitimated. As Carty puts it, liberal legality is characterized by "everywhereness" (1991: 196); it is a legal-ideological orientation in which law must encompass and justify every other dimension of society. This expansiveness is what Peter Fitzpatrick describes as the modern "grounds of law" (2001).

Third, liberal legality is predicated on a very particular understanding of rationality, in which the law is seen as a reflection of reason expressing itself in the public sphere. This is a rationality that is both individualist and technocratic. Finally, the liberal legality at the core of modern Bolivia is committed to the same range of utopian assumptions about mankind and its purposes as Enlightenment liberalism more generally: that mankind is ultimately perfectible through reason and the application of technocratic knowledge; that human progress is unilineal, predictable, and inevitable, despite the presence of barriers such as superstition, traditional folkways, and the darker angels of human nature; that the social and the physical are subject to human control and eventual mastery; and that the moral universe is subject to the laws of nature, so that moral or ethical systems become (ideally) just another expression of the natural universe's order and regularity.

Now the intent of arguing for the importance of liberal legality in understanding postcolonial Bolivia must not be misread. I am not saying that Bolivian encounters with law and liberalism should be seen as a triumph of Enlightenment liberalism expressing itself throughout Bolivian history, nor do I claim that even the initial enactment of modern Bolivia through law was a kind of uncontested or unitary event. There is, however, a basic fact about Bolivian history that has been overlooked by historians and critics who have constructed a picture of postcolonial Bolivia marked by unremitting political, economic, and legal chaos: The liberal legal framework within which Bolivia was conceived has been its *only* enduring legal-ideological framework. What I mean is that even if different periods of Bolivian history—indeed, long stretches of it—can be characterized as non- or even illiberal, Bolivia's essential legal-ideological framework nevertheless persisted and shaped history, even when it only served as a utopian mirror, or lighting rod for socialist or syndicalist agitation, or even the reason for national revolution. In other words, I argue that the modern Bolivian experience has always been shaped by the presence of liberalism expressing itself through law; that this legal-ideological framework is the lodestar of modern Bolivia, but a lodestar that has shaped Bolivia's trajectory even when—or especially when—Bolivians have resisted it, or worked to dismantle it, or held it up to ridicule. Another way of making this point is to say that liberalism expressed through law is the negative key to the Bolivian modern.[6]

We can see the presence of this pattern of intention on either side of different moments in Bolivian history, moments that have been described as marking qualitative breaks or profound disruptures in the trajectory of modern Bolivia.[7] Three particularly important moments illustrate this point: the 1880 Law of Expropriation and the subsequent push by the post–War of the Pacific governments to accelerate the process of land capitalization in rural areas; the 1952

National Revolution and 1953 Agrarian Reform; and the culmination of "ne-oliberal" consolidation under Gonzalo Sánchez de Lozada and the passage of Law 1551 (Law of Popular Participation). Klein's is a very good summary of the impact of the War of the Pacific (1879–80) on Bolivian social, political, and legal life: "The year 1880 marked a major turning point in Bolivian history" (1982: 149). Yet despite the fact that Bolivia lost its access to the sea and the fact that postwar governments happened to be at least nominally civilian (something that is usually invested with extraordinary importance), the basic legal-ideological foundations continued to shape many aspects of public life in Bolivia, even if only as a discursive foil or as the opposite side of what might be understood as a "negative dialectic" of Bolivian history.[8]

For example, the Law of Expropriation, which enacted a series of measures directed toward rural land tenure patterns, only made more effective what was a process of transformation in rural landholding that had begun long *before* 1880. There is no question that the emergence of Bolivia as a liberal abstraction would eventually have a more practical transformative effect on Bolivia's peasants, whose lifeways symbolized those antiliberal barriers described earlier; there is also no question that, as we will see in subsequent chapters, rural people in Bolivia have always been acutely aware of their position within this master narrative of Bolivian modernity. But this is exactly my point: The postwar changes to the Constitution and the Law of Expropriation did not introduce anything into Bolivian legal or political culture that was not already fundamentally present. Rather, the developments following the catastrophe of the War of the Pacific simply magnified a preexisting pattern of intention, whose shaping presence belies talk of turning points, paradigm shifts, epochal breaks, or other millenarian ways of narrating Bolivian history.

Similarly, the 1952 National Revolution and subsequent Agrarian Reform are usually described in the apocalyptic language of epochal breaks and historical shifts. Even if it is possible to use the analytical (as distinct from the political) language of revolution to describe this period, it is important to draw a distinction between a revolution *from* and a revolution *to*. If Bolivia's National Revolution is to be understood as a revolution "from"—as it normally is—then it must be a revolution away from something. In this framing, the National Revolution is seen as a profound turning away from a corrupt liberalism and its discontents, which had, the argument goes, created an elite of private capitalists and landowners who built their economic and social capital on the backs of the disenfranchised Indian masses, those anachronistic exiles from Bolivia's liberal aspirations. Yet despite the fact that Bolivia's major mines were nation-alized, and haciendas were seized by victims of the *pongueaje* (personal labor service) system, and even despite the fact that for a short period of time hacen-dados and their family members were forcibly expelled from their lands or, in some instances, killed, these acts represented a turning *toward* the legal-ideological principles through which Bolivia was constituted in the first quar-ter of the nineteenth century.

Take two of the most important reforms of the *Movimiento Nacionalista Revolutionario* (MNR): the elimination of the literacy requirement in national elections, and the creation of the Agrarian Reform Commission and promulga-tion of the 1953 Agrarian Reform decree. The first act resulted in an immediate five-fold increase in Bolivia's eligible voters. As Klein says, "in one stroke, the Indian peasant masses were enfranchised, and the voting population jumped from some 200,000 to just under 1 million" (1982: 232). However, universal suf-frage does not represent a turning away from the expression of liberalism through law, but the precise opposite. So despite the fact that Bolivia's "Indian peasant masses" (Klein 1982: 232) continued to suffer economically and politi-cally at the hands of elites, they were, after the National Revolution, at least re-cast as citizens defined by the bundle of interlocking human rights that lay at the bedrock of the nation's legal and ideological foundations.

The facts of the 1953 Agrarian Reform are equally at odds with the interpre-tation of Bolivia's mid-twentieth century revolution as a rejection of the coun-try's initial legal-ideological principles. The most important result of the land reforms was the almost total abolishment of the haciendas and a diminishment of the exploitative hacendado class, which had waxed and waned since it emerged in the second half of the sixteenth century in the wake of the Toldedan reorganization of the countryside, which led to the "reduction" of Indian com-munities into new towns and the subsequent explosion in available land (see Larson 1978; Santamaría 1988; Sebill 1989).[9]

But the hacienda system was a preliberal, colonial, semifeudal anachro-nism, and although the titling of rural land at the community level can be read as evidence of a socialist or antiliberal impulse behind the events of 1952–53, I would argue that the emergence of a new class of peasant landowners, and the intense focus on securing and registering titles within existing Bolivian law, should be seen as a struggle by peasants to reconceptualize rural land tenure patterns *in terms of* Bolivia's national liberal legal principles. Moreover, the fact that titles were registered at the community level—and then, as now, individual family lands were not alienable outside several different rural jurisdictions (hamlet, minor and major *ayllu*)—should not be seen as evidence of the emergence of a kind of autochthonous Andean socialism. Rather, the rush to title lands should be understood instead as an attempt to appropriate republican and utopian ideals within a cultural framework that was capable of both opening itself to the imperatives of national liberalism and maintaining its local integrity at the same time.

Finally, the lodestar of liberal legality can be seen shaping what in Bolivia (as elsewhere) is understood as neoliberalism. It is important to distinguish between two senses of neoliberalism. The first could be described as the historic-analytical. This is the use of neoliberalism as a historical or analytical category that purports to describe the period after liberalism has undergone basic changes to the principles and practices that define it. I have serious doubts about this way of employing neoliberalism to describe the post-1982 period in Bolivian history (i.e., after the restoration of civilian rule), because my study of contemporary Bolivia reveals liberalism expressed through law to be a constantly unfolding presence, or pattern, rather than a discrete historical moment or phase that has ended.

If it is indeed necessary to periodize the Bolivian encounter with liberalism, one could perhaps describe the post-1982 period as "late-liberalism," although I think this raises (or, perhaps, begs) as many questions as it answers. There is another sense, however, in which neoliberalism can be understood. This is neoliberalism as a category of critical public discourse, one that emerged in Bolivia during the mid- to late 1980s. As a discursive category, neoliberalism was a way of both celebrating the reengagement of Bolivia with the international financial system, and casting a critical shadow over the effects of this reengagement; it was a way of describing the aspirations of politicians and landowners who hoped to jumpstart—with the benevolent oversight of über-neoliberal Jeffrey Sachs, among others—Bolivia's economic development, and a way of lampooning the servile position of these same pro-market Bolivian elites; it was a way of heralding the embrace—especially by Bolivia's archneoliberal, Gonzalo Sánchez de Lozada—of several important international human rights provisions (e.g., International Labor Organization Convention 169), and a way of criticizing this same embrace of human rights as a cynical strategy to placate, in particular, Bolivia's increasingly militant indigenous movement. In other words, neoliberalism has been a discourse that has obscured as much as it has revealed about contemporary Bolivia over the last twenty years.

Even if neoliberalism was a category of critical public discourse that served different purposes in Bolivia over the last twenty years, its emergence did not signal the end of the broader patterns of intention that have shaped Bolivian history. In fact, neoliberalism should be understood as a way of marking the reintensification of Bolivia's legal-ideological foundations after a relatively long period (roughly twenty years) in which the framework of Bolivia's modernity was almost destroyed; that is, I am arguing here that the emergence of neoliberalism-as-discourse signaled the *reemergence* of a set of framing ideals and a continuation of the Bolivian encounter with liberalism expressed through law. Take the iconic Law 1551, the "Law of Popular Participation," which was promulgated in 1994, the year in which the discourse of neoliberalism—in all of its multifacetedness—crested. Although Law 1551 is typically understood as a response to the national experience of indigenous activism that had begun in Bolivia in the late 1980s (see, e.g., Van Cott 1998, 2000), an experience that supposedly transformed the way Bolivian elites responded to longstanding social demands, in fact the law itself tells a different story. The goal of Law 1551 was to

> incorporate the indigenous and rural communities and urban neighborhoods into the juridical, political, and economic life of the country. Its aim [was] to improve the quality of life of Bolivian women and men . . . by strengthening the political and economic means and institutions necessary for perfecting a representative democracy, facilitating citizens' participation and guaranteeing equality of representation at all levels between women and men. (Art. 1)

The law does this, in part, by vesting collectivities—the *Organizaciones Territoriales de Base* (OTBs), or Territorial Grassroots Organizations—with legal status and the right to eventually manage resources and resolve disputes according to the "ways, customs, and standards" to be found within the OTBs. The legal recognition of OTBs during the mid-1990s in Bolivia is usually read (again, see Van Cott 2000) as a fundamental shift in the trajectory of modern Bolivia, a reflection of a profound realignment in relations of power, and a transformation of those legal-ideological principles through which Bolivia emerged.[10]

However, in many ways, Law 1551—and the bundle of other neoliberal reforms in Bolivia during the 1990s, including the Law of Educational Reform (Law 1565, 1994), new Article 171 of the Bolivian Constitution (1995), and amended Article 28 of the Bolivian Code of Criminal Procedure (1999)—evoke the post–War of the Pacific Constitution and Law of Expropriation. Law 1565 created a system of bilingual education in which Bolivia's Amerindian languages were given equal status as vehicles for the education of Bolivia's citizenry. Article 171 of the National Constitution and Article 28 of the Code of Criminal Procedure were intended to broaden the range of permissible legal techniques for resolving conflicts, including techniques based in what Article 28 described as "Customary Indigenous Law." The meanings of these two articles will be discussed in subsequent chapters, including the ways in which the imperatives of liberal legality resurfaced in Bolivia in the 1990s cloaked in the language of a pan-Andean—and pan-Latin American—movement to recognize and validate what was believed to be a distinct indigenous legal tradition. But if there is any question about whether these other parts of Bolivia's so-called neoliberal reforms in fact signaled the reemergence of liberal ideals, rather than their fundamental transformation, one need only look to Article 2 of the Law of Educational Reform: Its basic objective is to "form the Bolivian man and woman by stimulating the harmonious development of all potentialities."

This wonderfully resonant statement of principles reflects the presence of most of liberalism's key markers: a belief in the ultimate perfectibility of mankind through reason; the primary role of education in a representative democracy (indeed, the statement is positively Lockean); a focus on the relationship between a liberal education and human development; and the all-important role of technocratic knowledge in shaping subjectivities, as expressed here in the use of findings from developmental psychology and sociolinguistics. Moreover, the legal redefinition of collectivities in Bolivia during the 1990s had the effect of *expanding* the categories of Bolivians whose subject positions were recognized within Bolivia's liberal framework, rather than transforming the framework itself. In other words, like the creation of a class of peasant landowners and the acceleration of land capitalization after 1880, and like the abolishment of the literacy and property requirements for suffrage after the National Revolution, the reconceptualization of Bolivia's different collectivities as rights-bearing juridical subjects during the 1990s simply reinforced Bolivia's basic legal-ideological framework by reinterpreting its principles in terms that reflected shifting political and social realities at the end of the twentieth century.

To conclude this chapter, it is important to make a final series of points about *how* patterns of intention shape social practice in Bolivia and why I think it is essential to foreground the chapters that follow within this analytical framework.

First, if liberalism expressed through law has been a key pattern of intention through which modern Bolivia continues to emerge, the effects of this pattern are not confined to any one sector or level of Bolivian society. This means that it is to the multifarious practice of everyday life in Bolivia that one must look for evidence of this broader frame, whether in provincial towns in the norte de Potosí, or in debates in the national media over capital punishment, or in the rap music produced in youth cultural centers in El Alto, or in the central plaza of the law faculty at the *Universidad Mayor de San Andrés* in La Paz. Moreover, in arguing that postcolonial Bolivia must be understood, in part, as a reflection (or refraction) of certain patterns of intention, I am not making the argument that there are particular centers (e.g., urban or intellectual) that have been historically more important locations for the diffusion of these shaping patterns. Rather, I see the influence of liberalism expressed through law as a much more disarticulated and ambiguous process throughout Bolivian history, but an influence that is nonetheless ever-present and therefore important to understand. As we will see, social practices at the "local" level in Bolivia are always, in part, an articulation or dialogue with broader assemblages; conversely, the national level in Bolivia must always be seen in light of this articulation or dialogue, which is another way of saying that the unfolding of modern Bolivia is also fundamentally a local process.

Second, the narrative of Bolivian encounters with law and liberalism not only ranges over the vertical axis, as it were, by tracing the impact of these patterns of intention up and down social, political, and legal scales; there is also what can be understood as the horizontal axis. So, as we will see in Chapter 5, when a rural legal services center opened its doors to women as a resource for protecting their human rights, the impact of this center owed as much to the future as to the past. If the legacy of spousal abuse was a reason for opening the center, the promise of a more "just" future—as defined by liberal conceptions of rights incorporated into Bolivia's national law—was equally important, both as a formal legal and moral justification for the *Servicio Legal Integral* in the province Alonso de Ibañez, and for the women and men whose lives were—at least for the years it was open—transformed by it.

Perhaps most importantly, in locating the study of specific Bolivian encounters with law and liberalism within a broader framework, I must emphasize that I am *not* making the argument that there is a deterministic relationship between this framework and the social practices that reflect its shaping presence. As I have said, liberalism expressed through law functions like a *negative* key to understanding modern Bolivia, and this means that the effects of this pattern of intention can be seen as much in social practices that resist or seek to transform Bolivia's liberal imperatives as in those that seek to reinforce them. I also do not want to overdetermine the basic argument that connects the book's different chapters and points of reference. This is not a book *about* Bolivian history, intellectual or otherwise, any more than it is a book *about* law, politics, or conflict in one province in the norte de Potosí. Rather, it is a book about the ways in which specific kinds of social practices in Bolivia reveal a set of dilemmas at the heart of the modern project itself, dilemmas that appear in stark relief through both legal practices and contemporary struggles over the meaning of the legal-ideological principles through which Bolivia emerged in the early nineteenth century. This is why it is necessary to move between registers: from the detailed discussion of law and the practice of everyday life in one area of rural Bolivia, to the transnational human rights movement; from an analysis of the highly gendered nature of one set of legal institutions in the province Alonso de Ibañez, to a discussion of what the coming of television programs like *The Simpsons* to rural Bolivia says about Bolivian modernity more generally; and so on. In other words, no matter how finely grained the analysis of a particular set of social practices in a particular region of Bolivia at a particular time, it must be located *in relation to* the broader currents of history and ideology that define modern Bolivia. To relate, however, is not to determine; it is not to understand local legal and political life dogmatically "in terms of" these broader currents. Indeed, it is all too easy, for any number of political, ethical, and even methodological reasons, especially in rural Bolivia, to try and understand the practices of everyday life through a kind of self-imposed myopia. This book is in part an argument for resisting this tendency.

3   The Making of a Legal Universe

Law and the Practice of Everyday Life

IN THE LAST CHAPTER, I developed in some detail the theoretical and historical arguments for understanding Bolivian encounters with law and liberalism telescopically, by alternating the angle of focus in order to view the practice of everyday life in Bolivia in relation to broader patterns of intention, and, conversely, to examine the way these patterns of intention are destabilized or reinforced by the practice of everyday life. In flipping the lens in this way, I do not want to convey the impression that I am making the argument for a better window into cause-and-effect relationships across different social, political, and legal scales in Bolivia. Rather, in moving between the legal and political, and between finely grained accounts of legal and political practice in one iconic region in Bolivia and broader frames of reference, I am committing myself to something like a theory of social refraction. What I mean is that there must be *some* way to account for the relationship between what is all-too-easily described elsewhere as the "global and the local," one that goes beyond mere categorical description. Here and throughout the book, I choose to see these relationships as refractive. The imperatives of liberalism expressed through law are refracted through legal practices in rural Bolivia, as we will soon see; national legal discourse in Bolivia is produced, in part, by refracting what is known about legal practices in rural and provincial Bolivia through national legal categories and expectations; legal norms associated with international human rights law are introduced into rural Bolivia by transnational actors and these norms are refracted through a long local history of external imposition of universalist legal and moral systems; these same human rights norms are appropriated and vernacularized by rural Bolivians and these epistemic changes then are refracted by transnational actors through their institutional commitments to "local" or "indigenous" knowledge; and so on. Refraction captures the essence of these relationships between scale because it assumes that there *are* influences between the local and broader scales in these ways, but that this influence is oblique and difficult to track with any certainty. The relationship between local legal and political practice in Bolivia, and national, international, and transnational networks is causal, in other words, but causal in only the most indirect, almost metaphorical, sense.

This chapter depends on this understanding of relationships, the linkages within the networks of ideas and practices that enmesh Bolivians and form the porous boundaries of their lives. Let us now turn to one point of articulation within these networks, one that will provide the grounding for many of the book's arguments about Bolivia's contested modern trajectory.

Law and the Production of Culture in Alonso de Ibañez

Sacaca is the seat of a *juzgado de instrucción*, where one *juez* instructor (literally "instructor judge") presides for a term of four years. The *juez* instructor is assisted by an *actuario* (clerk of the court) and a secretary. The juez instructor is selected in the following way. The *presidente de la Corte Superior de Distrito* (in Potosí), who is the highest judicial official in the department, sends a list of three names of lawyers (*una terna*) to the *Corte Suprema de Justicia de la Nación* ("National Supreme Court" in Sucre). This first list is made by choosing candidates for a vacant position from a larger list of lawyers. The process of drawing up this first list, then choosing three from it, is a secretive one and involves the typical networks of clientism that characterize other civic appointments in Bolivia. The Supreme Court in Sucre then makes the final selection from the group of three. The belief among judicial officials at the departmental level is that during this final selection the court in Sucre—which is not connected or subject to the specific departmental networks of influence—actually *does* select lower court judges based on a consideration of qualifications and other indicators of merit, even if the judges who appear on the list arrived there because of political, personal, or other nonjudicial criteria.

The juzgado de instrucción is technically the second lowest court in the jurisdictional hierarchy after the *juzgados de mínima cuantía*, but there are no *jueces de mínima cuantía* in Alonso de Ibañez, and the office is becoming obsolete because the juez instructor in most rural areas fulfills the same functions. The juez instructor is able to hear all criminal cases, although in practice most judges at this level would pass on hearing criminal cases involving financial dealings of extreme complexity, even though the Ley de Organización Judicial, the Bolivian code that regulates judicial jurisdictions, does not establish threshold monetary amounts for competence in criminal cases. In civil matters, however, the Ley de Organización Judicial removes the jurisdiction from the court in cases whose worth exceeds 10,000 pesos bolivianos (Title VI, Chapter 1, Art. 122[1]), and in cases that fall clearly within the purview of the Código de Familia (Family Code), like those involving divorce. Besides the normal adjudicative functions, the juez instructor also has investigative functions, which is somewhat unusual and marks the juez instructor as a special type of judicial official. Even though there is a police officer in Sacaca, the juez instructor and staff will investigate both criminal and civil cases by inspecting crime scenes, interviewing witnesses, and walking the boundaries of disputed land.

These peripatetic events are complicated legal and social moments for all the parties involved. The plaintiffs, defendants, judge and court staff, and any interested anthropologists who happen to be in the area, all make a tour of the property in dispute. Of course the way in which the location is described and the manner in which the judge is treated depend very much on the parties present and their ultimate intentions. Both sides of the conflict make their impassioned appeals right there in the courtyard, or outside the property walls, or in the field, while the actuario takes notes and the judge does his or her best to adopt a pose of detached neutrality. However, this supposed impartiality is soon disturbed by the prospect of the most luxurious of meals. Both sides jockey to have the walking inspection end with a grand meal at their own house, and the party who manages to convince the judge and staff (and any lingering anthropologist) to choose his house is usually the one who prevails later in court. After several plates of well-prepared meat of some kind, and especially several bottles of Huari (Oruro's well-liked beer), the favored party can be assured that the judge will have seen the nature of the disputed property in just the right way.

The next court up in the jurisdictional hierarchy is the *juzgado de partido*. This court serves as a court of appeal from the juzgado de instrucción for matters that it hears in the first instance, and the court of first instance for cases like divorce and civil cases whose worth exceeds 10,000 pesos bolivianos, as previously noted. After the juzgado de partido, the next court would be the corte superior de distrito, which in Potosí department is based in the capital; after the superior court comes the national supreme court, in Sucre.[1] There are also specialized courts in some of the larger cities in Bolivia, like the *juzgados de familia* and *juzgados de vigilancia*.

I should point out that in larger cities, most of the judicial hierarchy exists in the same place, and there is much more connection and functioning between the various courts. But in many of the provincial capitals in rural areas like the norte de Potosí, it is quite common that the only court will be a juzgado de instrucción, with the corresponding juzgado de partido located in another distant town. This distance has certain effects. For example, in towns where there is only a juez instructor, the judge will play a much more prominent role as a broadly active legal actor than he would in a city, where there is more judicial oversight. Also, when the juzgado de partido is in a distant town, the ability of parties to appeal is made more difficult and in some cases, it becomes practically impossible to appeal, especially for people from remote hamlets. This has the effect of making a juzgado de instrucción, the lowest court in the judicial hierarchy, paradoxically the state court of last resort for many people.

Although this framework describes the official jurisdictional structures in Bolivia and Alonso de Ibañez, the following officials in Sacaca also serve judicial functions: the subprefect (the highest political official in the province), the police officer, and the *corregidor* titular of Canton Sacaca.[2] In addition to these officials, there are other important nonjudicial legal actors in Sacaca, including the one titled lawyer, Lucio Montesinos, the *defensores* (lit. "defenders," private citizens who work as lawyers), the notary public, the civil registrars, and the priests.

Outside of Sacaca, there are literally hundreds of judicial and nonjudicial legal actors of importance. Their jurisdictions or mandates are derived from three broad social categories, which also divide public life in the province more generally: state, union, and ayllu. The category of "state" refers to positions or obligations that are understood to be associated with the Bolivian state and its purposes. The most important positions within this category outside of the provincial capital are the corregidores titulares of each provincial canton (there are eighteen) and their "auxiliaries," who are selected to work with the *titulares* in order to represent the interests of the canton to the wider province, department, and, when necessary, the nation-state. As a consequence of the 1952 National Revolution, almost every hamlet in Alonso de Ibañez is also coextensive with a rural peasant union, so that a hamlet like Jank'arachi also will be "Sindicato Campesino Jank'arachi" and participate on this basis within the regional umbrella organization of rural peasant unions—the *Federación Sindical Única de Trabajadores Campesinos del Norte de Potosí*, or FSUTCNP. Although *sindicatos* can have several different authority positions, the most important legal actor among them is the *dirigente* ("director" or "leader"). Finally, legal life in Alonso de Ibañez is shaped by authorities acting on behalf of different ayllus.[3] There are two types of ayllu official, and they perform a range of legal functions. *Jilanqus* are heads of minor ayllus, which is the highest ayllu level in the region. As with the officials in the category of state authority positions, jilanqus will often have seconds-in-command, who are known by the Spanish word *segundas* (literally "seconds").

Forms of Legal Practice

With this as a background, I can now examine the importance of legal practices and meanings in Alonso de Ibañez. Each of these different legal actors and institutions serve different roles within a larger framework of legality, one that is intimately connected with broader networks of ideas and practices. Law means different things at different times in the province. In certain cases, law describes the practical techniques and social expectations attached to particular disputes, which are invoked in the normal course of fulfilling the public roles assigned to the different parties to a dispute: the public authority responsible for managing the dispute, the disputants, family members, interested government officials, and so on. But because law in this sense is so common, so normal, it is difficult to define law only in terms of the techniques and ideas used to resolve disputes. It would be more accurate to say that legality frames the spaces in which public life can be performed, and culture produced, because the times and places where disagreements over land boundaries, or fights involving young men, or accusations of defamation, can be discussed, are also the times and places where a public sphere is most obviously and regularly present. Further, legal modes of debate and forms of knowledge provide the framework for the performance of political activities in the norte de Potosí, so that we might usefully view the political and the legal as mutually implicated spheres of public subject-making. Even so, with the exception of certain ritual performances, such as festivals celebrating Todos Santos (end of October/beginning of November) and Candelaria (February), and the ritual battles known as *tinkus*, most key acts of social life in provincial Bolivia are expressed through logics that have a decidedly legal orientation. And especially over the last ten years, with the rise of new political parties in the norte de Potosí—most importantly the *Movimiento al Socialismo*

(MAS), the *Movimiento Indígena Pachakuti* (MIP), and the regional *Movimiento Originario del Pueblo* (MOP)—politics has become even more formalized and elite, creating opportunities for very few men (and even fewer women) to become full-time organizers and, more rarely, candidates for public office.[4]

Every Sunday, the corregidor titular of Canton Sacaca converts a part of his house into a public meeting space.[5] Over the course of a typical year, hundreds of men and women from throughout the province come for an official visit to the corregidgor titular's house (see Figure 3.1). They come to have a *demanda*, or summons, issued against a person, a family, or sometimes an entire hamlet, for complaints ranging from defamation (a violation that is considered much more grievous in rural Bolivia than the Bolivian Civil or Criminal Codes recognize) to "land invasions" by animals, which can involve anything from a single animal wandering unattended across a person's fields without further damage, to cases in which much of a family's bean or potato crop has been eaten by sheep or goats (see Figure 3.2). They come to respond to demandas, to participate in hearings and tell their version of what are always multisided conflict narratives. They come as *testigos*, or witnesses, to support family or hamlet members out of a sense of obligation, or because their names have been listed on a demanda, or to protect their own interests in a case, which always unfolds in terms of a social context that is broader and more complicated than what can be observed or described in sessions in the corregidor titular's *sala de recepción* ("meeting" or "waiting" room).

For example, in late 1998, an old man came to make his case for a demanda that he had filed against his *yerno* (son-in-law) the week before. His son-in-law was present in response to the demanda that had been delivered to his hamlet. The *demandante* ("claimant" or "plaintiff"), who was about sixty years old, claimed that his son-in-law regularly beat his daughter. The couple lived in another hamlet (Kochipampa) and so he had no control over how his son-in-law treated his daughter, but the man said that because of the way his son-in-law abused his daughter, he had refused to give his blessing to the marriage. He said that the couple had been together for ten years and that the knowledge that his daughter, his only child, was being beaten all this time caused him great suffering.

Because the father had refused to give his blessing, the couple's marriage had not been registered in Sacaca and the father did not consider the couple legally married. Nevertheless, the old man still used the Spanish yerno to refer to the younger man and it was clear that their situation produced conflicting feelings

Figure 3.1. Parties wait to be heard on Sunday at the house of the *corregidor* titular, Sacaca (the corregidor is second from the right)

for him. The corregidor asked the *demandado* (defendant) if the charges were true and he denied them. He said that he did not beat the woman and that her father was unreasonable in withholding his support for ten years. All he wanted to do, he said, was to become officially married. The corregidor then asked why the daughter had not come, and the man said that his wife was working in Cochabamba and could not return for the hearing. The man also denied, contrary to the father-in-law, that the woman had wanted a separation in recent years because of the way he treated her. The corregidor responded that this discrepancy in their accounts made her presence even more necessary.

The corregidor then said that the parties should return in two weeks with *testigos* to corroborate their versions of the situation and that the daughter should come to testify herself. The father then began weeping and said that he could not ask people from another hamlet to come and testify against one of their own; he said that his daughter had always confided to him in secret about

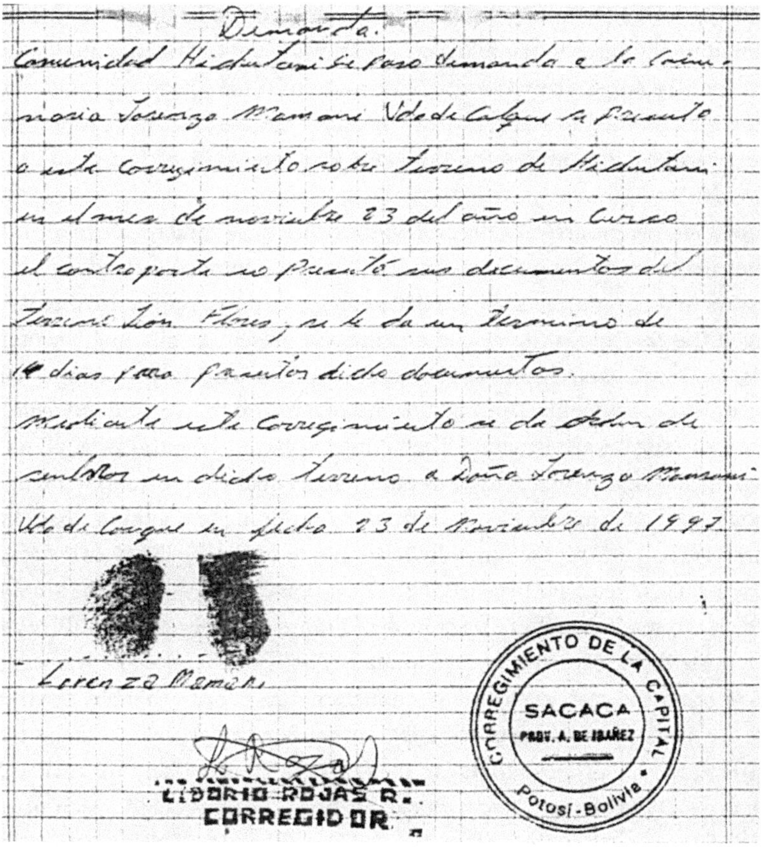

Demanda.

Comunidad Hilaticani se paso demanda a la comunaria Lorenza Mamani Vda de Calque se presento a este corregimiento sobre terreno de Hilaticani en el mes de noviembre 23 del año en curso el contraparte no presentó sus documentos del terreno Leon Flores, se le da un termino de 14 dias para presentar dicho documentos.

Mediante este corregimiento se da orden de cultivar en dicho terreno a Doña Lorenza Mamani Vda de Calque en fecha 23 de noviembre de 1997.

Lorenza Mamani

LIDORIO ROJAS R.
CORREGIDOR

CORREGIMIENTO DE LA CAPITAL
SACACA
PROV. A. DE IBAÑEZ
Potosí - Bolivia

Figure 3.2. A *demanda* from the *corregidor* titular of Sacaca to a member of hamlet Jilaticani to produce documents in a dispute over land

the beatings and that he doubted that she herself would even discuss it publicly in front of her "husband." The corregidor said that there was nothing he could do about that, but they would simply need to wait to hear from the woman. Further, the corregidor said that if the allegations of beatings were substantiated with witnesses, he would use an *acta de maltratamiento* (record of maltreatment), a rarely used acta, that would officially acknowledge the son-in-law's abusive behavior; the corregidor also would require the son-in-law to promise not to beat the woman anymore. The corregidor then would use an *acta de compromiso* (record of compromise), in which the couple would be formally reconciled. He said he would impose an unspecified amount as a fine if the son-in-law broke the future promise. The corregidor asked the father-in-law if he would finally agree to the marriage if, assuming the treatment could be corroborated, the son-in-law promised not to do it in the future. Through more tears, which seemed to indicate that the father felt the treatment would continue regardless of promises and threats of fines, the man said he would agree to the marriage.

However, people arrive at the corregidor titular's on Sundays for many other reasons that have nothing to do with disputes. They come to seek advice on the best ways to write contracts, advice that emerges through a collective discussion between the corregidor titular and anyone else present at the time (including resident gringo researchers). They come to receive help in preparing a wide range of legal documents, from certificates of baptism to a *renombramiento*, or intent to change a given name. They come to have declarations of all kinds drawn up and signed, which serve as public and, equally important, written, intentions to perform duties, or refrain from doing something they have acknowledged—within the same declaration—to be wrong. They come to pay *multas*, or fines, that have been assessed for various transgressions, the amounts of which are small enough to be considered more symbolic than punitive even in the norte de Potosí—the average multa is 5 bolivianos (about 65 U.S. cents). If, as is often the case, even this symbolic amount is not available, then they come to make arrangements with the corregidor titular, which range from everything from a promise to pay in the future to an agreement to work in his fields for a day. Although these work obligations are considered a sign of corruption by urban Bolivians, and are decried by transnational NGOs active in the province, in fact, an offer of labor as a way of canceling a monetary obligation is a culturally resonant and even honorable way of making restitution.

Over in the juzgado de instrucción (Figure 3.3), legal practice takes place within a more formalized context, one framed by the imperatives of Bolivian state substantive and procedural law. Because of this, the juzgado contributes different—but no less consequential—sets of ideas and practices to the broader repertoire that people in the province draw from in the course of negotiating rights and obligations, subtly contesting structures of power, pursuing more narrow self-interests, and otherwise engaging in public life. The court coexists with the corregidor titular and the other spaces of legal practice in terms of a set of open logics that suggest, rather than define, the ways in which law should shape this public life. In this way, law provides the means through which subject-making in the province is connected to—and influences—the historical

Figure 3.3. *Juzgado de instrucción*, Alonso de Ibañez

and discursive currents that invest the practice of law in Alonso de Ibañez with a wider significance, and which locate it firmly within—rather than apart from—the trajectory of modern Bolivia.

At one level, the juzgado de instrucción is like any other court in Bolivia and elsewhere. Court hearings are scheduled on a posted docket. People waiting to have cases heard as plaintiffs or defendants, or to appear as witnesses, or to pay fines because of earlier dispositions, or to drop off paperwork, must wait quietly and patiently in a reception area until called by the court's actuario, who functions as the clerk of the court, the person who transcribes court sessions, the court archivist (assisted, when present, by foreign researchers with a special interest in the province's legal history), and general steward of court tradition and protocol (see Figure 3.4). Like other courts in other places and times, Sacaca's juzgado de instrucción can be Dickensian: parties to cases frequently complain that they do

Figure 3.4. *Sala de recepción, juzgado de instrucción,* Sacaca

not understand the legal arcana that envelop them; they bemoan the long time that passes between hearings; they resent the cost in time and money of having to come to Sacaca over what can be many years; they are suspicious of the motives of the court as a symbol of the state; and so on.[6] As a result, the most formal legal space in the province, the one with the power to enforce judgments with the assistance of the province's one state police officer, the place reserved for the resolution of the most recognizably serious of *casos penales* (murder, attempted murder, rape, infanticide), is, ironically, the one whose role in shaping legal subjectivity is the most circumscribed. At one time or another, most people in the province have been involved in legal cases that are brought and, with luck, resolved *outside* of the juzgado de instrucción. But beyond this, most people in the province regularly invoke the mechanisms of law in order to protect interests, reestablish individual or family identity on a different basis, or publicly memorialize any number of important life-moments.

As I have already explained, beyond the expressions of "law" in these two more orthodox senses—to address conflicts and to meet civil or administrative obligations—most people in the province, to the extent that they participate in public life, do so in terms of what are understood as legal frames of reference. This can be seen in the way entries in public records are made, from the legalistic language to the use of seals, stamps, and the other symbols of an oathbased legal culture (Figure 3.5). This legal framing of public life also can be seen

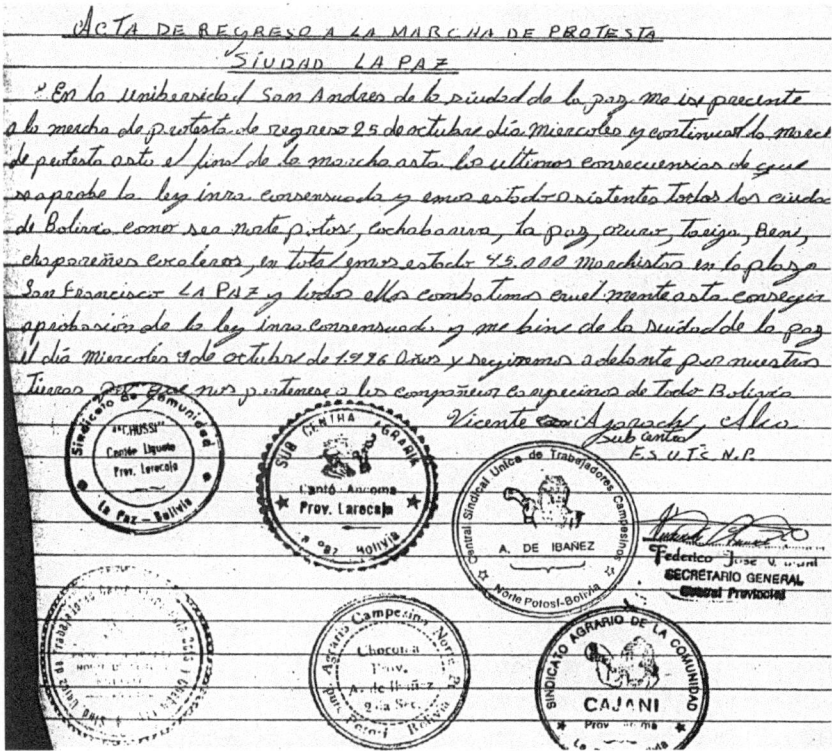

Figure 3.5. "Acta de regreso a la marcha de protesta, Siudad La Paz," *cuaderno de actas*, hamlet Molino T'ikanoma

in the way debates over everything from whether to participate in NGO projects, to how to use funds raised locally for the construction of a new school, take place in a discursive register that is essentially legal—people invoke the *la palabra* as a point of reference and testigos are pressed into service to support assertions.[7] Despite how common, even banal, however, all of this legal practice is in Alonso de Ibañez, most people have never participated in cases in the juzgado de instrucción. This is not because of its association with the power of a hostile state, but rather because of its specific location within what will be described later as a broader legal universe, one which extends well beyond the boundaries of the province.

Outside the provincial capital, an even richer tapestry of legality forms the basis for public life and connects even the most remote hamlet, to greater or lesser degrees, to the wider currents of ideas and practices that define modern Bolivia. Authorities from the three distinct public categories—state, union, ayllu—have many legal responsibilities and they serve many legal functions, even though there are no "titled" lawyers among the province's thousands of people (there are, however, notaries public in several of the larger cantonal capitals). Jilanqus, segundas, and dirigentes act as adjudicators in the course of resolving disputes between members of a single hamlet, between people from different hamlets, between different hamlets, between different ayllus, and, on occasion, between people/hamlets/ayllus from a different province or even department. The ways and means of resolving disputes within and among these different types of parties are open and have changed over time, but they are roughly patterned on what is known—or thought to be known—about dispute resolution by the corregidor titular in Sacaca (who, in turn, is inspired by what he believes to be proper legal practice in the juzgado de instrucción, although at a simple empirical level the modes of dispute resolution across the province are much closer to those at the corregidor titular than those at the corregidor titular are to those in the juzgado de instrucción).

Parties come together at a designated time and place, both of which vary according to a range of contingencies, such as weather, demands of work (for parties and authorities), time of the year (dispute resolution sessions usually are not held during important yearly ritual periods, nor during the heavy planting or harvesting seasons), the likelihood that Sacaca's legal institutions will eventually become involved, and the state of affairs in the provincial capital. (Is the juzgado de instrucción closed for a lengthy judicial holiday? Does the corregidor titular know about the case, and, if so, what is his disposition toward it? Are any of the parties inclined to take the case directly to Sacaca even though the case would normally be resolved within the hamlet?)

The jilanqu of Minor Ayllu Chaykina Abajo (in Fundación) told me that "at times [people from his ayllu] just don't want to bring their cases to him. They think it's more valuable to take their cases to Sacaca. They say they are going to resolve their disputes well in Sacaca." A *corregidor auxiliar* in Kachari explained that "some fights are so serious that we are not able to resolve them here [in the hamlet]. We have to take them to the corregidor [in Sacaca]. And if he's not able to resolve them, then they must be taken to the *subprefecto* [of the province]." However, the dirigente of hamlet/sindicato Jant'a Pallca rejected the idea that legal institutions in Sacaca were somehow superior, or that even the gravest of disputes could not be resolved either within Jant'a Pallca itself or through the collaborative efforts of hamlet and wider ayllu authorities (in this case, Ayllu Jilaticani Menor).

Once the parties actually meet at the appointed time and place (all things being equal, at the authority's house on a Sunday, the traditional day for such meetings), they chat about unrelated things and chew coca leaves by passing around the *ch'uspa*, or coca leaf pouch (which can be made of traditional textiles or a simple plastic bag). Although a period of small talk and coca-chewing precedes almost all public events, here it is even more important that the parties share their coca with the authority and, ideally, each other. There are no formal rules of procedure, but in most cases, the authority will begin by summarizing the reasons for the meeting, then asking the parties to describe their version of the events. No time limits are imposed at this point and I have seen people talk for periods ranging from between fifteen minutes to an hour (rarely longer at this point) without being interrupted. Each side, which can include testigos, speaks and argues with the authority and not to each other. Except for young children, parties or witnesses to disputes can be men or women of all ages, and it has been one of my consistent observations over the last ten years that women outside of Sacaca prosecute or respond to claims as often as men (see Chapter 4 for a full discussion of the relationship between gender and law).

After everyone has spoken, argued, wept, shouted, remained silent, equivocated, and testified, so that nothing more—at this point—is left to do, the authority does one of several things. He can render a judgment immediately, which can be anything from an order to one party to pay a fine to the other, to the design of a plan for restitution that is based on the underlying circumstances (and the authority's assignment of blame).[8]

In late 1999, there was a particularly acrimonious dispute between two brothers in Jank'arachi, a large hamlet far (about seven leagues[9]) from Sacaca in Canton Karkoma and within Minor Ayllu Tarawqa Cuerpo. The dispute was over the boundaries of the lands that were left to the brothers by their father, who had recently died. The dispute was heard by the jilanqu and even though there were different arguments on both sides about the exact location of the dividing boundary, the jilanqu settled the dispute by applying the principle that arable land should be allotted equally between surviving siblings. As he said, "we have to divide the land equally [in disputes like this], because that's how the father left it."

The corregidor auxiliar of Khea Khea, a large hamlet connected by a well-maintained road to Sacaca, emphasized that dispute resolution was most necessary during and after both weddings and festivals. As he said, "it's a problem when people get drunk. When young men fight we give them three lashes with a whip here [indicating the small of the back] . . . . But when the fight is really bad, we give [those young men who fought] an *orden* [or "official order"] so that they must go to either the subprefect or the police station in Sacaca." After one dispute resolution session in the hamlet of Molino T'ikanoma (Canton Karkoma), the corregidor auxiliar instructed a man and his son to provide a bag of potato seed to a neighboring family as restitution for allowing their animals to damage part of the other family's potato crop.

The authority can also ask for more information from the parties, which usually means asking testigos to appear at a later time. If the time of the year is conducive, the authority customarily will ask the parties to have the testigos appear the following week, and, if so, the case is resolved at that time (in the hamlets, legal practice is clearly less Dickensian). Much more rarely, an authority will not reach a decision or establish a concrete plan for future meetings. Although it is the obligation of authorities to convene meetings, conduct dispute resolution sessions, make decisions and assign responsibility, and, finally, to track the course of disputes and make sure dispositions are followed, there are instances in which the best course of action is a kind of permanent postponement. There are any number of complicated interpersonal and social dynamics that might lead to this, but sometimes during the initial meeting the authority senses that a formal decision itself—whatever the outcome—would create greater, rather than less, discord within a hamlet or between hamlets. In addition, there are times in which the act of meeting and discussing and arguing is itself a kind of resolution without anything more. An authority has to be extremely sensitive to these nuances to fail to come to a decision for this reason, which is why a nondecision of this type is so uncommon.

I suggested that this particular category of legal practice—dispute resolution—outside of Sacaca is a form of adjudication, and I do so with a certain amount of analytical trepidation. A long line of literature in legal anthropology has addressed the forms of law cross-culturally as a problem of classification. Indeed, cross-cultural definition and sorting were the initial raisons d'être for the empirical study of law and what is known in the literature as "law-like systems." All of this took place within either an explicit or implied evolutionary framework, in which law, like other forms of culture, was seen to develop chronologically from the earlier stages of normativity that corresponded with earlier stages of political development and modes of production. These different normative stages were sorted based on different variables, such as the presence or absence of an official enforcement mechanism (e.g., the state), the presence or absence of neutral third parties in dispute resolution, and the presence or absence of rules of procedure that ensured continuity and fairness across different cases.

Both the evolutionary assumptions that motivated this kind of legal anthropology, and the exercises in classification that were based on them, have long since become obsolete. However, for those who might be interested in locating dispute resolution in Alonso de Ibañez within these classificatory schemes, I can say that hamlet authorities act more like adjudicators, rather than like mediators or arbitrators. Mediators assist different parties in negotiating problems without the right or obligation to render binding decisions. Arbitrators *can* make binding decisions, but the defining difference is that the parties must agree in advance to be bound by these decisions. In both mediation and arbitration—that is, according to the orthodox classification literature—parties to disputes imbue a third party with a set of powers that he did not already have. By contrast, adjudicators (e.g., judges) possess the preexisting right, and, equally important, obligation, to render binding decisions. How well they exercise these rights and perform these duties is another question; so is the problem of enforcement, which can run the gamut from a system in which the full weight of a state's police arm can be brought to bear in support of judicial decisions, to those in which the adjudicator must rely on less institutionalized forms of pressure. Because authorities outside of Sacaca *do* possess preexisting rights and obligations to make binding decisions over disputes that fall within their jurisdictions, they act much more like judges than mediators or arbitrators.

Still, dispute resolution is only one category of legal practice throughout the province. Jilanqus, segundas, and dirigentes function much more broadly during their time in office, which is usually one year, but often longer. From the vantage point of the hamlets outside of Sacaca, the legal universe appears more complicated than in the provincial capital itself and the jurisdictional problems are more acute. People who live in the provincial capital have really only one formal option for harnessing the discursive and procedural machineries of law: the juzgado de instrucción, as I have already described. On occasion, *sacaqueños* try and use the town's *alcaldía*, or mayor's office, as a kind of quasilegal public space, but this does not happen very often, especially now that the province's political sphere has become more professionalized, elite, and directed toward political processes at the national level. However, for those who live in the province's hundreds of hamlets, legal practice-as-public life unfolds within a much more diverse, and contested, set of expectations (and counterexpectations). There are nine distinct—but fundamentally interconnected—spaces of legal practice within the broader legal universe that encompasses hamlets outside of Sacaca, which can be designated either by reference to nominal location or the authority who exercises a separate set of legal rights and obligations: dirigente, segunda, jilanqu, cantonal corregidor titular, corregidor auxiliar, corregidor titular of Canton Sacaca, office of the provincial police officer (see Figure 3.6), office of the province's subprefect, and, finally, the juzgado de instrucción. I have made this list by purposely mixing the different legal spaces associated with the different social categories in order to underscore the point that these separate nodes of legal articulation are not related to each other within a rigid jurisdictional hierarchy—nor is it possible to rank or order them according to orthodox understandings of power distribution, degrees of legal formalism, degrees of jurisprudential refinement, and so on. Rather, people from the hamlets must navigate within this legal universe based on a range of idiosyncratic moral, political, and social interests, and it is the role of jilanqus, segundas, corregidores auxiliaries, and dirigentes to provide guidance, which comes attached to different kinds and degrees of pressure.

A hamlet authority acting in this capacity serves as a kind of legal-moral counselor, providing advisory opinions to people so that they can make a decision about which points of access are most appropriate given historical precedent, the changing relationship between the nine different spaces of legal practice, and, especially over the last fifteen years, the heightened imperatives of a broader liberal legal framework that shapes even the most apparently localized legal problems. In this way, authorities outside of Sacaca fashion a blueprint of legal subjectivity for those who fall within their scope of responsibility (a scope that depends on the category of authority [state, union, ayllu], location in the province, and other, more contingent, factors). It is important to emphasize both how pervasive this kind of legal practice is—that is, the interplay between authorities acting as legal-moral counselors and the ordinary social actors who seek their advice— and how, even more so than what in classical legal anthropology is known as the "trouble cases" (Llewelyn and Hoebel 1941), it serves as a key means through which legal (and thus public) identity is shaped and challenged.

A former corregidor titular of Canton Iturata who lived in Sak'ani—one of the largest hamlets in Alonso de Ibañez (ninety-five families) and one of the

Figure 3.6. Police station, Sacaca

farthest from the provincial capital (8.5 leagues, though located on a major in-terdepartmental road)—explained that in order to be able to provide this kind of legal-moral guidance, an authority must possess certain characteristics. He must "not be in debt over land to anyone. He should be able to write and have some education. He should be the right age. And more than anything he should have a capacity." By capacity, he meant more than simply the proven ability to resolve disputes within the community; he meant a kind of analytical capacity, the ability to both envision the broader legal universe of which the social space of Sak'ani occupied just one node, and be able to navigate jurisprudentially within it.[10]

The corregidor auxiliar of Kamacachi (Canton Wila Wila), however, emphasized the need for authorities to respect the tight interconnections between the hamlet and judicial and political officials in Sacaca: "for any problem that is at all serious, we advise [the parties] that they should go to Sacaca. There they receive medical treatment [in the case of fights], agree to repair damaged property, agree to pay for medical treatment [when at fault], and [when appropriate] they must pay fines."

The jilanqu of Minor Ayllu Jilawi Cuerpo (living in Kachari) underscored the importance of always thinking beyond any one dispute or legal problem and keeping the future as much in view as the unfolding present. As he put it, "when I have to resolve a dispute, I try and have patience, so that [the parties] do not act foolishly in the future."

I should emphasize that it is not my intention here to try and account for *all* of the forms of law in Alonso de Ibañez (or elsewhere in Bolivia); rather, the purpose is to give the reader a concrete sense of both the importance of law as a primary means through which public identity and meaning are shaped, and enough information to begin to see *how* law functions in these ways. Needless to say, there are other legal actors of some importance in Alonso de Ibañez and other forms of legal practice, some of which I will return to at different points and in different ways in subsequent chapters. I have already mentioned notaries public, who play a much more expansive legal role in Alonso de Ibañez—both in Sacaca and in several cantonal capitals (e.g., Karkoma)—than they do in Bolivia's cities, in that they give legal advice and otherwise shape the parameters of legal practice well beyond their nominal capabilities under Bolivian law. Most intriguingly, there are the defensores, who are also known by two other historically significant names: *tinterillu* (which is a Quechua-inflected version of *tinterillo*, a very difficult word to accurately translate, but which means something like a "scribe-lawyer" or, more derogatorily, "hack-lawyer") and *qhelqeri* (which appears to be an Aymara-Quechua hybrid that is intended to mean either "writer," or, even better, "scribe").[11]

The category of defensor is created by Bolivian state law, which allows people to essentially practice law without a license in rural provinces with less than four titled lawyers (Art. 103, No. 3, Ley de Organización Judicial). There are no formal educational requirements for certification as a defensor and people who want to embark on this controversial but potentially lucrative career must meet only the most basic of criteria, which involve a set of notarized self-assertions about character, professional fitness, knowledge of the law (which means here state law), and support of provincial officials. After this certification is returned from the Corte Superior of the relevant department, the newly minted defensor is able to provide the full range of legal advice and services, represent clients in the local court in both civil and criminal cases, and otherwise tend to the legal needs of the province's citizens (for more on the province's defensores, see Chapter 4).[12]

Strategies and Tactics

If the forms of legal practice in Alonso de Ibañez provide the institutional and discursive frameworks through which public identity is shaped and contested, and this process, in turn, interconnects law and the practice of everyday life to the broader currents, those patterns of intention that have shaped Bolivia's postcolonial trajectory, then we must ask some further questions. What is the relation between legal institutions—understood as both "actual" institutions and those public authorities whose duties are institutionalized—and the hundreds, if not thousands, of ordinary social actors for whom law is the primary means through which they enter—and resist—the "modernist sublime"? Although I have already suggested that traditional ways of understanding the distribution of power in Bolivia cannot begin to capture the complex relationship between town and hamlets, men and women, old and young, indigenous and mestizo, and so on, in Alonso de Ibañez (and elsewhere, I am suggesting), we must nevertheless examine the reasons for the unpredictable and counterintuitive expression of interests through law. Finally, it is important to consider the implications of this subversion of traditional understandings of power for the more general relationship between local practice in Bolivia and the historical and ideological frameworks within which these practices necessarily take place.

Institutions in Alonso de Ibañez can be usefully understood as examples of what Michel de Certeau (1988) described in the context of the industrialized north as "strategies": expressions of authority whose ultimate purpose is to perpetuate themselves through the things they make, whether these things are laws, discourses, language, art, or—what de Certeau was most concerned with—mass-produced consumer goods. To say that institutions are constituted in this way is simply to recognize their essential structure, the way they must exist in relation to both *what* they make (legal decisions, guidelines for legal subjectivity) and *who* makes them (court officials, the peasant farmers who become literally institutionalized while they serve as public authorities). One of the implications of thinking of legal institutions in Alonso de Ibañez in this way is the fact that the dynamic, creative forces that make the practice of everyday life so consequential are not likely to be generated by institutions, regardless of the political, moral, or other intentions of individuals who might want to reform the institution or change its purpose (which is its own continued existence). Indeed, this essentially conservative understanding of institutions-as-strategies helps explain why, over the course of the last 150 years, legal institutions in the province (both in the capital and hamlets) have not been a location of social change or formalized resistance.

Rather, we must look to the noninstitutional legal actors themselves, those thousands of people who encounter law as a primary means through which public identity—and thus subjectivity more generally—is shaped and reshaped. This is the side of the encounter that de Certeau described as the "tactical," the everyday encounters with institutions/strategies that are fragmented, ad hoc, noninstrumental, and whose purpose (if one can be articulated) is simply to find meaning in these encounters because this is where meaning is to be found. This is a way of understanding law and the production of culture as a kind of low-level guerilla warfare, in which social actors-cum-legal actors generate meanings beyond those contemplated by institutions merely by engaging with them. This also means that a jilanqu of a minor ayllu who thinks and acts strategically one year will—after rotating through what is known in the Andean studies literature as his "fiesta cargo" position (for Bolivia, see, e.g., Abercrombie 1998a; Albro 2001)—think and act tactically the next. This is how de Certeau (1988) redefined "subversion": Although it is "unmappable," as he so compellingly and perplexingly described it, real subversion is to be found in the ways in which people find concrete and creative meanings through encounters with the institutions of formal meaning-making.

To understand the relationship in Alonso de Ibañez between legal institutions and ordinary legal actors in this way is also to begin to understand the reasons why the diffusion of power cannot be explained through all of the usual dichotomies. These depend on what I have already described as a concentric approach to power, in which its distribution is concentrated in cores—defined in terms of location (city versus countryside), ethnicity (mestizo versus indigenous, "white" versus mestizo), mode of production (urban office worker versus campesino), and so on—and then radiates, and weakens, as it spreads outward. As applied to Alonso de Ibañez, this would mean that sacaqueños have more power than members of (for example) Minor Ayllu Jilawi Cuerpo, the juez instructor has more power than the corregidor titular of Canton Sacaca, the *vecino* (or neighborhood) shopkeepers who line the plaza have more power than the campesinos who walk for hours to sell them their potatoes and beans, and hamlet authorities have more power than the members of their jurisdictions for whom they attempt to resolve disputes or provide advice on navigating among the different nodes within the broader legal universe.

However, if "power" is concentrated in the strategic, the institutional, this is a false kind of power, one that can be mobilized only in order to support the continued existence of status and authority (i.e., the institution itself), but not, I would argue, domination, which would require a kind of dynamic or creative power that is lacking in legal institutions in the province. Rather, this creative power is expressed through the tactical, through the intellectual and practical engagement by ordinary people—here both sacaqueño and *runa*—with legal institutions through the different forms of legal practice. This is the creative source—which is both actual and potential—of resistance to the conservative imperatives embedded in legal institutions in Alonso de Ibañez and, by extension, the broader patterns of intention of which they are, in part, a local expression. So here we come to something like a conclusion: If I am correct in that a particular form of law—liberal legality—forms one of the main pillars of modern Bolivia, and this form of law expresses itself through cultural, political, and economic relations that interconnect all regions and time periods in postcolonial Bolivia, then this pillar is anything but solid. Instead, it is destabilized—and is destabilizing—through its sheer persistence over time, through its expression within the practices of everyday life, in Alonso de Ibañez and elsewhere in Bolivia. In other words, it is in the everyday encounters with law and liberalism—rather than in the spectacular marches, the dramatic elections, and occasional acts of symbolic public violence—that we must look in order to understand the subtle shifts in the social, economic, and political plates that run beneath the surface of modern Bolivia.

The Making of a Legal Universe

It is somewhat counterintuitive to think of law in Alonso de Ibañez as forming one node in a wider legal universe. This counterintuition is not primarily—or most consequentially—analytical; it is easy enough to envision the significance of law and the practice of everyday life in the province within a broader framework of the historical, political-economic, or even jurisprudential kind.

Rather, when the claim is anchored in the experience of the empirical, the ethnographic research encounter that always unsettles as much as it clarifies, it is difficult to believe that a meeting between several men in a hamlet far from the provincial capital, a meeting to discuss and resolve a conflict over the shifting—and unmarked—boundaries of family land, has any greater meaning beyond the specific circumstances of the dispute. Indeed, the intuition runs in the opposite direction: It is much more likely, one would suppose, that a meeting to resolve a dispute over land boundaries in Jank'arachi (a growing, but still quite remote hamlet) takes place exclusively in light of the most local of concerns and expectations. Again, the concentric circle approach to understanding (in this case) legal relations would seem to explain the effects of this kind of distance: The patterns of formal "law" in Bolivia radiate out from the urban centers and, like radar signals, weaken with each successive kilometer, until "law" merges and then is subsumed within "custom," which then gives way to the idiosyncratic normative practices of single clusters of hamlets, then individual hamlets, then, finally, at the far reaches, perhaps groups of families. This intuition suggests a kind of double distance between dispute resolution in a place like Jank'arachi and the cases at bar in the courtrooms of La Paz or Cochabamba: in the way Jank'arachi's corregidor auxiliar listens to the two family heads argue over the disputed reach of their eroding fields; in the way he listens to testigos talk about historical patterns of land usage; and in the way he decides to establish a new boundary that results in roughly equal land between the two disputants. All of this—intuition suggests—has nothing substantively or procedurally in common with the law of the state; in fact, it is not even law, however corrupted.

However, all of this intuition about normativity in Alonso de Ibáñez, those social processes through which people envision and perform right conduct and the patterns for a proper life, is wrong. As it turns out, when the corregidor auxiliar of Jank'arachi brings these disputants together in a remote corner of a remote province in one of Bolivia's least "coeval" (Fabian 1983) of regions, he both contributes to, and destabilizes, the same legal universe that includes the group of elite *paceño* men who might at that exact moment be sharing drinks, legal gossip, and a game of billiards in the clubby confines of the *Ilustre Colegio de Abogados de La Paz*.

To describe the group of men chewing coca leaves and engaging in small talk about the rainfall or the latest NGO incursion, and the group of paceño lawyers shooting pool and indulging the Latin America–wide legal-culinary passion for canapés, as coequal constituents of a broader legal universe, is to make several empirical, analytical, and critical claims, all of which reinforce the more general methodological argument that runs through each chapter—that we must use a telescopic lens in order to understand the importance of law and liberalism in shaping Bolivia's modern trajectory. In order to explain what is meant by "legal universe," and to understand how this framework captures the context of law in Alonso de Ibáñez as much as in La Paz—as well as provides a basis for connecting the two, the intercontext—recall Malagón Barceló's aphorism that "[Latin] America was born beneath the juridical sign" (1961: 4).

Bolivia, like other Latin American countries, was both conceived and constituted in terms of legal categories and frames of reference. This was not simply true of republican Latin America: from the laws that established racial categories in colonial Latin America (see, e.g., Appelbaum, Macpherson, and Rosemblatt 2003; Wade 1997), to the legal frameworks that created new forms of sociopolitical space—for example, Viceroy Toledo's program to "reduce" the native Andean population into Spanish-style towns—legality has always formed the foundation, and provided the subsequent means, through which culture, politics, and eventually history itself were given new shape and meaning. Now what is critically important to underscore at this point is the fact that law becomes foundational in this way for Bolivians by unfolding both outward and inward, from the top down and from the bottom up. Again, it has always been thus, as historians of colonial Latin America like Steve Stern have demonstrated (see Stern 1982a). Almost immediately, native Andeans became primary producers of legal categories and meanings, not in isolation from, or in opposition to, the law of the colonial oppressors, but in a kind of diffuse symbiosis with it.

"Law," understood in this way, becomes the ill-definable sum total of all of this complicated normativity, which emerges as much as it is imposed, pacifies as much as it justifies social change, and reinforces structures of power as much as it destabilizes them. And "universe" is a metaphor that perhaps best captures this ill-definable sum total. There is no question that our universe—that is, *the* universe—is comprised of many different parts that are connected to each in ways that are both understood and not understood; there are, unquestionably, patterns among the universe's different parts, but what these patterns are and what they mean are subject to debate. One can artificially isolate distinct dimensions of the universe—say, life on earth, or the moons of Saturn—for certain purposes, but there is no question that this isolated dimension is subject to broader forces and cannot be understood, in the end, apart from them. Something like cause-and-effect forces are at work in the universe, but how causes and effects are related to each other, and where the centers of power or gravity are (if there *are* any centers of power or gravity), are difficult to specify with accuracy; yet for all of this uncertainty, debate, and ontological ambiguity, there is no question that the universe exists at some meaningful level, that patterns can be detected, and that, more than anything else, what sociocultural anthropologists call "holism" is the best analytical framework for trying to come to terms with these meanings and patterns.

Scholars and others interested in understanding the dilemmas of legal complexity, including the relationship between discrete—but essentially interconnected—legalities, have come forward with a number of different theoretical models, most of which suffer from one defect or another. These models have gone by different appellations—"legal pluralism," "legal polycentricity," "sociolegality"—but they all fail, in different ways, both theoretical and empirical, to provide much useful guidance for explaining contemporary legal constellations, which have become even more difficult to locate analytically in light of the rise of transnational legal regimes like human rights and transitional justice since the end of the Cold War. Perhaps the best recent attempt to capture the processes and meanings of law within late-capitalist global formations can be found in the writings of the Portuguese sociologist Boaventura de Sousa Santos (see, especially, Santos 1995 and Santos and Rodríguez-Garavito 2003). Santos's framework, which he describes as "interlegality," recognizes the two dimensions that are usually missed—or conflated—in orthodox accounts of legal pluralism or multiplicity: the way legal subjectivity, the ability of law to shape self-identity, is constituted both outwardly and inwardly, and the way that people experience the presence of multiple legal regimes—with their different sets of expectations—in the same social space as a kind of normative mélange, as a mixture of codes and discourses that resists easy analytical parsing at the same time it manages to provide a basis for purposive action. As Santos explains, his approach:

> is not the legal pluralism of traditional legal anthropology, in which the different legal orders are conceived as separate entities coexisting in the same political spaces, but rather, the conception of different legal spaces superimposed,

interpenetrated and mixed in our minds, as much as in our actions, either on occasions of qualitative leaps or sweeping crises in our life trajectories, or in the dull routine of eventless everyday life. We live in a time of porous legality or of legal porosity, multiple networks of legal orders forcing us to constant transitions and trespassings. Our legal life is constituted by an intersection of different legal orders, that is, by *interlegality*. . . . Interlegality is a highly dynamic process, because the different legal spaces are nonsynchronic, and thus result in uneven and unstable combinations of legal codes (codes in a semiotic sense). . . . (1995: 473; emphasis in original)

When I describe Alonso de Ibañez as occupying one point or node in a wider legal universe, I similarly mean to emphasize the way people experience the semiotic mixings and unstable combinations of law, as well as the essential porosity of the distinct legal *orders*—such as they are—that have claims on people, and, equally important, are claimed by them in return. However, beyond the analytical, to describe law in Bolivia in this way is also to make empirical and critical claims. It is to recognize would be considered heretical within Bolivian legal circles: that "law" in Bolivia is more complicated than supposed (though not essentially indeterminate); it is diffuse; and it is to be found outside the control of those institutions that are charged with codifying *the* law, which—as in other Latin American countries whose legal traditions also are directly connected (jurisprudentially, if not historically) in an unbroken chain to the Platonic certainties of Roman law—is understood to exist in a kind of parallel intellectual universe that can only be accessed by an enlightened few. Alonso de Ibañez, however, has sat at the crossroads of a different kind of legal history, one that was constituted by—among others—the Catholic church (present in Sacaca since the sixteenth century), local debates over constitutionalism in the early part of the nineteenth century, resistance to the late nineteenth century Law of Expropriation, the subtle and more obvious shifts associated with the incomplete National Revolution of 1952, and, over the last fifteen years, the coming of western human rights discourse to the province through transnational development.

Finally, if this way of understanding law—and the place of Alonso de Ibañez within it—is a radically alternative *descriptive* account, it is also radically *prescriptive* or critical. During the height of neoliberalism in Bolivia during the 1990s, frameworks like "customary law" and "customary indigenous law" (as in new Article 28 of the Code of Criminal Procedure) were adopted as part of a specific political project to recognize alternate legal systems and forms of legal knowledge (see Postero 2007a; Van Cott 2000). However, these frameworks did not challenge the basic understanding of law itself. Instead, the discourse of "indigenous law" that emerged in Bolivia during this time was due in large part to the willingness of certain progressive (but nevertheless elite) lawyers and politicians to expand the existing categories to include new expressions of a very orthodox law. The recognition of something like official legal pluralism in Bolivia, therefore, was at the same time an attempt to reinforce what I am arguing is a fundamentally mistaken account of the reality of law, which exists for people not in terms of distinct systems conveniently nested within institutional and intellectual hierarchies (however expansive), but through the "legal spaces superimposed, interpenetrated and mixed in . . . minds, as much as in . . . actions, either on occasions of qualitative leaps or sweeping crises in . . . life trajectories, or in the dull routine of eventless everyday life," to again draw on Santos's formulation.

To conceptualize law in this way is to critically undermine both the traditional who and where of law in Bolivia. "Law" and its consequences are no longer centered in urban sites of law-making, those courts, classrooms, and clubs that have long been seen as the professionalized sites where Themis is to be found. In other words, canapés must now take their place alongside ch'uño as the preferred repast of choice for Bolivian jurisprudents and legal actors. But even more subversive is the assertion that rural provinces like Alonso de Ibañez occupy a location—geographic, institutional, conceptual—that is every bit as essential within the broader Bolivian legal universe as La Paz or Sucre, the nation's traditional legal capital (like South Africa, Bolivia divides its branches of government between multiple cities).

Before the first period of extended research in Bolivia in 1998, I had hypothesized the existence of a category of rural-legal intellectuals I called "Andean lawyers." In the dissertation that resulted (Goodale 2001), I rejected this hypothesis, arguing instead that men who pass through the fiesta-cargo system do not obtain a level of specialized legal knowledge sufficient to describe them as "lawyers" in the conventional sense. Yet I now see that in making this argument I was adopting a much too restrictive conception of "law." Moreover, I did not fully understand at the time the relationship between law and the wider historical and ideological patterns that have shaped the emergence of modern Bolivia, and the extent to which law and legal subjectivity in places like Alonso de Ibañez both reflected and shaped these patterns. In locating the practices of law in Alonso de Ibañez within this profoundly different framework, places like the juzgado de instrucción and the meeting area in front of the house of the corregidor auxiliar of Molino T'ikanoma must take their place as essential sites of law, as public spheres in which the imperatives of Bolivia's troubled modernity are encountered, appropriated, and refracted.

4 Courts of Desire

Gender, Power, and the Law

GENDER IS A QUINTESSENTIAL CATEGORY of late modernity, one that reflects the ways in which social practices both shape, and are shaped by, broader imperatives of global economics, political ideology, and law, among others. Like other modern categories, gender expresses a set of aspirations that must be understood in relation to broader frames of references—aspirations about ideal social relations, the way men and women ought to conceive of themselves, and the way they are supposed to think and act in relation to each other. Moreover, the use of gender in this dual sense—to refer to cultural or social constructions of sex (as opposed to its simple biology) and the disciplinary intent of the category itself—is decidedly quite recent. Only around the 1950s did medical researchers and then social scientists in the United States and Europe begin to use the term *gender* as a way to distinguish between the biological fact of sex and ways in which this fact was filtered through the lens of culture. In addition, it wasn't until the late 1960s and early 1970s that feminist theorists and political leaders began to locate the sex-gender nexus within wider networks of economic, regional, ethnic, and other forms of power, so that the analytical and ethical focus on gender came to be seen as one of the key means through which inequality was identified and subverted.[1]

There is a certain irony in the fact that the category gender emerged in this way, although its irony can only be appreciated in terms of another peculiar feature of modernity. The word gender itself has sociolinguistic roots that go very deep, all the way into the proto-Indo-European past, in which *gen-os* was used as a way to refer to "kind" or "race." This root can be seen across a large number of words in many languages that indicate neutral classification, including genus, genre, *gens* (the Roman clans that shared a common name), kin, and so on. The word gender had been used (in English) to refer to a simple class or type from the early Middle period (Chaucer uses it in this way, for example), which shows that the word entered English through either Latin or Anglo-Norman French, or some combination. For about 900 years, gender was a word used to specifically cut through all of those subjective frameworks of meaning that were differentially applied to people, plants, nouns, and anything else that could be subdivided. In other words, for centuries gender meant something like category and category connoted objective classification, or, even more, a classification that represented the mere formal recognition of differences that were objectively present and observable in the natural world. The contemporary Spanish *género* is even more closely connected to its Latin (and then proto-Indo-European) roots. The twenty-third edition of the Royal Academy's *Diccionario de la Lengua Española* does not even recognize a meaning for gender that reflects profound recent shifts, preferring instead to preserve for the word its essential value neutrality.

However, by the 1960s the very idea of a neutral category—linguistic, social, or otherwise—was itself under attack on a number of different fronts. Formal categories of language were believed to obscure more subtle meanings, some of which reflected wider cultural or political imperatives. And supposedly neutral social and political categories like class, ethnicity, and race were seen to mask even deeper, and often even more insidious, historical truths about relations of power and the structures of domination that maintained these relations. The critique of categories as such, in other words, marked the onset of a peculiar kind of postwar modern malaise, in which the neutral techniques of scientific classification and sorting were exposed as tools at the service of the powerful.

So the word itself—gender—that had its roots in words that meant simply "type" or "kind" was turned on its head. From a way to distinguish between— among other things—the two biological sexes of humans, it came to refer to the many invidious social dynamics that were obscured by the very act of distinguishing in this way. If gender categorization was a means through which power inequalities were established and justified, then it was simply a short step from the critical to the normative: henceforth, gender would be the analytical means through which these power inequalities were identified and undermined. By an odd twist in intellectual—and perhaps political—history, the emergence of gender as a site for these wider debates was also an attempt to restore an essential—but quite different—kind of neutrality to the concept itself.

If relations between men and women (and other genders) could eventually be made equal, or at least stripped of their bases in wider struggles over economic, political, legal, and other forms of power, then gender would regain some of its original proto-Indo-European mojo.

However, that moment is a long way off. In the meantime, the struggle over—and through—gender in Bolivia illustrates several of the dilemmas of modernity that are expressed in different ways throughout this book. One of these is the dilemma of competing narratives. The problem of multiple narratives of gender coexisting in the same social spaces poses problems for *both* social actors and the social scientist who wants to understand their lives and experience of everyday life. And of course the observer also is imbued with his or her own gender expectations, those idealized frameworks that provide a set of working guidelines for male-female relations, some of which harden into bright lines (a man shall not physically or verbally abuse a woman in any way [and vice versa, although this line is not as clear]), some of which are certainly normative but more ambiguously (women and men should earn equal pay for equal work).

Collisions

It did not take the reflexive turn in anthropology in order to understand how much the sight of a campesino in the norte de Potosí beating his wife and dragging her on the ground by her long braids would cause me, whose understanding of male-female relations is anchored—even if unconsciously—in the dim mists of medieval European courtly romances, to play the part of the chivalrous knight and boldly intervene. And what if at least one of the multiple narratives of gender in the norte de Potosí tells a *runa* man that it is acceptable to beat his wife if her behavior crosses certain lines, for example, if she flirts with another man or is lazy in her housework or devotion to the children?[2] At the exact moment the drunk and cursing man (*"¡gringu caraju!"* or "damn gringo!" the man growled as I threw him to the ground) was prevented from acting as he believed he was supposed to toward his wife, at least four separate narratives of gender violently collided in that dusty alley in Sacaca's lower district.

First, there were the variations on the narrative that structures relations between men and women across the two hundred hamlets in Alonso de Ibañez. These are complicated enough, because gender relations in the province have been the target of intense discursive intervention for centuries (even if these were not treated *as* "gender" relations until only recently). From the ever-present influence of the Catholic church, in which men and women are both equally children of God, to the arrival in the early twentieth century of the rhetoric of revolutionary Marxism, which exhorts both campesinos and campesinas to join together in a common struggle, the ways in which men and women understand themselves *as* men and women have never been disconnected from wider patterns of intention.

Second, both of us—to greater or lesser degrees—were aware of the way Bolivian state law envisions gender relations, in large part through the way certain types of behavior either are expressly prohibited or tacitly condoned. There is no question that the Bolivian Penal Code prohibits the use of physical violence against an adult woman, regardless of the reason (it makes an exception for the "reasonable" punishment of children). The rationale behind this goes back to the Enlightenment foundations of the nation-state, in which the protection of bodily integrity was a natural consequence of the liberal and rational individualism that set the parameters for large portions of Bolivian law. However, this same penal code shapes a quite different set of expectations in the area of "crimes against sexual liberty," in which the crime of "violation" is almost never brought against a man when the victim is his wife (Title XI). In legal practice, if not in legal theory, a husband has the presumption of consent from his wife, which means that violence—by definition, a lack of consent— can never be the *cause* of "carnal access," one of the elements of the crime.[3]

Third, our desperate tussle was informed by another narrative of gender relations, one that had begun to impact social practices in rural Bolivia by the mid-1990s, the highpoint of "neoliberalism." This was the narrative that refracted relations between men and women through the prism of human rights, both generally—human rights-as-idea, what I have described elsewhere as the connotative expression of human rights (Goodale 2007b)—and specifically, through a series of legislative reforms that were intended to put into effect provisions of international human rights that focused on gender violence.[4] As I describe more fully below, Alonso de Ibañez was one of the few places in rural Bolivia where a *Servicio Legal Integral* (SLI) was established, which was a legal services center for women who had been victims of violations that were recognized by international human rights law but which had—until then—been ignored or rejected by Bolivian state law and judicial tradition.

Of course given the liberal legal foundations of Bolivia itself, and the patterns of intention that had emerged over the preceding 180 years, it would not be accurate to say that Bolivian law and human rights represented opposing frameworks for understanding gender relations. Instead, the much more recent rise of human rights discourse and consciousness in Bolivia in places like Alonso de Ibañez has served to heighten, and expand on, imperatives that had been present—but obscured or ignored—in Bolivian law and moral discourse since the early nineteenth century. Given what I know about the workings of the SLI in Alonso de Ibañez, there is a very good chance that the man I struggled with had been present while SLI officials explained its purposes to people in his hamlet and described more broadly why *derechos humanos*, or human rights, represented a new vision for Bolivia and its people. In other words, as he dragged his wife by the hair across the ground, he must have known, at some level, that what he was doing violated the norms of more than simply Bolivian law, which, in any case, had always turned a blind eye in practice to "reasonable" levels of physical violence against married women by their husbands, as much in Sacaca as in La Paz.

Finally, in this collision of discursive categories and bodies, a fourth set of gender expectations was invoked, even if unconsciously: my own idiosyncratic hodge-podge of ideas and understandings, which for whatever reason compelled me to act in the first place. (I have never intervened in this way during the many *tinkus* I have observed, in which men beat each other senseless and, on occasion, hit each other on the head with large rocks, which leads to death every few years.) In many ways the contradictory bricolage of gender expectations that produced my response represents the future for every man (and woman) in Alonso de Ibañez, what the concern with *roles de género*, or "gender roles," in Bolivian law and moral discourse is leading toward.

I was raised in southern California to moderately conservative children of the Eisenhower generation. I broke away from the stifling intellectual and moral climate of the Reagan years through a study of Marxist political theory at UCLA. I underwent a conversion of sorts in the early 1990s as a graduate student in London, which included a study of *The Anti-Social Family* (Barrett and McIntosh 1991), an example of Marxist feminist writing that reinterpreted the traditional western nuclear family in terms of class conflict. And I had spent most of the 1990s refining a progressive and cosmopolitan sensibility, while in practice my relations with women resembled much more the kind of *Leave It to Beaver* world I had vehemently rejected than the one envisioned by Barrett and McIntosh.

So there I was: a progressive, educated man with feminist training and sympathies, yet with a stubbornly instinctive appreciation for tradition (in other words, not too progressive). My understanding of gender equality was informed by both American civil rights law—via a stop for law school in the mid-1990s—and the history of international human rights work in Bolivia against gender violence in the late 1990s. Interestingly, both of these bodies of norms emphasize what is described in the United States as "formal," rather than "substantive," equality; again, a vision of gender relations that settles into the workable middle, just as I apparently had. And of course in my case, any reaction to what I encounter in Bolivia is always filtered through what I know—and passionately appreciate—about both the diversity of worldviews in Bolivia, and, even more important, the way imperatives of power shape, deny, support, and are otherwise expressed through these worldviews.

Was I, in that moment, an instrument of this power? By preventing the man from doing what another gender framework suggested he do, was I liberalizing him at the end of my well-worn Timberland boot? Everyone knows that gender equality—which includes the right not to be dragged through the dirt by the hair—is justified by a set of assumptions expressed in national, international, and transnational law. But does that settle it? Do we simply say that he was wrong and I was right to have intervened in the way I did, in a brief moment of violence that also could have been justified as an ethically uncomplicated act of defense on behalf of a victim of assault and battery?

The dilemma of multiple narratives of gender can be seen in other, perhaps less dramatic, ways in contemporary Bolivia. In her collection of previously published essays, Olivia Harris (2000) presents what is among the most wide-ranging and deservedly influential bodies of work on gender in rural Bolivia.[5] Although her many analyses add important qualifications, she argues—across different essays and themes—that relations between men and women express an underlying complementary unity, a structural relationship that has its roots in a broader traditional Andean culture. This kind of complementarity can be compared to the yin-yang of Taoism: two elements are recognized to be both ontologically distinct but inseparable; they ideally should coexist in balance or harmony; and their complementary presence symbolizes, or even expresses directly, a complementarity among pairs of structural opposites throughout the wider universe.

The complementary unity of male-female relations in Bolivia invokes a quite different idea than dualism, in which structural opposites are not necessarily joined toward a wider—and, ideally, harmonious—purpose (think of the profound conceptual differences between, say, Manichaeism and Taoism). In the norte de Potosí, this essential unity of opposites is expressed by the Aymara concept of *chachawarmi*, which is a substantive created by combining the Aymara word for man-husband with the word for woman-wife (Harris 2000: 164, et seq.). This idea also is found in the broader Quechua expression "*tukuy ima qhariwarmi*," or "everything is man-and-woman."[6]

But complementary unity as the basis for gender relations, and, by extension, wider social relations throughout the rural Andes, is also the source of conflict. As we will see, and as Harris shows, conflict arises from the gap between ideal gender relations and what we might call the social practice of gender. Yet this is not primarily what I have in mind here. The conflict that I will, in part, explore throughout this chapter is rather the one between two ideals: the complementary unity of traditional highland culture, and the essential sameness that is both assumed and demanded by liberalism, especially as expressed in recent human rights and development initiatives in Bolivia. The social ontology that forms the foundation for transnational human rights work in rural Bolivia redefines the social being in ways that carry profound, if subtle, implications for the structure of male-female relations.

At a conceptual level, complementarity depends on three assumptions: first, that men and women are fundamentally different (though interdependent) kinds of beings; second, that although men and women are fundamentally different, they are both functionally and structurally necessary across the range, from the maintenance of the household and family economic unit, to the harmonious unfolding of the universe itself (whose structure the male-female dyad, in part, reproduces); and third, the essence of male-female relations is centripetal, in that it is in the nature of men and women to think and act in ways that actualize their dyadic unity. (An important corollary to this is that disrupture and strife result when male-female relations become centrifugal, because by pulling apart, men and women actually threaten—however modestly—the structural integrity of the wider social universe.)

The rational individualist ontology that undergirds the modern liberal project, by contrast, depends on a quite different set of assumptions. Men and women are fundamentally the same kind of being; nothing can be said about men and women *as* men and women, because their essences are not meaningfully distinguishable in this way; men and women are not conceived in a necessary relation to anything, whether each other or the wider universe; and because men and women do not play different but integral roles within the framework of modern liberalism, conflicts between men and women—again, *as* men and women—do not necessarily affect the wider structure in which their relations are embedded. This is the wider ontological system implied by liberalism and not the universe of traditional Andean culture, which Frank Salomon (2001) describes as a "unified biological-technological productivity unfolding seamlessly from human–telluric bonds through matrimonial alliance outward to very wide regional alignments and toward cosmological forces" (p. 654).

When the SLI in Alonso de Ibañez proselytized throughout the province as part of its strategy to transform people's consciousness, its director was most concerned that men and women come to see themselves first and foremost as *humans*, that they understood they were part of this more elevated category of social being whose essence was defined by a basic equality and who was imbued with a set of rights (derechos humanos) that transcended—morally, if not practically—all existing normativities. In other words, within a liberal ontology, the moral universe is reproduced through the individual, degendered person, rather than through the complementary male-female—or any other—pair, and certainly not through the collective social body. In developing this argument more fully below, we will see that the anthropological account of gender relations in Bolivia is reinforced in unexpected ways that demonstrates its continued conceptual and ethnographic strengths.

Power and Pragmatism

Before discussing the relationship between gender, law, and broader patterns of intention more specifically, it would be helpful to make some general observations about gender in Bolivia. Given the discursive history of the concept itself, it is not surprising that "gender" has become a way of describing relations between men and women in Bolivia and, more specifically, a conceptual framework for analyzing male-female relations in terms of power. Power has its own peculiar discursive history, of course, one that tracks very closely gender's recent transformations. However, within discussions of gender in Bolivia, power refers to at least two things: first, the ability of one gender (usually, but not always, men)[7] to secure greater access to resources—economic, intellectual, political—in part through the way the productive labor of women is mobilized; and second, when power is invoked in relation to gender, the mere fact of unequal access to resources and the differential ability to employ labor usually is followed by a critical analysis of the social conditions that have led to, and which perpetuate, these facts of inequality.

As both a concept, and ordering principle for social and political action, gender entered Bolivia in the early 1990s as part of the broader liberal renaissance, which unfolded, as we have seen, under the banner of "neoliberalism." Gender was, and continues to be, the vanguard category for human rights mobilization in Bolivia, something that has only recently begun to change with the electoral triumph of Evo Morales and the *Movimiento al Socialismo* party and the political apotheosis of indigenous rights discourse. The 1995 United Nations World Conference on Women in Beijing was a key moment in this history because the event was preceded by several years of international legal and political outreach that sought to embed so-called women's issues—like domestic violence, child support, and education—within a human rights framework, represented by foundational documents like the Convention on the Elimination of All Forms of Discrimination Against Women (CEDAW).[8] Bolivia did not ratify CEDAW until 1990, after which the successive governments of Paz Zamora (1989–93) and especially Sánchez de Lozada (1993–97) took steps to implement provisions of CEDAW through the creation of governmental agencies and municipal initiatives dedicated to gender. For example, in 1993 the Subsecretariat for Gender Issues was created within the new Ministry for Human Development. As a direct response to Bolivia's ratification of CEDAW four years earlier, in 1994 the Ministry (in Resolution 139/94) adopted the National Plan for the Eradication, Prevention, and Punishment of Violence Against Women.

At the same time, transnational NGOs also brought the discourse of gender and women's rights to rural areas like the norte de Potosí. (The role of development within broader patterns of intention in Bolivia will be discussed more fully in Chapter 6.) In the norte de Potosí during the late 1990s and early 2000s, there were at least four international or transnational organizations whose activities focused, at least in part, on gender issues, including the education of women, which had been codified within international human rights law in places like CEDAW's Article 10.[9]

UNICEF, which had focused on potable water projects in the norte de Potosí until about 1992, began a series of women's literacy and education initiatives.[10] This shift reflected the heightened transnational receptivity to gender at this time within the development community, as well as the increasing demand by Bolivia's small, but influential, elite activist community for international agencies like UNICEF to broaden their focus to include more complicated "human development" problems. In 1999, a first-ever fair was organized in Sacaca by many of the NGOs active in the region in order to promote an awareness of gender inequality and continue the didactic process of explaining the concept of women's rights that had been slowly expanding over the previous decade. As always, there was a certain ambivalence at this event over whether gender issues—like violence against women, or greater reproductive choice—should be treated as human rights problems, or problems of public health, or perhaps both (see Figures 4.1–4.3).

All of this was happening against a backdrop of what might be called "actual" gender relations in rural Bolivia, by which I mean relations between men and women as they were, not necessarily as they were conceived of within the relatively recent *discourse* of gender and women's rights. As a way of describing certain basic features of actual gender relations in a place like the norte de Potosí, it is helpful to view them through the lens of political and legal practice. Although woman are not formally excluded from serving in authority positions where they would have official legal and political duties, in practice they are almost never elected or chosen for such positions. This distinction between formal or ideological prohibitions and practice is very important here. People in hamlets in Alonso de Ibáñez, as elsewhere in the rural Andes, tend to place a high value on pragmatism. Cultural institutions, in

Figure 4.1. Transnational NGO feria, Sacaca (demonstration of the moral and health benefits of the *wawa wasi*, or kindergarten)

Figure 4.2. Transnational NGOs market their discursive wares during a feria in Sacaca's plaza

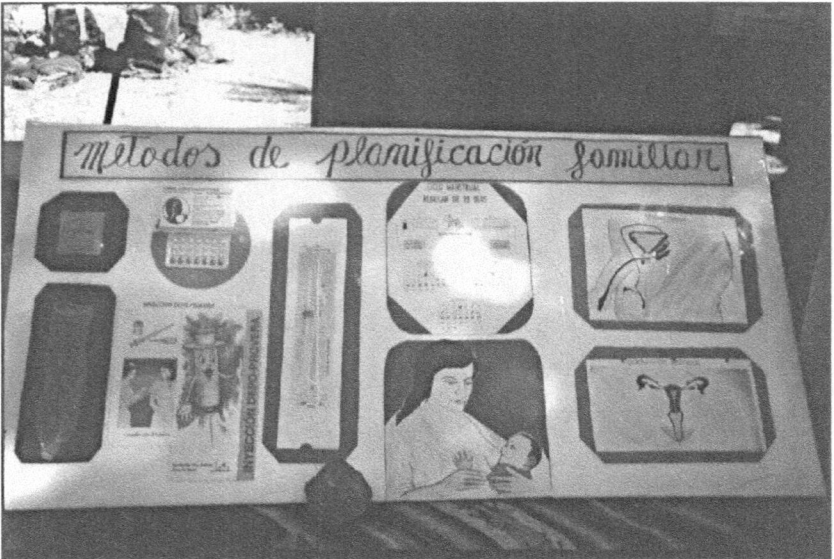

Figure 4.3. A transnational NGO feria exhibit, Sacaca, explaining the methods for family planning, another expectation of Bolivian modernity

turn, reflect the importance placed on finding pragmatic solutions to problems; this means, among other things, that rigid local ideologies are uncommon and flexibility is one of the hallmarks of local cultural practice. Because
of this, there are very few formal or explicit cultural prohibitions in hamlets in
Alonso de Ibañez. There are, of course, trends, patterns, and tendencies, but
these reflect what could be understood as an ongoing process of negotiation
within hamlets and *ayllus* in the face of constant pressures—both internal
(poverty and its implications) and external (NGOs' demands, penetration of
western discourses)—rather than the presence of rigid preexisting dogma.

In terms of women and authority positions, people in hamlets never say
that "women cannot serve," but rather that "women do not serve," and there is
a crucial difference between these two, because the first would demonstrate a
formal rule that disadvantages women while the second, actual response simply reflects an effect of certain current realities. The *jilanqu* of Minor Ayllu
Chaykina Abajo (living in Fundación, Canton Sillu Sillu) emphasized that the
main community principle was "equality," in both participation in legal and
political duties and in the division and use of land. However, women from
Fundación (and throughout the minor ayllu) eventually marry and when they
do, they are "carried away," which means—among other things—that they
cannot serve in local cargo positions away from their affinal hamlets. The *corregidor* titular of Canton Sillu Sillu argued that if women did not participate
equally in hamlet and ayllu affairs, it was "not according to custom," but because "men and women have different work."

An important factor that weighs against the selection of women as legal and
political authorities in the province is the fact that hamlets are in most cases
functionally exogamous and follow a patrilocal postmarital residence pattern.
This means that almost all the adult women living in a particular hamlet are
nonlocals; their parents, brothers, and their lands are located in their birth
hamlets, which can be located throughout the province, in different provinces
throughout north Potosí, and even in different departments.[11] One effect of patrilocality in this context is that women are not part of the same political and
economic networks as their husbands, who were born and usually live in the
same hamlet their entire lives.

As the jilanqu of Minor Ayllu Chaykina Abajo explained:

> The father divides the land among his children, but not equally. He gives a little
> less to the daughters and a little more to the sons. When the women [of a hamlet]

marry, they leave, and so they don't get much land. Those that remain, the sons, they seize the land so that they can sow it. But among the sons, the division of the lands is equal, with a little remaining for the daughters.

The corregidor titular of Canton Iturata also emphasized the ways in which geography amplified the practical effects of patrilocality:

The father passes his land equally to his children. Both his sons and daughters receive land equally, the girls don't receive less. But a woman from Iturata will marry a man from another community, [and when this happens] her land is given to another, but also together with [this other], no? Because when she lives in another place that's far away she is not able to return to work [on her land]. For this reason, her brothers or neighbors [in her birth hamlet] sow and work on her land.

However, despite the problem for women of patrilocality, the coming of human rights legislation at the national level, and the local implementation of institutions authorized under this legislation (see the following chapter), have to a certain extent altered the implications of postmarital residence. As the cor-regidor titular of Canton Iturarta in Sak'ani described it, the national legisla-tion dedicated to *asuntos de género* (gender issues) was shifting the balance of power toward women in their use and ownership of land: "Before, more im-portance [in the division of land] was given to the boy. But now, with these new laws, it isn't this way anymore. The situation has changed."

Nevertheless, postmarital residence continues to matter. The importance of residence patterns in determining who does (not *can*) assume authority posi-tions is shown in the case of the *segunda* of Ayllu Qolque Menor Abajo, who lived in Enguyo during 1998–99. The segunda was a fortyish woman who had never married and thus had never moved away from her birth hamlet. It is un-common for a woman not to marry at some point in her life; some women do return to their birth hamlets after divorce or the death of their husbands, but this typically happens after an interval of many years. Moreover, an older woman moving back to her birth hamlet faces hostility from the hamlet's mar-ried women, who will see her, somewhat ironically, as an outsider and a threat. In these cases—because of the mistrust and long absence—women returning to their birth hamlets will not be able to suddenly participate in local politico-legal networks. However, a woman like the Ayllu Qolque Menor Abajo se-gunda had two factors weighing in her favor: First, she had lived in the hamlet

all her life and had participated—only unofficially before her election to
segunda—in many of the hamlet's legal and political activities; second, she did
not have any brothers (see Figure 4.4).

She was a quiet woman, but eager to talk about her official duties. Her term
would last for one year and during this time she attended courses in "*capac-
itación*" (or "technocratic writing") in Sacaca and consulted with the corregidor titular in the capital on the proper strategies for resolving disputes. She was

Figure 4.4. A dramatically uncommon sight—the *segunda* of
Ayllu Qolque Menor Abajo (Enguyo) entering her cargo

quick to point out that although it is not common for a woman to hold one of the "natural authority" (i.e., ayllu) positions, there had been a female *dirigente* of her *sindicato*. She said that women from her hamlet had an obligation to return home to work their lands, even if their lives made this difficult. When conflicts within the ayllu became especially serious, she always worked in collaboration with the ayllu's jilanqu (who lived in Kochinipampa). When asked about the unusual—and delicate—fact that she was not married, she said that a woman who is not married and does not have any brothers "must serve" the community in the way she was doing.

Although this convergence of factors (a woman remaining unmarried with no brothers to represent the family in authority positions) occurs quite infrequently, it does happen, and when it does, politico-legal authority positions can be filled by women. A useful example is the case of land tenure. In all hamlets in the province, women and men are able to inherit land equally from their fathers. This rule is acknowledged by the authorities who are called on to resolve disputes over inheritance; in most cases such disputes are relatively quickly and easily resolved because authorities simply divide the disputed parcels equally among the contesting parties. Yet even though men and women *must* inherit land equally (that is, fathers do not have the right to create unequal divisions), the fact remains that daughters move away from their birth hamlets—and their future inheritance—while sons remain; the sons, not the daughters, are the ones who work the land, nurture it through ritual, and the ones who are present with the father during all decisions regarding it. Moreover, because daughters usually move away from their birth hamlets while they are still quite young—usually younger than twenty years old—and their fathers have twenty years of life or more left before death forces a division, a daughter's connection with the family's land—as with her birth hamlet—is quite tenuous by the time she returns to reassert her rights in it.

As we have seen, the result is that in practice sons' shares of family lands are much greater than the shares that daughters receive. However, because this result is not due to a formal *ideology* of gender inequality, but rather to the variable effects of patrilocality, it is not possible to give a general description that holds true across the province. In some cases, married women make a concerted effort to return to their birth hamlets during the planting and harvesting seasons each year in order to exert more control over their future allotment;[12] and in some families, daughters maintain an especially close relationship with their brothers, who then agree to a later equitable division. Finally, some brothers agree to an equal division of land irrespective of the presence or absence of their sisters simply out of a personal belief that an equal division is fair and appropriate. However, based on my own research in many of the province's hamlets over a ten-year period, I can say that a de facto gender inequality in land division exists. Further, both women and men are aware of this practical tendency toward inequality in land tenure. Women complain about it openly; men, on the other hand, tend to emphasize the general principle of equality while admitting somewhat sheepishly that a woman's long-term absence from a hamlet means that the rule is difficult to apply in practice.

Although the cases in which women become legal or political authorities are far fewer than those cases in which women manage—despite significant obstacles—to retain control over family lands and inherit equal plots at division, the principle is the same in both: Formal rules do not prohibit women from assuming authority positions or exercising control over land in the same way that men do, but practical factors work to make both outcomes unlikely in specific cases. It is important to underscore this formal equality versus practical inequality dynamic because participation in authority systems and control over land are the two most important routes for the accumulation of personal power and prestige within hamlets, as well as in the provincial capital. Power within gender relations, however, cannot be understood without taking wider imperatives into consideration. In other words, despite the way a more recent gender discourse has shifted traditional structuralist approaches to male-female relations in the Andes, it is simply not possible to explain them in terms of prefigured categories, which see male-female relations in rural Bolivia as local expressions of more global phenomena.

This also does not mean that actual gender relations in rural Bolivia reflect a basic set of conditions either assumed, or desired, by competing discourses of modernity like human rights, which deny the legitimacy of inequality as measured in very specific normative or material terms. As I have said, gender relations are essentially pragmatic, which means, among other things, that they are not exclusively or rigidly derived from formalized norms about men and women as such. Rather, even if the ways in which male-female (qhariwarmi/ chachawarmi) is expressed in social practice is in part a response to preexisting— and changing—cultural expectations, it is also in part a response to—equally changeable—economic, political, and social conditions. More provocatively, my research leads to another unsettling conclusion: In relation to landholding, women *must* be unequal to men in Alonso de Ibañez, not because this is compelled by local legal or moral discourse, but because a pragmatic inequality is necessary for sheer survival.

For the 25,000 people spread throughout the province—whose lives mirror those of people all across rural Bolivia—productive land is the basis for social participation. Yet at a more basic level, productive land is also the foundation for continued existence. Without access to land, people in rural Bolivia (as elsewhere in the Andean countries, see, e.g., Lund 1994) must migrate to the urban poverty traps of El Alto and La Paz, where life conditions are even more tenuous, or try and find work in the mining towns of Potosí or Oruro (an option that has almost disappeared since the economic reforms of the mid-1980s). So even if daughters have a right—one that is a formal part of local normative discourse—to inherit and then control a portion of family lands after the death of their fathers, the scrupulous enforcement of this right would have obviously damaging consequences, because it would mean letting significant portions of available land lie fallow and possibly become barren. Through a kind of ownership through usufruct, brothers eventually take control over land that had been only symbolically maintained for absent sisters. This and the other effects of patrilocality mean that women do not, and cannot, have as much "power" as their husbands—but it also means that men and women can survive in the norte de Potosí, as elsewhere in agro-pastoral rural Bolivia.

Gender and the Legal Subject

Within what has become a transnational discourse, scholars, activists, government officials, and others assume that the truth-value of gender analysis—combined with its critical skepticism—reveals cultural ideologies for what they are: elaborate mechanisms in which gender expectations or "roles" obscure unequal relations of power. These roles or expectations often are qualified with the euphemism "traditional," which usually indicates that what is being described does not seem to accord with numerous emerging visions of gender relations, especially those embodied in international human rights law. In this framing, the whole range of modern dichotomies usually is employed in one way or another: progressive versus reactionary; dynamic versus static; cosmopolitan versus cultural; democratic versus authoritarian; and, of course, traditional versus modern. This can be seen in examples from diverse regions in the contemporary world. Female genital circumcision/cutting/mutilation (even the naming of these practices shapes and reveals) is a mere "tradition" (translation: it cannot be justified by either reason or recourse to universal moral principles):

By canonizing traditional and cultural restrictions on women and girls into official policy and law, the Taliban leadership of Afghanistan has created the most notorious example in the world of state denial of basic rights of women and girls. It is little consolation that these regulations are enforced unevenly at different times and in different parts of Afghanistan. The dilemma faced by concerned individuals and agencies is in finding a strategy that will result in real and lasting improvements in the lives of Afghan women. Righteous indignation and distant protests are inadequate. (Barker 1999)

Chinese women whose beliefs and experiences reflect traditional norms that limit gender equality may be at increased risk of being subjected to intimate partner violence. (Hollander 2005)

Traditional gender roles are slowly undergoing change. This change is bringing about a vast number of positive outcomes for both genders including: [1] freedom for both men and women to explore and develop new roles based on personal choices rather than gender stereotypes. For example, females can be independent, strong and successful; males can be nurturing, emotional and intuitive; [2] equality of interaction between genders; [3] and increased social, domestic and career opportunities. (State of Queensland 2005)

In other words, to the extent that transnational gender discourse shapes the understanding of actual gender relations, the local, the traditional, and the cultural are ways of describing all of those conservative, rigid, and dogmatic forces that have historically prevented change and worked to maintain gender inequality by suppressing the potential of one gender (usually women) to the benefit of the other (usually men). However, in the norte de Potosí, it is not traditional gender relations that are rigid or dogmatic; as I have shown, they are characterized by an essential pragmatism, one that in part reflects a set of rough-and-tumble contemporary realities, such as the impact of patrilocality and the need to keep available land under cultivation.[13]

Rather, among the set of competing narratives of gender in contemporary Bolivia, it is those derived from transnational human rights that present themselves to ordinary social actors as unyielding sources of normative knowledge that admit of no exception or nuance. Of course, it does no good to simply invert the dichotomies in order to explain the complicated cultural and conceptual interconnections between gender categories in Bolivia: tradition is dynamic, modern liberal notions of gender static; cultural practices respond to difficult contemporary circumstances, those linked to international (or "universal") frameworks tend toward a reactionary moral imperialism that seeks to shape the world's normative alterity into recognizable forms; traditional gender relations in rural Bolivia are imbricated in the entire fabric of local life, if not seamlessly, then, to a certain extent, organically, while ideas of gender that are just another expression of what Ferguson (1999) called the "expectations of modernity" are hopelessly abstracted from local social life; and so on. The interrelationships between categories of gender in Bolivia are much too complicated for this kind of conceptual sleight-of-hand.

This complexity can perhaps best be seen through the ways in which changing ideas about gender come together in the course of ongoing legal struggles, because the logics of the law, even in provincial courts and public meeting places in rural Bolivia, only partly reflect the wider currents from which the different narratives of gender are derived. I mention this here in order to remind the reader that any study of the relationship between law and wider political, economic, or ideological currents must come to terms with certain basic characteristics of what the social historian E. P. Thompson called the law's "own logic and criteria of equity" (1975: 263). At the same time, Thompson's point goes the other way, which is why it bears on the discussion of gender and the law in Bolivia. The logics of the law constrain progressive social impulses as well, including those that seek to reform the law in order to transform legal and social relations between men and women. This means, among other things, that the law is not *essentially* gendered, let alone the mere expression of gender relations in other terms. But it is the case that legal struggles in Bolivia often are interpenetrated—and, in certain cases, motivated—by broader social struggles over relations between men and women, which means that the legal subject is shaped, in part, by wider gender categories, and these categories, in turn, are in part shaped by the law.

The conventional wisdom within the wider Andean studies literature is that if relations between men and women are characterized by separate but equal principles of structural complementarity, then women's presence most often is to be observed in private or semiprivate spheres—the home, informal inter-hamlet or regional exchanges, the mining camp's slag pile, around the loom. Men's contribution to complementary unity, on the other hand, is expressed through dramatic acts in the public sphere, in particular through the legal and the political. The tendency to divide men and women in this way through yet another modern dichotomy—private/public—is linked to certain facts about the differential roles of men and women in public life. For example, as in Alonso de Ibañez, women do not "rotate through"—as the phrase goes, with all of its allusions to culture as a kind of Swiss clockwork—cargo positions. They do not serve (except in exceptional circumstances) as dirigentes of sindicatos campesinos. They do not negotiate with representatives of transnational NGOs when their late-model SUVs come roaring into hamlets in a cloud of benevolent dust. Women do not organize rituals related to irrigation canals or lead pilgrimages to the high places (although they accompany men on these journeys). All of this, and more, is true. Nevertheless, I consistently have found quite different patterns of gendered social practice within what are perhaps the most dramatic of all the public spheres—the arenas of law, where the very fabric of peasant life is exposed, repaired, and, at times, irrevocably ruptured.

Table 4.1 shows the percentage of women who utilized legal institutions in Sacaca as a function of the total over a seven-year period (1998–2005). I have already described Sacaca's *juzgado de instrucción*, its office of corregidor titular, and the province's only titled lawyer, Lucio Montesinos, who was also the director of Sacaca's SLI between 1995 and 1998. However, before exploring what these numbers mean for our understanding of the relationship between gender, law, and broader patterns of intention, let me explain what the "D" refers to here. The *defensores* were mentioned briefly in Chapter 3, but here I must describe them in greater detail. Very soon after returning to Bolivia in 1998, I was told there were six lawyers in Sacaca, which surprised me given the fact that Cesar Ayaviri—who had first directed me to Sacaca—had said in 1996 that there were no lawyers in the town or province. People in town, however, did not refer to these legal specialists as *abogados*, the Spanish word for lawyer; rather, they called them defensores, or "defenders."

I soon discovered that defensores are a peculiar and controversial group, and they form an almost unknown (and certainly unacknowledged) class of legal intellectuals within wider legal circles in Bolivia. Bolivian law (Art. 103, No. 3, Ley de Organización Judicial) authorizes defensores; the idea is that in

Table 4.1. Percentage of women at Sacaca's legal institutions*

JDI	Corregidor Titular	D #1	D #2	D #3	D #4	D #5	Lucio Montesinos
25	60	30	30	50	50	70	70

*These data are based on archival research (where possible), interviews with legal officials, and observations over the relevant time period.

rural provinces with less than four titled lawyers, certain people can be authorized to work as de facto lawyers. There are no requirements for defensores in terms of education or training. A person simply has to be granted permission by the local juzgado—usually a juzgado de instrucción—and then receive a letter of certification from the *Corte Superior* of the relevant department (see Figure 4.5). The declaration to the Corte Superior must state that the person asking to be certified as a defensor has worked in that capacity and has experience with legal matters, assertions that are not verified or corroborated by the court. After that, a person can work as a certified defensor with all the rights—but few of the responsibilities[14]—of a titled lawyer. Defensores can represent clients before the police and judicial officials; they can draw up contracts and other legal documents; they can give legal advice; and finally, they can charge fees for their services using the current *arancel*, or fee list, for lawyers published by departmental authorities.

As of 2005, there were five defensores working in Sacaca. The quality of legal representation provided by these defensores is highly variable. Most have a passing knowledge of the law, which in this case means Bolivian law because they only work with Sacaca's juzgado and not with the corregidor titular or with hamlet authorities outside of Sacaca. As a result of this, the defensor functions as a kind of hybrid legal specialist. They represent their clients' interests in front of the judge and in private consultations, but they work more as lay advocates than professional ones. So, for example, most defensores know what a marriage certificate is supposed to look like or what court documents should formally contain—signatures, stamps, the requisite legalese—but when in situations, particularly court sessions, where the result is not absolutely certain in advance, their level of competence drops dramatically. Because of this, the province's one titled lawyer—Lucio Montesinos—has frequently complained to me about the defensores' inability to effectively represent clients in different situations or to solve problems by applying legal principles. He does not really blame the men in town who work as defensores—they are only taking advantage of a situation they did not create—but rather the law itself, which establishes a system that Montesinos sees as an obstacle to what he has described as general social development (*el desarrollo social*).

The image of the defensor in Sacaca is a complex one. To people from the hamlets, they are lawyers plain and simple; they do not draw a distinction between them and Lucio Montesinos, for example. People from the hamlets use the honorific "doctor" when addressing a defensor. Among themselves, the

SEÑOR PRESIDENTE DE LA RESPETABLE CORTE SUPERIOR DE JUSTICIA

PIDO SE CONSIDERE PARA AUTORIZACION

Otrosies.-

Yò, ARMANDO ALVAREZ ARENAS, mayor de edad, vecino de la localidad de Sacaca, precariamente en esta ciudad, con R. U. N. No. 1001-280432V. y con capacidad jurídica plena, con el debido respeto expongo y pido:

Señor Presidente, ocurre que hace tiempo atrás, trabaje como DEFENSOR en Sacaca, por lo cual he adquirido bastante experiencia en aspectos judiciales en defensa de los habitantes de esa localidad, en vista de que no existen profesionales abogados que cumplan esta función en ese lugar, razón por la cual nuevamente he iniciado estas actividades, y vengo cumpliendo con esmero y dedicación, por tal motivo es que SOLICITO, muy respetuosamente se me otorgue AUTORIZACION para este trabajo que me permitirá seguir cumpliendo como DEFENSOR . Por mi parte protesto cubrir lo recaudos de ley necesarios.

Será Justicia, etc.

OTROSI.- (DOMICILIO) La Stría. de su Despacho.

Potosi, 20 de agosto de 1997

Dra. Mirtha Romay Ojpada
ABOGADA A.D.A
RU. ...... M.C.A. 000281

INTERESADO

Presentado por el interesado a horas ante con cuarenta icinco minutos en ficha veinte de agosto de mil novecientos noventa y siete años.

Figure 4.5. A *defensor* certificate, in which the applicant certifies that he has been working as a lawyer with "careful attention and dedication," Sacaca

defensores also use "doctor," though somewhat ironically at times depending on who is present. Montesinos and the juez instructor are likely to refer to them in derogatory terms, either by using tinterillo, or, more commonly, the Quechua *qhelqeri*, which is not derogatory in itself but becomes so when used as a substitute for *tinterillo* (see Chapter 3, n. 11). I became aware of the complexity of the defensor's image when I met two of them greeting each other one time in Sacaca's plaza with "*¡buenos días*, doctor!" ("good morning, doctor!"). They saw me right as they were exchanging this greeting with knowing smiles and they immediately became silent and clearly embarrassed because they had been caught in some sense self-consciously playing a role.

Now look again at Table 4.1. Taking all of Alonso de Ibañez's defensores as a group, roughly 50 percent of their clients are women. Over half of all the people who travel to Sacaca's corregidor titular each week in order to prosecute legal claims of one kind or another are women. Most strikingly, 70 percent of Lucio Montesino's clients have traditionally been women.[15] It is only in the juzgado de instrucción (JDI) that we see a marked departure from this extraordinary and counterintuitive pattern within the legal practice in this part of rural Bolivia. I will discuss gender and the JDI in greater detail in the next section, but several things must be said about what these numbers reveal.

First, when I say that a certain percentage of people are women in particular legal institutions, these are instances in which women become legal actors alone or in collaboration with other female family members (sisters, mothers, daughters). Depending on the case, a women might initiate a legal proceeding in collaboration with a man (husband, brother, father), but if she is the one who attends the hearings, delivers the *demandas*, discusses the cases with potential witnesses, and so on, then she is listed as the primary legal actor. Using these criteria, women make up over 50 percent of the legal actors in the province—but this number is actually higher, because the total number of active cases in the JDI is relatively lower than the number of "cases" or clients or legal proceedings in the other legal institutions in Sacaca. For example, there are on average 250 to 270 dispute resolution sessions at the house of the corregidor titular on Sundays over the course of a year. Even though these figures include some multiple sessions related to the same case, they still show that the number of cases—and thus legal actors—at the corregidor titular is considerably higher than those at the JDI, where the average is about 120 cases per year.

Second, although Table 4.1 does not include data on gender and legal processes outside of Sacaca, more anecdotal evidence suggests that women participate at about the same rate—50 percent.[16] Keep in mind that the vast majority of legal actors in the provincial capital come from hamlets spread across the province. This means that a woman must leave her hamlet and make what can be a long and arduous journey to Sacaca in order to visit, for example, the corregidor titular. After initiating a case, she then might make repeated visits to Sacaca over the course of months in order to move it along. As I described in Chapter 3, this typically will involve the issuance of demandas, the appearance of *testigos*, a finding of culpability by the corregidor, the levying of a multa, and the inevitable follow-up proceedings when subsequent problems arise. In other words, when a woman becomes a legal actor, she makes a profoundly public and consequential decision, one that can result in equally profound—even if subtle—shifts in social relations within and between families, ayllus, and other categories of identity.

So what do these data tell us about the important presence of women as legal actors in Alonso de Ibañez? More than anything they show that much of the conventional wisdom about gender and power in rural Bolivia must be reconsidered. On the one hand, ethnographers and theorists have made a convincing case for using a complementarity model for understanding male-female relations, even if such a model can harden into an overly structuralist conceptual framework if taken too literally. But on the other hand, complementarity has often not been taken literally enough. As I have said, a common argument is that although oppositional equality is a traditional feature of Andean culture and social relations, one that is expressed in idealizations of male-female, in practice, this structural equality gives way to male dominance, as women suffer physical and emotional violence at the hands of husbands, women are excluded from positions of legal and political power, and women face the burden of having to provide both productive labor and most of the daily child care. All of this has been used to paint a picture of women in rural Bolivia as beaten down and even submissive, content to exert what little power they have in their nonnatal hamlets behind the scenes, in the so-called private sphere.

But how can women be both beaten down and at the same time such vigorous legal actors, well beyond whatever cases might arise from domestic violence or spousal abandonment or other problems that obviously afflict rural women in Bolivia? Women are eager, knowledgeable, and persistent advocates for whatever rights are to be found within the range of normativities at their disposal. A woman who does not read or write and speaks Spanish with only the greatest difficulty, a woman who faces the prospect of having children for her entire childbearing years,[17] a woman whose adult years are passed among people who are, in a sense, strangers, a woman whose "life choices" (as the United Nations would describe them, in its peculiar argot) are, by any measure, severely restricted, also is a woman who can argue convincingly at a public dispute resolution session, is conversant with demandas, *órdenes*, *multas*, testigos and the other finer points of rural legal procedure, and is, finally, a woman who turns to the most powerful institution in Bolivia—the law—without fear or hesitation. All of this means, among other things, that orthodox gender analysis can only partially explain what I have described as Bolivian encounters with law (and liberalism). As we will see in the following section, men and women also are affected by discourses that intersect ambiguously with those of "gender" in Bolivia, and these shift relations of power in yet more problematic ways.

Courts of Desire

The JDI is located in the *casa de justicia* on the western side of Sacaca's plaza (see again Figure 3.3). To enter, one passes through a small passageway that continues on to a garden, owned by the JDI, which usually is planted in corn. One enters the JDI in the passageway to the left and immediately enters the first of four distinct rooms that make up the juzgado. The principal room of the JDI is the *sala de recepción*, or reception room (see again Figure 3.4). This room has chairs for people waiting for court sessions, or to speak with one of the court officials, and a bar that formally separates the court and its personnel from everyone else. On the western wall, the court posts a *lista de audiencias* (list of hearings), *cedulones*, or official notices, and the most recent *arancel*, or list of prices for various court services that is set by the *corte superior de distrito* in Potosí. Also on the walls of the JDI are tourist posters from Potosí and posters that explain the rules related to the law of the *defensa del público rural*, a law intended to provide free counsel to campesinos charged with certain crimes, like rape or murder, who cannot afford to hire counsel on their own. The court also puts on public display notices directed to the JDI from the corte superior de distrito relating to matters like vacation time, or the recognition of public holidays.[18] Behind the bar sit two of the three court personnel, the *actuario* and the secretario. Behind them are *expedientes* (case files) from the current year and files from the previous year that have not been moved back to the archives, which are located in two dusty rooms behind the judge's chamber. Looking down on them are portraits of Simon Bolívar and Antonio José de Sucre, two of Bolivia's greatest national heroes.

In all of this, there is nothing surprising or unusual about Alonso de Ibañez's JDI. In its functioning, architecture, and lazy presence, it is not unlike most of the provincial juzgados scattered throughout rural Bolivia. However, beyond the case files and fee lists, the empty chairs and the relentless sound of the actuario's typewriter, there is something else about the court that does not seem to fit with the image of Bolivia's staid, marginally efficient, and often dreary judicial bureaucracy. On both the walls above the heads of the actuario and secretary, and out among the correspondence from departmental officials, are one or more photos of women, usually topless, but sometimes fully naked (Figure 4.6). The most common source for these photos are the business calendars that are ubiquitous throughout shopkeeper Bolivia. In both urban and rural shops alike, owners hang the calendars produced by the bigger Bolivian companies, from breweries to cement manufacturers, calendars that will feature the saints' days below and the erotic pose of a naked woman above. Although they are more or less readily available, I have never seen one hanging from adobe walls in hamlets in Alonso de Ibañez (although other mass-produced calendars and posters *are* common). They are, in other words, the product and reflection of what might be described as Middle Bolivia: the vast middle and lower middle classes of mestizo Bolivia, which include indigenous campesinos who have moved to places like El Alto and have become, in the jargon of modern sociology, "urbanized."

Here, as in other parts of Latin America, the female body is sexually objectified in all the usual ways. On the one hand, a woman is a sister, daughter, wife, and mother, a social person whose power and presence depend on the whole range of idiosyncratic factors—age, education, social class, ethnicity, and so on. On the other hand, the depersonalized female body is the subject of intense and ever-present sexualization. Although highland Bolivian women in their social roles do not normally self-objectify or trade in dangerous sexual preoccupations as do women in other parts of Latin America (and, to a certain extent, in the Bolivian lowlands)[19]—Bolivian women regularly draw this distinction between themselves and the "hotter" parts of the continent, such as Brazil and Venezuela—they nevertheless confront an undercurrent of sexualization through public images, common slang, and the knowledge that husbands can be expected to seek sexual gratification outside of marriage on a regular basis.

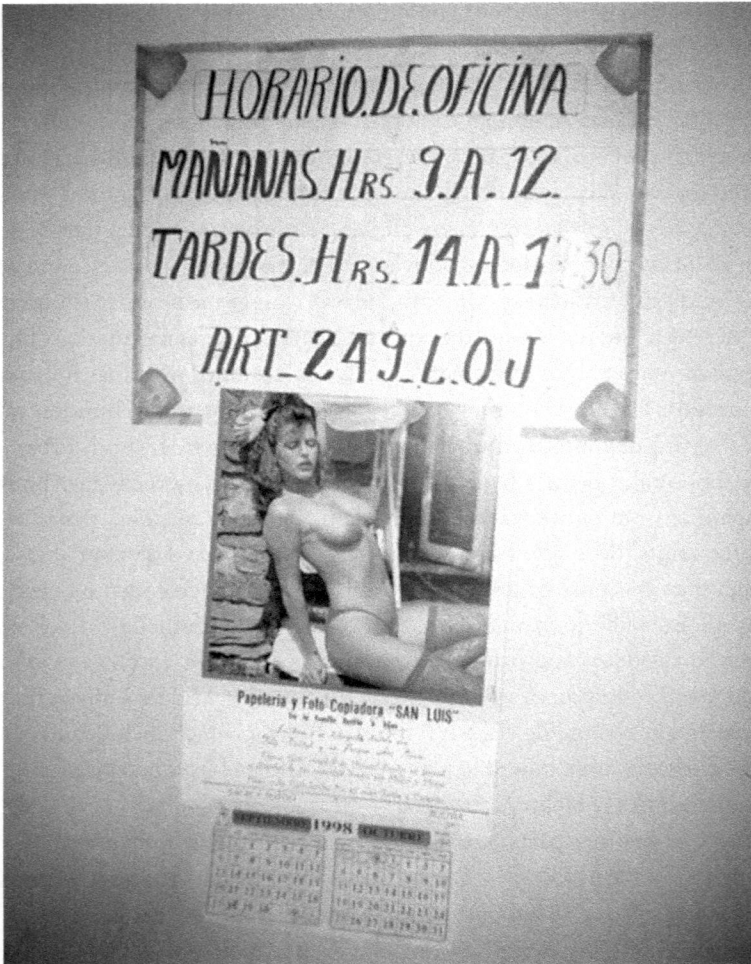

Figure 4.6. Official court hours are announced as per the Ley de Organización Judicial, above an erotic calendar photo

Although the sala de recepción is the main room in the JDI, the place where all of the tedium and ambiguities of small-town court life are to be found, it is not the most important, or most incongruously sexualized, of the juzgado's public spaces.[20] When one is permitted to pass through the gate that separates the laity from the grandeur of the *law*—which is embodied here by both the court's three officials and the judicial archives—one enters the judge's chamber. This room is smaller than the sala de recepción and is divided into even smaller subspaces, where the different distinct legal actors take their places and play their parts in the province's legal (and thus social) dramas. There are spaces for the *demandante* (plaintiff) and *demandado* (defendant); spaces for the *promotor fiscal* (public prosecutor), whose presence is required during hearings for criminal cases; there is a small desk adjacent to the judge's desk where the actuario transcribes, after a fashion, the proceedings (and also, when the judge does not speak Quechua or Aymara, sits as translator); there are a few chairs for lawyers (or defensores) and witnesses (though never enough to accommodate everyone); and finally, there is the relatively magisterial desk of the judge himself, from which he interrogates parties and counsel, thunders out his decisions, and rises, oversize crucifix in hand, so that everyone present can "kiss the cross" at the moment when solemn oaths are required.

But on the wall, looming down on everyone and everything, are posters and photographs of the judge's favorite Brazilian porn star. These are much more graphic than the relatively innocuous business calendars, although he has several of these on his chamber walls as well (Figure 4.7). In all my years of conducting research on legal and social processes in Bolivia, I have never had a more surreal experience than watching an elderly runa woman rise from the floor in order to kiss the massive crucifix, while in the same visual field I was confronted with a display of photographic images clearly not authorized anywhere in Bolivia's Law of Judicial Organization. Imagine the scene. A woman from, say, Iturata, makes the thirteen-hour walk to Sacaca in order to appear as a plaintiff in a case of sexual abuse that her brother-in-law allegedly committed against her thirteen-year-old daughter. In a case like this, hamlet and ayllu authorities would be most likely bypassed altogether, especially since Iturata is— for reasons of unfortunate location—slowly dying, losing some of its people to Oruro and Cochabamba and its young men to the army or the coca fields of the Chapare; this despite the fact that the hamlet/town is a cantonal capital almost as old as Sacaca itself, one with a chapel that probably dates from the early sixteenth century.

This would be at least her second visit to Sacaca for this purpose, because it is first necessary to convince the court that sufficient evidence exists for it to open a case in the first place and issue to the accused and any other parties demandas, which are written on wispy and slight pieces of paper that must be carried back to hamlets and personally delivered by the accusers themselves. With the exception of cases of murder or perhaps attempted rebellion against the state (a charge that has been leveled with surprising frequency over the years),

Figure 4.7. Chambers of the *juez* instructor, Alonso de Ibañez. The full symbolic array of secular and sacred Bolivia is visible at center. At top right one can see the beginning of the judge's pornographic montage.

there is almost nothing that would cause Sacaca's one police official to make the long trip to a distant hamlet like Iturata in order to serve judicial papers, secure the presence of parties or witnesses at legal proceedings in the provincial capital, or otherwise perform the type of enforcement and judicial support duties that are expected of police officers in Bolivia's cities and larger towns.[21] Then there is the problem that the accused man from Iturata would need to make one or more initial trips to Sacaca, *after* being served with a demanda, in order to se-cure the services of the one of the town's defensores. This depends, as I have al-ready mentioned, on a number of contingent factors, including the time of the year, the willingness of an individual defensor to take on a case like this, and, perhaps most importantly, the ability of the demandado and the defensor to come to acceptable terms for payment, which in a case of this magnitude and likely length would consist of an extended work obligation.[22]

So assuming all of this—and more—happens, and the woman from Iturata is able to secure a hearing date at which she will face the man who abused her daughter, what will she herself be confronted with in return? Unlike everything she knows—or feels—about male-female relations, those complementary sets of gender expectations that give men and women in Alonso de Ibañez the best structural framework for survival, when she walks into the JDI, she will enter a world in which power is sexualized and the law is a means through which the healthy cacophony of multiple gender narratives to be found outside the court is abruptly silenced as soon as the judge's gavel is slammed on his desk. The separate-but-equal gender narrative of indigenous hamlets, and the universalist narrative of liberalism and human rights, are both excluded from the disciplinary gaze of Sacaca's court.

The juzgado is the embodiment of the law, *la palabra*, and the word was enacted by and for men. Here women are not the complementary opposites of men; even less are they morally or legally identical to them. Indeed, within the court, women are hardly even social agents, something that is reflected in the fact that their numbers as parties drop dramatically compared with other legal institutions in the province. And no wonder. After waiting for her court session to begin under the watchful gaze of several bare-breasted Venezuelans (or Peruvians or Mexicans), she is brusquely ushered into the judge's chambers, where the judge tells her to sit down (and he means on the floor). Although she perhaps has never seen such images in her life, she cannot help but notice the sexual array on the wall over the judge's left shoulder—and of course she is the only woman in the room: the court's officials are men, the two defensores are men, the promotor fiscal is a man, and the accused is a man. Moreover, her Spanish is very rudimentary in the best of circumstances, which means during a highly charged public meeting like this she is even less likely to try and use it; she must plead her case in Quechua (or much more rarely Aymara), which has become a literally feminized language, because many more women than men are likely to use it as a first and enduring mode of communication, something that only further antagonizes the judge.

Despite all of this, she must try and convince the men present that her brother-in-law sexually abused her daughter and should be punished for it. No matter what the Bolivian Penal Code says, the pornography on the walls, the dismissive attitude of the judge, the vigorous (though incredible) denials by the demandado, all tell her something quite different: that what Bolivian law might describe as sexual abuse, many men—including those present—would consider something *just* over the boundary of both what is acceptable and desired. How can any of the dominant modern narratives of gender address these problems if they are unwilling to turn the rock over and examine what's beneath? What if there is something even deeper and more unsettling than what's underneath the rock? After all, reformers like Lucio Montesinos have had the courage to turn it over from time to time, as we will see in the next chapter. And if what's at the bottom cannot be explained by anything like "power," so that it is not enough to simply have the courage to speak truth to it, what then?

Conclusion: A Different Complementarity

I began this chapter by exploring the way "gender" emerged as a category for social analysis and political action, first as a transnational discourse in the post-war period, and then, more recently, as part of Bolivia's liberal renaissance over the last twenty years. Within the Andean studies literature, the application of gender analysis has given us a wealth of deeply nuanced studies of different aspects of male-female relations, which explore the structural and conceptual aspects of complementarity as well as the economic and political factors that cause the social practice of gender to deviate from the cultural ideal. I would like to end here, however, by suggesting that the study of gender and legal subjectivity suggests another kind of complementarity, one that is both parallel to the male-female opposition and which illustrates, yet again, the dilemmas that mark Bolivia's modern trajectory.

There is no question that the majority of men and women in rural Bolivia envision themselves as only aspects of a wider cultural system, that "unified biological-technological productivity" that opens out from "human–telluric bonds," as Salomon has characterized it. There is also no question that this system must increasingly confront other systems or narratives that have their origins in radically different ontological assumptions. We can see, therefore, how a different complementarity emerges in Alonso de Ibañez, one in which the cultural stands in opposition to the legal. Transnational human rights discourse opposes complementary unity because the latter actually demands that men and women be understood as different, though structurally equal, kinds of social beings, whereas the entire moral and legal edifice of human rights is built on the assumption of a gender-less universal sameness. Both of these distinct narratives, however, coexist in rural Bolivia and men and women must find ways to navigate within and between them.

Finally, there is something else. Because the concern with gender is fundamentally a concern with power, it is necessary to see power for what it really is, and, perhaps more important, what it really isn't. The multiple narratives of gender in contemporary Bolivia, some of which coexist in a kind of rough complementarity, cannot completely capture—even taken together—all of the different ways in which expectations attach themselves to men and women, and to their relations with each other. There is also the fact of a pervasive sexualization of male-female relations, one that gender analysis (at least as it has emerged in contemporary Bolivia) only barely acknowledges. If power means something like the differential ability to mobilize labor, or force decisions, or acquire political or social capital, then we will never be able to understand the almost gothic juxtaposition of crucifix and judicial pornography in Alonso de Ibañez. The dominant narratives of modernity offer to replace tradition with equality and a respect for universal principles, but these noble aspirations tell us nothing about the tears, the fear, and the complicated forms of desire in the juzgado de instrucción.

5 Human Rights and the Moral Imagination

Becoming Liberal in the Norte de Potosí

WHEN LUCIO MONTESINOS IS ASKED to officiate at a civil wedding in Alonso de Ibañez, the young couple and their *padrinos* (godparents) are both hopeful and apprehensive. They are hopeful because they know that Montesinos, one of the most well-known and respected public intellectuals in the norte de Potosí, will honor both the local cultural traditions that structure wedding ceremonies and the provisions of the *Código de Familia* that must be followed in order to have a valid marriage. For example, Article 68 specifies that a statement be read out loud to all present, one that is meant to encapsulate in very few words the rights, duties, and social importance of the act of matrimony. People know that Montesinos can be counted on to read this statement in the clear *castellano* of educated urban Bolivians, something that reflects the fact that he spent many years away from the campo in order to work in law offices and then, relatively late for most Bolivians, study law and obtain his professional credentials (Figure 5.1).

Yet if the couple and their *testigos* can be certain that the presence of Montesinos at their wedding will lend the occasion a significant amount of gravitas and create assurances that the proper forms will be presented and the correct words solemnly intoned at just the right moments, his necessary role at weddings also is cause for a particular kind of unease. Since the late 1990s, Montesinos has modified civil wedding ceremonies in the province in ways that extend the time they take to complete, but also, more importantly, reflect what I will describe more fully below as a liberal renaissance in Bolivia, one that accompanied the different variations of human rights discourse that had become firmly embedded at the national level by the early 1990s.

Figure 5.1. Lucio Montesinos (center): lawyer, human rights activist, rural-legal intellectual, and moral philosopher

The typical civil wedding ceremony in Bolivia, in the norte de Potosí as elsewhere, should take about thirty minutes. The competent official must make sure that the proper documents are presented (Article 56), and they are what would be expected: identification papers, birth certificates, proof of legal annulment or divorce (if applicable), and so on. The law even gives "peasants and indigent persons" an exemption from these documentary requirements if it would be "difficult or costly" to provide them, as long as their testigos are willing to make a formal declaration at the time of the ceremony.[1] The couple and their assembled guests are always impatient for the documents to be accepted, the oaths to be given, and the words of Article 68 to be read, because the most important events are yet to come, and they must await the signal from the official. The party following the ceremony is, at least in rural areas, usually held in the same room as the ceremony itself, and the table must be cleared away so that the *ch'allas*, or ritual toasts, can begin, the food distributed, and (after that) the music and dancing can commence.

However, after collecting the documents and signatures, accepting the *declaración jurada* (sworn declaration) from the witnesses, and informing all those present (among other things) that "marriage . . . perpetuates the species, and is the foundation of the family, society, and the State" (Art. 68), Montesinos then inserts what has become his own "annex" (as the required oral statement from Article 68 is called) to the standard civil marriage protocol.

As the wedding couple shifts nervously in front of him, he tells them—and everyone present—that the rights and duties outlined in the *Código de Familia* are not the only norms that apply to married people. Apart from the simple civic requirements embodied in Bolivian law, and apart from the cultural expectations that are created through the ritual web of *compadrazgo* (or "ritual kinship"), there is another layer, one that transcends all the others: the layer of *derechos humanos*, or human rights. Montesinos then proceeds to lecture on the topic of human rights, both as a general concept—rights we have, as he says, "as humans"—and in what Sally Engle Merry (2006a) would describe as "the vernacular." As Merry explains, when the idea of human rights is rendered into the vernacular it becomes "ornamented by local cultural signs and symbols and tailored to local institutions" (2006a: 216). Elsewhere, Merry develops a theoretical model that locates the process of discursive localization on a continuum, with what she calls "replication" on one side, and "hybridity" on the other. As she describes it:

> [v]ernacularization falls along a continuum depending on how extensively local cultural forms and practices are incorporated into imported [human rights] institutions. At one end is replication, a process in which the imported institution remains largely unchanged from its transnational prototype. The adaptation is superficial and primarily decorative. At the other end is hybridization, a process that merges imported institutions and symbols with local ones, sometimes uneasily. These differences are a matter of degree. (2006b: 44)

The vernacularization of human rights is a discursive process that Montesinos has mastered, yet he does not invoke local cultural signs and symbols as much as pots and pans and *q'epis* (carrying bundles). He tells the couple that men and women are equal in human rights and that this equality entails certain reciprocal duties (a normative linkage that is not emphasized in the Universal Declaration). Among these are the need for men to help their wives with domestic chores, such as washing pots and pans and helping to prepare food. Even more interestingly, he makes derechos humanos the source of redress for highly specific grievances that he has encountered during his legal career in the province, grievances that are not recognized within any section of Bolivian law. Among these is the complaint of many women that their husbands do not bear a greater burden on the trails that connect hamlets across the province's towering mountain passes and plunging river valleys.

The relative distribution of loads is structured by the kind of gender expectations examined in the last chapter: men carry, among other things, agricultural tools and alcohol; women carry babies, food, and weaving materials. Men and women do share the load for certain items, like produce bound for market in the provincial capital, but if, as is often the case depending on the season, men do not have a need to transport their tools, they will not offer to help carry babies, for example, even if this means their wives are heavily burdened and the men carry nothing but a bag of coca. Montesinos embeds this profoundly specific set of circumstances within a different universe, one that would, among other things, compel a man to carry babies or anything else that would foster equality between men and women—and all of this is explained at great length to the waiting couple and their guests, until finally Montesinos decides he has done all he can do (for the moment).

In another part of the province, the *corregidor auxiliar* of Molino T'ikanoma is doing his best to relocate himself and his hamlet within the same reborn liberal universe that is invoked by Montesinos during wedding ceremonies in Sacaca, although the means and effects are quite different. The corregidor auxiliar is in many ways a quintessential rural-legal intellectual in contemporary Bolivia: mid-30s, the oldest male in his family, and someone whose intense personal ambitions have their roots in multiple discursive traditions from different periods in Bolivian history, including rural *sindicalismo* (or "unionism"), peasant nationalism, and, more recently, indigenous and human rights (Figure 5.2). What connects each of these traditions for the corregidor auxiliar is the fact that they are made instrumental as an expression of law, as a means through which binding norms are articulated and put into play at the service of wider projects (especially political ones). Something as seemingly insignificant as the fact that the corregidor auxiliar scrupulously maintains a *cuaderno de actas,* or record-keeping book, in which he uses mundane forms of low-level administrative law that he has picked up during trips to La Paz and Oruro, must be understood as

Figure 5.2. The *corregidor auxiliar* of Molino T'ikanoma: peasant union activist, community leader, archivist, and legal visionary

an expression of broader historical and discursive shifts in contemporary Bolivia, some of which, I will argue, have the effect of renewing the dominant patterns of intention that always been present in modern Bolivia.

In order to explore these complicated interconnections between law, a renewed liberalism, and modernity, this chapter will focus on the coming of human rights discourse to Alonso de Ibañez. Human rights discourse has become an example of what might be described as a contemporary global superliberalism, meaning a discursive form that brings together in itself and then expresses to a high degree the very essence of liberalism itself (see Koskenniemi 2006; Kymlicka 1995). Another way of making this point is to say that contemporary human rights discourse has become the summarizing key symbol (Ortner 1973) par excellence of (late) liberalism, in that liberalism is symbolized through human rights discourse in ways that discourage analytical parsing (of human rights discourse-as-symbol), encourage emotional and even messianic devotion (as with a nation's flag), and, above all else, establish clear lines of discursive demarcation, what I like to think of as universes of inclusion and exclusion.

As Ortner explains about summarizing key symbols in general, "they operate to compound and synthesize a complex system of ideas, to 'summarize' them under a unitary form which, in an old-fashioned way, 'stands for' the system as a whole" (1973: 1340). In much of contemporary Bolivia, human rights discourse compounds and synthesizes a complex system of ideas that is both partly old—indeed, coextensive with postcolonial Bolivia itself—and partly new (or, we might say, emergent). As a summarizing symbol that functions in this way, human rights discourse must, of course, be embodied. As we will see, it is, through the work of key public intellectuals like Lucio Montesinos and the corregidor auxiliar of Molino T'ikanoma; in the institutional presence of transnational human rights NGOs and the cosmopolitan elites who carry out their technocratic mission in rural Bolivia; and, more ambiguously, through the presence of engaged foreign researchers, who are often called upon to intervene in local social struggles precisely because it is assumed that they, in a way, "stand for" the system as a whole (even if, as I have argued throughout this book, they might actually be critics of a system local leaders hope to appropriate and eventually reproduce).

Human Rights and the Moral Imagination

The region that is now the province Alonso de Ibañez has always been at crossroads of various kinds. Zorn recapitulates much of this history in her

1997 dissertation, in which she explains that the provincial capital, Sacaca, was "once a stop along the important silver route between Sucre and Cusco" (1997: 70). A highly anticipated book by a group of international scholars documents in considerable detail the importance of the region as a center for precolonial political and military organizations (Platt, Bouysse-Cassagne, and Harris 2006; see also Arze and Medinaceli 1991; Izko 1992).[2] But what concerns me here are not the political, economic, or even military histories that locate the province and give its more recent developments meaning and context; rather, I am concerned with how the coming of human rights discourse over the last fifteen years is embedded within a longer flow of discursive currents that have swept through—and lingered in—the region, and how the idea of human rights represents both a continuation of, and break from, this history.

Since the early colonial period, the province has been the site of intense religious prosetylization, beginning with the Catholic church (Bustamante 1985). The church itself in Sacaca has been the regional seat of Christian missionizing since it was built, most likely during the time the regional indigenous population was "reduced" as part of Viceroy Toledo's dramatic transformation of the Andes during the 1570s. Although the exact dates are difficult to document, the two strategically located churches (or chapels) in the old cantonal capitals of Iturata and Karkoma were most likely built during the late-sixteenth century (see Figures 5.3 and 5.4). The locations were chosen at roughly equidistances from Sacaca so that the province's disparate populations and different *ayllus* would be enclosed within the boundaries of a Christian religious and social space, even if these boundaries would prove to be porous over the centuries.

The Catholic church in the region has been a source of ideas and practices derived from both a western colonial worldview, and a moral ideology that is universalist, submissive, and directed toward the hereafter. Even though there have been periods in Bolivian history when the Catholic church in Alonso de Ibañez fell into near obsolescence—most notably during the paroxysmal time of the National Revolution at mid-twentieth century—it has always served as a foundation of moral, legal, and religious discourse and has been an institution that has shaped, to greater or lesser degrees, subjectivity and identity among both the region's mestizo and *runa* populations.

But beginning in the late 1960s, the position of the traditional Catholic church underwent a profound change. In 1971, in the wake of Vatican II and the liberation theology movement, the Claretian Order, made up of priests from the Basque region of Spain, assumed control of *Misión Norte de Potosí*, which

Figure 5.3. The old cantonal capital Iturata, Alonso de Ibañez. By the early 2000s, Iturata was a dying hamlet. Only several elderly people remained; the rest had left for Oruro, Cochabamba, or the coca fields of the Chapare.

now includes parishes in Sacaca, Caripuyo, Acasio, Torotoro, and San Pedro de Buenavista. The Claretian Order, which was founded in Spain in 1849, received new impetus and focus during the liberation theology movement of the 1960s. The first priests who arrived in Sacaca were Roman Catholic missionaries officially committed to developing the province's poor and serving as agents for social justice, focuses that continue to characterize the Claretian mission in Bolivia and elsewhere.[3] Almost from the very beginning, the Basque priests in Sacaca began intervening in local affairs and, in particular, engaging in development projects with the support of mostly Spanish organizations with whom they were able to form links (see Figure 5.5). Indeed, many of the significant infrastructural changes in the province from 1971 to the present can be traced to the involvement of the Claretian priests, in particular Padre Esteban, who has been in Sacaca from the beginning of the Claretian mission in north Potosí and who speaks fluent Quechua and Aymara and is also an amateur collector of local archaeological artifacts.

Figure 5.4. The old cantonal capital Karkoma, Alonso de Ibañez

For example, the Claretian priests took an active role during the 1970s in negotiating with the Bolivian government for electricity in the province, which was thought necessary for, among other things, a functioning hospital, another project that was begun by the Claretians during the 1970s. According to Bustamante, in 1978 Padre Esteban traveled to Puerto Villarroél in the Chapare to receive a shipment of equipment necessary for the installation of a transformer and to sign the final contract with Bolivian government officials on behalf of the town (1985: 209–10). The transformer became functional in 1981, making Sacaca one of the only towns with twenty-four hour electricity in north Potosí.[4]

Between 1974 and 1983, there was a small health post (*puesto médico*) in Sacaca, run by nuns from the order of the *Hermanas de la Providencia*, who also came to Sacaca from the Basque region of Spain at the request of the Claretian priests. Between 1983 and 1997, the Claretians secured financing to build the

Figure 5.5. Younger Claretian priest from the Basque region of Spain, *Misión Norte de Potosí*

Centro de Salud Sacaca, which was staffed by a full-time doctor paid for by the Bolivian government. In 1997, after three years of construction, a new hospital was built in Sacaca (Hospital "San Luis") with funds provided by Medicus Mundi Navarra, a health NGO from the Navarra province in Spain (see Figure 5.6). Medicus Mundi became involved in north Potosí at the request of their fellow Basques in Sacaca, and now there are Medicus Mundi–built hospitals throughout the entire norte de Potosí (in Bolívar, San Pedro de Buenavista, and Torotoro).

The Claretians also were responsible more directly for the opening (and then closing) of a human rights center in the province. But what is most important at this point is to recognize that the church—in its different iterations,

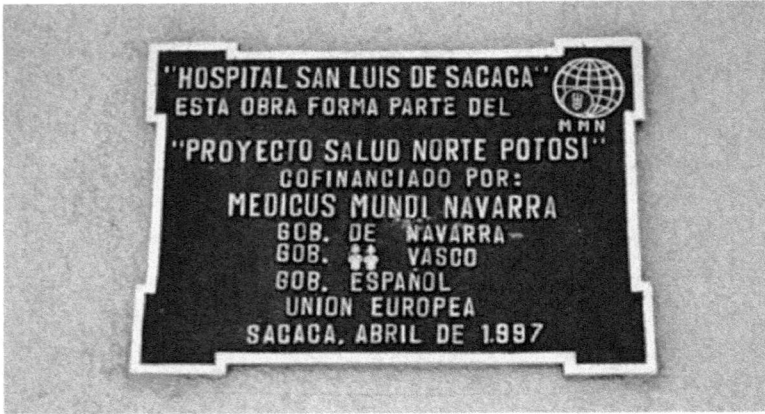

Figure 5.6. Plaque describing the financial support for Hospital San Luis de Sacaca, which vividly displays the extent to which the *"extremo"* norte de Potosí is fully embedded in the networks of transnational modernity

both orthodox and progressive—has been a conduit for discursive exchange in the region, a means through which different visions of life (and after-life) have been brought together within a broader framework of moral and spiritual development. The church has sought to mediate—and even dominate—the constitution of subjectivity in the region, which has been a mission understood in terms of conflict and confrontation from the very beginning. As it turned out, the church was never able to monopolize or transform personhood along its lines completely; the result, as we saw in the last chapter, is that multiple discourses of personhood have coexisted in the province in a complicated jumble of power and ambiguity. But within this ambiguity and multiplicity, there are patterns and lines of discursive coherence, so that even though the moral, legal, and ontological positions of the church over the years must be sharply contrasted with the much later secular worldview that gave birth to the liberal nation-state and then postwar human rights, there are points of convergence: Both emphasize the universal sameness of mankind; both are thoroughly normative; and both deny the possibility of coexistence—in theory, if not in practice—with opposing visions.

Besides the discursive contributions of the church in Alonso de Ibañez, there is one more current that must be mentioned at this point, before I explore human rights discourse in greater detail. This is one associated with the coming of sindicalismo to the province in the form of *sindicatos* campesinos, or peasants' unions, at the time of the 1952 National Revolution and Agrarian Reform of the following year. The sindicato campesino originally was meant to replace existing political, legal, and social structures throughout rural Bolivia and serve as a single ordering principle within which the reform of Bolivian society—especially in the countryside—would take place. Like sindicatos throughout the rest of Latin America during the first part of the twentieth century, the Bolivian sindicato had its ideological roots in the sindicalismo that was brought to Latin America by European immigrants from countries like Italy (Alba 1968; Burnett and Tronsoso 1960; Godio 1983).

As with the sindicalismo of countries like Chile and Argentina, the Bolivian trade union movement sought to reform unequal relations of power through collective representation and action, mutual support across all sectors of Bolivia's working classes, and the active pursuit of structural change in Bolivia through civil disobedience. The problem was that with the exception of certain key mining centers (some in the norte de Potosí), Bolivia has experienced a different type of industrial development than its more Europeanized neighbors to the south; so even within the context of agrarian reform, the sindicato campesinos never did fulfill their original purposes.

However, despite the fact that sindicatos in Alonso de Ibañez never developed into institutions for political and social change, they did become both an important source of what might be described as organic social theory, and a structure within which especially younger men take their first steps as public intellectuals. As I explained in Chapter 3, for most people in the province the hamlet is first and foremost a sindicato, rather than an estancia or *ranchu*, the other ways in which nucleated settlements in this part of Bolivia have been traditionally categorized. So although "sindicato" has long been denuded of its original connotation as an alternative political, legal, and social structure, one intended to confront and transform relations of (especially economic) power, there are implications to the fact that it was the sindicato—rather than some other category—that came to be an important alternative means through which people locate themselves and their families in local political space.

First, even if most hamlets-cum-sindicatos are only nominally part of the regional umbrella organization of rural peasant unions—the FSUTCNP—this larger organization does mobilize, at times, in order to function as a politically engaged workers' union. When this happens, members from individual hamlets/sindicatos will travel to the departmental capital, for example, in order to participate in marches or to protest outside of governmental buildings.

People who participate in these events from hamlets in Alonso de Ibañez absorb the syndicalist rhetoric of equality, struggle, and workers' rights by virtue of the fact that it is an organization of *unions* that serves as the ordering principle for political action, rather than political parties, or the church, or even the ayllu.

And second, sindicalismo in Alonso de Ibañez serves as a source for a very specific kind of moral and political discourse, one that young men learn to employ during their time as *dirigentes*, usually the entry level among the different politico-legal authority positions in the province. Unionism in rural Bolivia, like elsewhere, represents a particular modern impulse, one that exists as a counterpart to the dominant liberalism that has shaped postcolonial Bolivia. Both are committed to historical progress and human enlightenment and both are anchored in a scientific rationality that is dismissive of other ways of knowing.

But despite sharing a common historical trajectory, there are important differences between liberalism (which, in a renewed version, will be the source of human rights discourse) and sindicalismo. While liberalism emphasizes individual liberty, unionism (whose intellectual history includes at least small roots in Rousseau's General Will) makes the collective the unit of political and social action; liberalism views the social contract in largely negative terms— what Isaiah Berlin (1958) has called "negative liberty"—while sindicalismo places a burden on individuals (within the collective) to act in the world in order to change it; and, perhaps more than anything else, liberalism is an essentially skeptical political, legal, and social discourse, one that assumes that the modern world has unfolded pretty much as well as it is able, while the discourse of unionism in rural Bolivia (as elsewhere) is essentially utopian, in that it assumes that the true potential of mankind is yet to be realized, if only the bonds of alienation can be broken.

Young men who embrace the discourse of sindicalismo straddle multiple discursive universes, so that they might speak of human rights, *la lucha* (simply "the struggle"), and the imperatives of tradition depending on context. The corregidor auxiliar of Molino T'ikanoma is in this—as in other matters—a singular example. Before serving as the corregidor auxiliar, he had been his sindicato's *secretario general*. He explained that more than anything, his primary obligation to the community was to guide it: in its internal conflicts, in its relations with Sacaca and transnational NGOs, and in its understanding of the "new laws," by which he meant the laws derived from international human rights norms. He saw himself as both the "defender of his peasant comrades," and a learned man who had some formal education (in the mining center Siglo XX, where he was born before later moving back to his father's ancestral hamlet). As a new political authority second only to the *corregidor* titular of the canton (Karkoma), he saw it as his duty to familiarize himself with different provisions of Bolivian law and the language of international human rights treaties so that he could serve as an intermediary between the different jurisdictional spaces in the province and beyond. Even more broadly than this, the corregidor auxiliar was a servant of the truth—the kind that comes from understanding how different discursive systems are both interconnected and potentially strategic. As he put it, "[my job] is to advise that which is true."

What is important to recognize here is that the more recent advent of human rights discourse in Bolivia took place within a broader field that, at least in part, anticipated it. Yet despite the fact that different discursive currents have swept across Alonso de Ibañez since at least the early colonial period—so that it would be highly misleading to treat the emergence of human rights discourse over the last fifteen years as a kind of extraordinary event without either precedent or discursive resonance—there are certain aspects of human rights discourse that distinguish it from what has come before. The most important of these is the fact that it brings together the universalist assumptions of a secular modernity with a transcendent mysticism that suggests the worldview of the Catholic church (and, more recently, evangelical Protestantism).

Moreover, although the language of human rights is formally legal, when used in social practice in rural Bolivia it also becomes an important moral discourse. The advent of human rights tends to overwhelm coexisting frames of normative reference; indeed, this is one of the most important findings from the anthropology of human rights (Englund 2006; Goodale and Merry 2007; Merry 2006; Speed 2008; Tate 2007; Wilson 2001). In this way, human rights discourse functions in practice as a kind of liberal vanguard of the contemporary imaginary. It rides roughshod over existing moral and legal alternatives, which are redefined in opposition to human rights as vaguely sinister impediments to human progress, a discursive encounter that Berta Esperanza Hernández-Truyol (2002) has called "moral imperialism."

But if the practical effect in Alonso de Ibañez is that more men help their wives on the trail or hesitate before resorting to physical violence against their children, what are we to make of this moral imperialism of late (or, in Bolivia, *renewed*) liberalism? If Lucio Montesinos, the corregidor auxiliar of Molino T'ikanoma, and, more recently, emerging indigenist political leaders in the norte de Potosí have become over the last fifteen years Locke's willing liberals, how are we to understand what for many elite critics (like Hernández-Truyol) would be seen as the self-transformation of the moral imagination? Here we come back to the dilemma of polyvalence. Montesinos knows as well as I where the idea of human rights comes from, and what its messianic insertion into the practice of everyday life bodes for the people of rural Bolivia. There are no illusions in Sacaca's dusty alleys and one-room adobe offices about the transformative aspirations of human rights discourse and the desires of those who are its messengers. The coming of transnational human rights discourse to rural Bolivia is not like some normative cargo cult, in which the avatars of moral progress are mistaken for gods. Rather, the problem is both clearer and more complex. Montesinos and others simply disagree (with me, for example) about how to value—or judge—this quite intentional embrace of liberalism.

A Liberal Renaissance

The 1985 election of Víctor Paz Estenssoro marked an important moment in Bolivian history, one that is believed to have given birth to a new epoch. Soon after his election, Paz Estenssoro announced to the nation that major economic and social changes would be implemented over the coming years.[5] His dramatic national diagnosis, "Bolivia se nos muere" (or "Bolivia is dying on us"), would become the rhetorical symbol for what later would be described as "neoliberalism," although its meaning would eventually become ironic, as it would be the reforms that Paz Estenssoro—and his Torquemada, Gonzalo Sánchez de Lozada—initiated that would do the most long-term damage to Bolivian liberalism (indeed, would set in motion a series of events that threaten to break the patterns of intention that have defined modern Bolivia). In August 1985, the promise of a new era in Bolivian history became a reality through Decreto 21060, which formally launched what came to be known as the *Nueva Económica Política*, or New Economic Policy (NEP). The decree unleashed structural and social forces in Bolivia that would have far-reaching implications; there is a direct line, for example, from the Decreto to the 2005 election of Evo Morales. Under the NEP (Klein 2003: 245):

> the national currency was devalued; a uniform and free floating exchange rate [was] established; all price and wage controls [were] eliminated; public sector prices [were] substantially raised; government expenditures [were] severely restricted; and real wages of government employees [were] reduced.

Even more consequentially, Paz Estenssoro attacked Bolivia's mining sector through a series of institutional, tax, and price reforms that had the effect of draining places like Siglo XX and Catavi of thousands of mining families, who—without the ability to return to rural hamlets and resume a traditional agropastoral lifestyle—poured into El Alto and the Chapare, the first in order to try and find work of some kind in La Paz (or, over the years, in El Alto itself), and the second in order to participate in different ways in Bolivia's exploding coca/cocaine economy (see Léons and Sanabria 1997).

Paz Estenssoro's right hand during his twilight regime was Gonzalo Sánchez de Lozada, the American-trained businessman who served as the minister of planning between 1985 and 1989. This job, with its Orwellian title, gave Goni (as he is popularly known) the ability to implement the so-called shock therapy approach that was being pushed most notably by Jeffrey Sachs (who would later take his program to the newly emerging democracies of eastern Europe) as *the* prescription for bringing developing countries like Bolivia quickly into line with the expectations (and desires) of global capital.

Despite the highly ambiguous economic results of the NEP, and the more obvious social costs associated with the profound institutional and financial restructuring that it initiated, what concerns me most here is something else made possible by the emergence of so-called neoliberalism in Bolivia. The presidency of Jaime Paz Zamora (1989–93), which followed immediately after Paz Estenssoro's, coincided with a period in which international (and, later, transnational) human rights suddenly expanded in different ways, in part because of the end of the bipolar Cold War system that had formed an insurmountable barrier to the actualization of the postwar human rights system. For example, it was during Paz Zamora's administration that the Bolivian Congress ratified International Labor Organization Convention 169, the "Indigenous and Tribal Peoples Convention," a piece of international human rights law that reflected a recent expansion within the United Nations of human rights categories to include a full range of collective rights (especially those whose status was linked to historical marginalization).[6] Bolivia also opened the door to another important provision of international human rights law during the Paz Zamora administration: In 1990, it ratified CEDAW, the international women's bill of rights.[7]

The human rights floodgates were opened even wider during the first presidency of Gonzalo Sánchez de Lozada (1993–97), a period that was both the peak of what were understood as neoliberal economic, social, and legal policies, and the time in which "neoliberalism" was converted into a discourse in Bolivia, one in which the *idea* of neoliberalism—and the critique of that idea—began to separate from the underlying economic and political conditions from which the idea was derived.

More important than any specific political or social reforms during this period—most notably the Ley de Participación Popular (No. 1554) and the Ley de Reforma Educativa (No. 1565)—was the fact that Goni's administration outsourced the moral education of Bolivia, first to international development agencies like UNICEF, then, even more consequentially, to the network of transnational NGOs that had by the mid-1990s reformed the Green Revolution development model and reinscribed it within a wider global project of human rights activism. By the late 1990s, even after Goni had been replaced by the less-liberal presidency of Hugo Banzer Suárez,[8] a wholesale moral transformation was under way in Bolivia, in which existing norms, expectations, and categories of belonging were being radically reinterpreted in terms of human rights, from rural areas like the norte de Potosí to the major urban centers (which would, somewhat later, form the epicenter of national political mobilization).

But the key question—at least at this point—is what this radical reinterpretation signals for locating this period within the wider sweep of Bolivian history. As I have said, 1985 is believed to mark an epochal break in Bolivia, after which a "new" (and thus qualitatively distinct) form of liberalism was made the foundation for what was hoped would be a qualitatively new (and better) period for Bolivia. Indeed, to the extent that *neoliberalismo* was eventually converted into a discursive cipher, one that served many different interests at the same time, it took on an even more distinct sense of what Fredric Jameson (1998) describes as "epochality," the (post-)modern preoccupation with newness as a historical condition. Even if the apparent onset of neoliberalism was the subject of intense critique by antineoliberals as much as it was the cause of a kind of sigh of relief by neoliberals like Goni and the coterie of well-known intellectuals who (at least at first) supported him, the important thing is that both sides of the debate over neoliberalism agreed that it represented something historically and epistemically different.[9]

I think neither the impact of human rights discourse over the last twenty years, nor the rise of political and social movements based, in part, on transnational notions of indigenousness (and the rights associated with these notions), can be best understood by taking "neoliberalism" at face value, as an analytical tool for describing and explaining a new phase in Bolivian history.

Rather, the time after 1985 can be better understood by seeing it as a period in which preexisting patterns of intention were suddenly clarified and validated in new ways, a time in which the liberal roots of modern Bolivia, those epistemic foundations that have been coextensive with the idea of Bolivia itself, were relocated in relation to dominant categories of meaning: political, legal, cultural.[10]

As in western Europe during the fifteenth and sixteenth centuries, the period of neoliberalism in Bolivia was a time in which different kinds of knowledge—moral, legal, political, ideological—were rediscovered, in a sense, or reborn. It took a thousand-year interregnum before Europe returned to its classical foundations, but does anyone doubt that these foundations were ever-present, even if they were submerged beneath hundreds of years of so-called darkness? Bolivia's liberal foundations were never really submerged in this way, although one can point to many moments (even years or decades) that could be described as *interliberal*—pauses in the (apparently) inevitable unfolding of the Bolivian modern.

Klein writes that "[t]o the surprise of all, Paz Estenssoro adopted the principles of . . . liberalism and rejected the . . . nationalist and state capitalist ideology, which he himself had been fundamental in implanting earlier in Bolivia" (2003: 244). Seen in a different light, however, Paz Estenssoro was simply taking steps that would end the most recent period of interliberalism in Bolivia, one that had become very dark indeed during what Dunkerley (1984) calls "the long night," in which the army turned its bazookas and machine guns on women and children, neofascism became the order of the day under the banner "peace, order, work," and the Butcher of Lyon (living under the alias Klaus Altmann) became a trusted advisor to the president.

This means that the apotheosis of human rights discourse in the mid-1990s was neither a historical accident nor evidence that Bolivia was now under the sign of a new episteme. Everything distinctive about the idea of human rights that was given new momentum after 1989 was present in every Bolivian constitution since 1825. It was present during the reforms of the late-nineteenth century, which must be seen as an essentially conservative attempt to bring the country back onto its original liberal trajectory (rather than, again, initiate a new phase in Bolivian history). Even during the period of the National Revolution, reformers turned *toward*, not away, from the philosophical assumptions of Bolivia's liberal foundations (although this truth is often obscured by what seems like the antiliberal *economic* moves of the revolution). Bolivia is as much a child of the liberal Enlightenment as the United States—even if, like the United States, what came before (culturally, politically, historically) necessarily shaped the way this guiding framework of modernity was grounded within Bolivia's complicated and shifting reality. To see the coming of human rights discourse to Bolivia as a return, rather than as a sign of an epochal break, allows us to understand specific encounters with human rights in places like Alonso de Ibañez, where the evidence of Bolivia reborn is thick on the ground.

Technocracy and Tea

If there were any doubts about the relationship between contemporary human rights discourse and the modern patterns of intention that it both symbolizes and reinforces, look at the seemingly mundane *programa* for a July 1997 *taller*, or workshop, that was part of a broader campaign to transform social relations in the norte de Potosí in terms of human rights (see Figure 5.7). Before one even

PROGRAMA

DIA VIERNES 25 DE JULIO

9.00 a 9.15 ----> Palabras de bienvenida a cargo del Subprefecto
                  de la Provincia Alonso de Ibanez
9.15 a 9.30 ---> Explicación de objetivos, metodología y
                 organigrama por la Técnica Basilia de León.
9.30 a 9.45 ---> Inaguración del Taller a cargo de un personero
                 de la H. Alcaldía Municipal.
9.45 a 10.00 ---> Presentación de participantes
10.00 a 10.45 ---> ¿Qué es la violencia? (Lluvia de ideas) ·
10.45 a 11.00 ---> Refrigerio
11.00 a 12.30 ---> Organización de sociogramas
12.30 a 13.30 ---> Almuerzo
14.00 a 14.30 ---> Alcances de la ley 1674 con enfoque de género
14.30 a 15.00 ---> Roles de género (sociogramas)
15.00 a 16.00 ---> Plenaria (Preguntas y respuestas)
16.00 a 16.15 ----> Té
16.15 a 16.30 ---> Compromiso de trabajo entre autoridades
comunales y Servicio Legal Integral Sacaca
16.30 a 17.00 ---> Evaluación y clausura

Sacaca, 24 de Julio de 1997

Figure 5.7. The program for a *taller*, or workshop, intended to introduce the province to both the *Servicio Legal Integral* and the idea of human rights

knows what kind of institution the SLI is, or what its objectives are, one thing is clear: It is a mechanism for developing a kind of technocratic knowledge. The entire range of technocratic knowledge practices are brought together within the four corners of this humble little brochure at the service of, as it turns out, what has become a kind of meta-technocratic knowledge—human rights.

Start with its structure. The day's activities are tightly scheduled in increments of time that have been carefully and rationally chosen based on an assessment of the relative importance of each segment and its relation to the whole. Why not run an event like this with a kind of free association dialogue, or by using mind-altering substances to open up the participants' consciousnesses to the ideas to come? Instead, the kind of organizational principles that are expressed here have the same roots as those that led the Jacobins to scientifically reinvent the calendar.[11]

And what about the name of the event itself—the *taller* (workshop)? There are no moral or ideological values in a workshop, just good, clean, hard work—and the work itself is done by experts. Those who would learn the technical knowledge necessary to become experts in their own right must apprentice themselves for a period of time, must don the smocks of the guild and put nose to grindstone. The techniques of this particular workshop are the epitome of social scientific planning and organization. There are *sociogramas*, for example, charts that depict social relationships as they are in the province, and, more important, as they should be if they are to be restructured in accordance with the expert knowledge to be (re-)produced by the workshop's leader, whose professional credential is itself revealing—*técnica*, or technician.

Why *sociogramas*? Because (we can only assume) visual schematics are the most effective way to teach people about complicated relationships—social, moral, institutional, and so on. Between 10:00 and 10:45 A.M., the assembled group of hamlet authorities will be asked to freely explore the complex question "What is violence?" through what in Spanish is known as a "rain of ideas," which is a much more poetic (and less anatomical) way of translating the English "brainstorm." Here technocratic knowledge and human rights come together even more directly, because group learning is facilitated by collaborative and participatory exchange, in which participants feel they have a substantive role to play, and ILO 169 tells us that indigenous people (the assembled hamlet authorities would qualify) have a human right to "decide their own priorities for the process of development as it affects their lives, beliefs, institutions and spiritual well-being" (ILO 169, Art. 7).

After more sociogramas, and more opportunities for the workshop leaders to ensure that the provisions of Article 7 have been complied with—in part through the Habermasian question-and-answer session, in which knowledge is produced through a communicative exchange between equally construed citizens—there is tea: not *mate de coca*, the preferred (nonalcoholic) beverage of the province's runa, which can be made with only hot water and a few *hojas* from the coca bag, but real tea, that symbol of *la buena gente* and the idea that despite it all, civilized people will pause during the day if only to reaffirm their own sense of self-worth. When the fifteen-minute pause has ended, the participants are given another fifteen minutes to reinforce the quintessentially modern and technocratic nature of this workshop. The assembled hamlet authorities are asked to enter into a promise with the SLI, a promise to work together to mutually ensure that its objectives are met. Again, we are, at least in part, within Article 7 once more: Indigenous people must voluntarily and freely choose to be coequal participants in their own development, including, as we will see, their moral development.

But beyond ILO 169, this *compromiso de trabajo* takes the participants to the very heart of Bolivia's renewed liberalism. There will be no coercion of any kind here. The SLI might have arrived in the province with the awesome power of the transnational human rights regime behind it; it might be the passionately supported project of the region's most distinguished citizens; and support for its grand mission might hold the promise for individual hamlets (and even individual authorities) of other, less-metaphysical benefits, like the promise by the Servicio's director to point NGOs in the direction of certain hamlets (and thus steer them away from others). Nevertheless, after learning about the Servicio and what it intends to do for the region, a fundamental condition remains: Every man (for they were all men) present of whatever age or position is "[o]ver himself, over his own body and mind . . . sovereign," as John Stuart Mill famously put it in 1859. In other words, the SLI will not be legitimate, will not serve as the means through which human rights consciousness is inculcated in the province, unless those whose participation is essential for its success freely agree to exercise, as it were, some of their essential sovereignty, for the Servicio will also be an instrument of moral and legal discipline.

Finally, the workshop ends with a sustained technocratic flourish. The modern science of program evaluation—which is part sociology, part organizational psychology, with perhaps a dash of public policy and management thrown in for good measure—tells us that for a "program" (a modern term of art) to be instrumentally effective (what other kinds of effectiveness really matter?), it must be the subject of a "continuous feedback loop," in which the evaluation of a program is made an essential part of the program itself. Once the feedback loop has been created, there is, as there always should be, *closure*. The workshop must come to an end, of course, but even here the description and rationale are products of a particular epistemology. Here's what the University of Nebraska–Lincoln's Department of Special Education and Communications Disorders has to say about closure: "Learning [including moral instruction] increases when lessons are concluded in a manner that helps students organize and remember the point of the lesson. Activities used to conclude a lesson are often referred to as 'closure' " (Project PARA 2006). What, then, was (and is) the point of the Servicio Legal Integral?

The Servicio Legal Integral

The *Servicio Legal Integral* (SLI or center) was a human rights legal services center focused on woman that operated in Sacaca between 1995 and 1998. The SLI was authorized by the Ministerio de Desarrollo Humano, Subsecretaría de Asuntos de Género (SAG).[12] The Claretian mission in Sacaca made the formal application to La Paz and when the approval was given, they were designated as the managing agency. They also provided initial funding for the center, along with UNICEF and Sacaca's *alcaldía*. The Claretians continued as official managers of the SLI until April 1998, when they withdrew their support. The management then passed to the alcaldía until August 1998, when the SLI was closed. While it was open, it had a staff of two: Lucio Montesinos, as administrative director and legal counsel; and a *promotora* (or "skilled assistant") who moved to Sacaca from La Paz. She was a young university graduate in agronomy who had an interest in human rights and specifically the rights of women and children. She had many duties at the center—which was located in a two-story house near Sacaca's plaza—including processing new arrivals, giving advice and counsel to women who decided to stay at the center, and in general serving as a house mother to the group that was living at the center at any one time. She also was responsible for maintaining records related to the center's activities.

Montesinos worked with the promotora during interviews of new arrivals. He was responsible for all legal functions of the center including giving legal advice to women who came to the center for help, making decisions regarding the validity of cases at intake interviews, planning legal strategies for cases that were deemed worthy of prosecution, and, finally, prosecuting cases as they made their way through the *juzgado*. Montesinos underwent extensive training in human rights and family law both prior to, and during, the operation of the SLI. The center only handled cases that fell within its mandate; normal criminal or civil cases were not processed.

Besides serving as a legal resource center for women and children in the province, the SLI was also a refuge for women who were fleeing from abusive home environments (see the statistics in Tables 5.1–5.6). The center allowed women and their children to live there for extended periods of time; part of the center's funding included a subsidy for food services, which were contracted out to an adjacent family, who cooked for the women and children living at the center. There were no time limits imposed on women and their children; the only restriction was that there had to be beds for every adult. The maximum capacity was seventy women, and the center quickly filled up with women and their children. It turned out that some of the women who were able to stay the longest were the ones who had arrived the earliest; many stayed for more than six months while their cases were processed and then concluded in the court. Many women even stayed at the center without actively pursuing their cases; while the legal or moral dimensions of their situations were often misunderstood, the fact that they could live in Sacaca away from abusive husbands or boyfriends meant that the center's role became more complex than first envisioned.

Records from intake interviews show the remarkable diversity of the women who came to the center, and the different circumstances that brought them there. A fifty-six-year-old woman, for example, with three grown children, complained of being frequently "damaged" by her husband, with whom she fought over his inability to provide for the family. An unmarried seventeen-year-old was sexually abused while walking from one hamlet to another and feared she was pregnant. A fifty-one-year-old woman with ten children (between the ages of nine and thirty-four) had been the victim of physical violence at the hands of her husband for over twenty years (she had been married for thirty-five). She felt that alcohol caused her husband to abuse her and their children so regularly. A twenty-year-old unmarried woman claimed to have been tricked into having sexual relations with a young man from a neighboring hamlet. She wanted him to keep his promise to marry her and sought the help of the center in bringing him to account.

Although the center served broad functions, its main purpose was to provide legal protection to women and children, and to this end Montesinos began presenting cases processed through the center to the *juez* instructor very soon after the center opened in 1995. Records from the JDI show that in 1995, the court opened forty-five new criminal cases, which represented almost a 50 percent increase over the average total number of criminal cases in the previous ten years.[13] Almost all of the nineteen additional cases above the previous ten-year average of twenty-six were cases filed by Montesinos on behalf of women who had come to the SLI.

The following tables give a statistical sense of the SLI's activities for the years 1995 through 1997.

In its first year, 400 women arrived at the center. Out of this group, the types of violence complained of were divided between physical and psychological aggression, with twenty-five cases of sexual aggression being distinguished

Table 5.1. New arrivals to SLI, 1995

No. of New Arrivals	1st Quarter	2nd Quarter	3rd Quarter	4th Quarter	Total
Combined	132	140	214	188	674
Women	59	68	104	169	400
Men	17	4	44	21	86
Children	2	5	3	2	12

Table 5.2. Types of cases processed by SLI, 1995

Type of Case (W, M, C)*	1st Quarter	2nd Quarter	3rd Quarter	4th Quarter	Total
Physical aggression	30W	34W	52W	42W	158
Psychological aggression	42W, 3M, 2C	33W, 5M, 4C	60W	81W	230
Sexual aggression	4W	5W	6W	10W	25

*W = women, M = men, C = children; when no figure is given for a category, no data were available.

Table 5.3. New arrivals to SLI, 1996

No. of New Arrivals	1st Quarter	2nd Quarter	3rd Quarter	4th Quarter	Total
Combined	389	195	154	106	844
Women	235	147	133	79	594
Men	154	48	21	27	250
Children	9	6	5	5	25

Table 5.4. Types of cases processed by SLI, 1996

Type of Case (W, M, C)*	1ˢᵗ Quarter	2ⁿᵈ Quarter	3ʳᵈ Quarter	4ᵗʰ Quarter	Total
Physical aggression	69W, 1M	63W	38W	29W	200
Psychological aggression	314W	147W	109W	32W	602
Sexual aggression	6W	13W	7W	9W	35

*W = women, M = men, C = children; when no figure is given for a category, no data were available.

Table 5.5. New arrivals to SLI, 1997*

No. of New Arrivals	1ˢᵗ Quarter	2ⁿᵈ Quarter	Total
Combined	119	89	208
Women	58	48	106
Men	49	31	80
Children	12	10	22

*Statistics were not compiled by the SLI for the last two quarters of 1997 for unknown reasons. The statistics given here are through June.

Table 5.6. Types of cases processed by SLI, 1997*

Type of Case (W, M, C)	1ˢᵗ Quarter	2ⁿᵈ Quarter	Total
Physical aggression	28W	31W, 8M	67
Psychological aggression	20W	13W	33
Sexual aggression	7W	5W	12

*Statistics were not compiled by the SLI for the last two quarters of 1997 for unknown reasons. The statistics given here are through June.

from the general category of physical aggression. By its second year, the SLI's impact was even more striking: In 1996, almost 600 women arrived at the center, and, as seen in Table 5.4, the number of cases of psychological aggression is three times greater than the cases of physical aggression. In 1996, the number of cases of sexual aggression has risen to thirty-five from twenty-five. However, by the first two quarters of 1997, the numbers had fallen steeply: 106 women as new arrivals compared with 382 in 1996; and, most strikingly, only twenty cases of psychological aggression reported by women in the first quarter of 1997 compared with 314 in the first quarter of 1996. The cases of reported sexual aggression, however, remain more or less constant between the first quarters of 1996 and 1997 despite the large drop in overall numbers between the two years.

At one level, these numbers tell a story of both failure and success (understood in terms of the center's statutory objectives). In the last year of the SLI's existence in Sacaca, the number of people arriving to the center dropped dramatically from the first two years. This happened for two reasons. First, as the center quickly filled to capacity, Montesinos and the promotora were forced to turn women and their children away beginning in the second part of 1996. In 1996, almost 600 women arrived at the center to have existing conflicts reprocessed within the framework of human rights that guided the center's functioning. However, of these 600, only a small fraction were able to stay even one night, let alone remain while their cases worked their way through the system.[14]

This had a discouraging effect on other women who were willing to face the enormous risks an extended visit to the center posed. Although women throughout the province are vigorous and sophisticated legal actors, and accustomed to leaving their families in order to press their cases in Sacaca's different legal institutions (preferably, as we saw in Chapter 3, the corregidor titutlar), the idea that they would stay for days or even weeks in Sacaca for this purpose would have been previously unthinkable. Even the best students of gender relations in the Andes understandably have struggled at times to really convey the day-to-day struggle that rural woman face at the most basic of levels, and to give a tangible sense of the nearly insurmountable material, educational, and ethnic barriers that prevent a woman from a hamlet like, say, Ñuñumayni, from moving too far outside the cultural and structural parameters of her experience, let alone radically transforming them.[15] Still, hundreds of women from throughout Alonso de Ibañez did push through the social fabric, at least for a time. Yet because the center's physical, financial, and human resources were so limited, it is difficult to know for sure just how transformative—at this level—it could have been. To this extent, it failed hundreds of other women, perhaps the majority of those whose difficulties in life meant they *would* have come, if given the chance.

The second reason the center failed is at least partly related to the reasons why—from a different, and broader, perspective—it served to unsettle and then relocate categories of subjectivity in the province as part of a clarification (and renewal) of those pervasive patterns of intention that have shaped the unfolding of postcolonial Bolivia. Although the *claretianos* in Sacaca, who were the initial sponsors of Sacaca's SLI, like to think of themselves as progressive reformers who have a unique connection with their indigenous congregation, they are still committed to a worldview in which the source of justice, hope, dignity—and other theoretically transnormative values—is the Catholic God, and not anything as heretical as the mere fact of humanness. This means that the initial support of the priests for the SLI was yet one more example of a broader case of what we might call mistaken identity. Even though all of the Claretian priests in Sacaca come from well-educated, solidly middle-class backgrounds, they often will say that because they are Basques, and thus marginalized to a certain extent within wider Spanish society, that they identity with the plight of Bolivia's rural indigenous poor, that they *understand* them because they have—structurally, if not personally—faced similar obstacles in their own country.

Of course, from a certain perspective, this kind of identification is absurd. It is very difficult to see what a thirty-eight-year-old Basque priest, with a master's degree in theology from the University of Navarra, someone who has traveled and taught throughout Latin America, has in common with a thirty-eight-year-old peasant agropastoralist whose entire life has been circumscribed by the boundaries of Alonso de Ibañez. The priest speaks the Spanish of the *Real Academia* and Euskara (as well as French, German, and some Church Latin); the peasant speaks Quechua as a first language, and a rough third-grade Spanish as a second. It is difficult to even say these two men share a common language. Still, the priests of Sacaca believe that they are uniquely suited to their pastoral mission in the norte de Potosí and, at the very least, this earnest belief is what brings them to the region (although it cannot keep them there—the turnover for assistant priests beyond the indefatigable Padre Esteban has been rapid over the years). So despite the church's early enthusiasm, the SLI came to represent a fundamental challenge to it. The SLI became—as all secular human rights institutions do—a kind of moral Ockham's razor that threatened to sever the church from what it has always most demanded—relevance. Once the funding and institutional support passed from the church to the alcaldía, it was only a matter of time before the SLI's material lifeline was cut off.

Even more devastating, the mission of the SLI was vehemently opposed from the very beginning by the province's juez instructor. Perhaps it is not surprising that a judicial official who adorns the walls of his chamber with explicit pornographic images is not to be counted on to eagerly support the idea of women's rights-as-human rights or the presence of a novel legal and social institution committed to such an idea in his own jurisdictional backyard. And so it was (or wasn't). At the level of jurisprudence, the judge believed that existing Bolivian law provided ample protection for problems like rape, spousal abuse, and spousal abandonment (something that in rural Bolivia can have profound consequences for sheer survival). The coming of human rights was an intrusive inconvenience, one that had the effect of both reproducing categories of law that already existed (within a different framework), and, more mundanely, clogging the court's docket and making Montesinos and his "lady clients," as the judge described them, an even more suffocating presence than they already were. The result was predictable. Although, as we have seen, the number of new cases in the *juzgado de instrucción* spiked because of the activities of the SLI, the cases themselves went nowhere. The rise in the number of cases filed in the local court within the SLI's human rights model—based, however, on existing Bolivian law—did not lead to a corresponding rise in the number of convictions or other legal sanctions for violations of human rights implemented through Bolivian state law.

A reading of the impact of the SLI in Alonso de Ibañez based solely on its rise and fall, however, would miss its deeper meaning for people in the province, the way it marked the beginning, not the end, of a broader process through which people in the province continue to relocate themselves in relation to what Ferguson (1999) would call their "expectations of modernity." The coming of human rights discourse to Alonso de Ibañez cannot be understood only in terms of the number of prosecutions or the extent to which expectations were disappointed, or as a rural passion play that pitted the forces of darkness (the juez instructor) against the forces of light (the noble Montesinos). Rather, the saga of the SLI, and the rise of human rights in Bolivia over the last fifteen years more generally, must be understood through much subtler shifts and reorientations of identity, which show that the coming of human rights discourse is as much a form of discursive return as anything else.

6 Modern Dreams

An Ethnography of Grandeur

FOR A PROVINCIAL TOWN in the *extremo* norte de Potosí, Sacaca is certainly a busy place. Indeed, at different times of the year it becomes almost cosmopolitan in the way it fills with people (and their vehicles) who see the region illustratively more than anything else, as just one node within *some* global network—of the crushingly poor, of the nobly indigenous, of the spiritually fertile, of those who are morally and discursively ready to receive the message of human rights. The transnational tribes who move into the norte de Potosí are marked by their symbols: late-model SUVs emblazoned with the logo of the organization, accompanied by the inevitable Masonically impenetrable acronym; and roving groups of men and women in the uniform of the transnational development worker (baseball cap, again with the organizational logo, all-weather jacket or safari vest, also with acronymic logo, *Top Gun* aviator glasses, which have, by an odd coincidence in world fashion, become highly stylish once again, khaki slacks or knock-off jeans, and, finally, either polyurethane running shoes or nonleather hiking boots, one of those models that crowds the shelves of an REI Coop or its western European equivalent).

The times when Sacaca fills with these clans of transnational elites and their Bolivian counterparts are also the times when the town becomes crowded with groups of campesino leaders from throughout the province. The presence of large numbers of development NGOs at any one time means either massive meetings—usually held on the new basketball court at the alcadía—or NGO ferias, which are extraordinary events in which Sacaca's plaza is turned into a marketplace of liberalism, a place in which the moral and ideological assumptions of an entire discursive universe are peddled to the benighted masses like so many bags of potatoes (see again Figures 4.1–4.3, Chapter 4). To watch the coming together of transnational development NGOs and their intended beneficiaries is to come as close as possible to having an empirical encounter with modernity encapsulated.

But after (or before) these encounters, everyone has to eat. This presents some problems, because the number of *pensiónes* in town fluctuates between zero and about three, depending on the time of the year and any number of personal and economic contingencies. A pensión in Sacaca usually consists of a room adjacent to a house, which is filled with long tables, chairs, and benches. Meals are served twice a day at very specific times: usually 12:30 P.M. and 5:30–6:00 P.M. The food almost never varies: A bowl of soup to begin; the *segundo*, or main (literally "second") dish, which is either a piece of meat or fried egg, rice, and potatoes (either boiled or as *ch'uño*); and the *postre* (or dessert), which is often just a cup of mate, but (if one is lucky) can also be a cup of tea and something sweet, like rice pudding. If there is actually a choice among pensiones at any one time in Sacaca, people do not choose between them based on the quality of food or the price, which are always nearly identical. Rather, they do their very best to eat at the place that has a television.

In pensiones that merely have radios—and they always have some form of entertainment, either a radio or television—the diners must listen to a program like Radio Pio XII, which broadcasts the latest news from this one slice of provincial Bolivia and includes Norman Rockwellian segments like the series of very individualized announcements in which mothers remind their sons to return to their hamlets for birthday celebrations, or one brother exhorts another to return to the province safely after finishing a stint in the army (usually, but not always, in the *Regimiento Camacho* in Oruro). But those who are most eager to watch television during their meal—and, by extension, not listen to a program like Radio Pio XII—are the campesino authorities, who see a lunch or dinner at a pensión in Sacaca as both a mark of prestige and a rite of passage, since for much of Sacaca's history "indios" would never have been allowed to take a meal in one of the town's private homes. Even so, it is usually only a small subset of a hamlet or *ayllu* delegation that does, in fact, eat at a pensión; the rest find a grassy spot on Sacaca's plaza and nosh on whatever they have brought with them on their trip to the capital.

The programs that are broadcast on Sacaca's televisions span the range from Peruvian or Mexican *telenovelas* to CNN Español, from the (usually disappointing) World Cup–qualifying matches involving the national team to Japanese anime. But in a moment that was paradoxically rich in both ambiguity and clarity, I found myself alone in a pensión with a large group of men from Canton Iturata, a distant region of the province from which men (or women) do not frequently journey to the capital. The gathering of transnational NGOs in Sacaca this time was clearly important, especially since (this was July 2005) the upcoming national elections had shifted the terms of engagement ever so slightly. Yet despite the tension hanging over the entire province, the men sitting at the tables waiting for their soups did not say a word—not about the meetings they had attended that day, not about how long their journey back to their hamlets would take, and not about whether they had managed to convince the man from the Belgian forestry NGO to begin a project in their part of the province, despite its relative remoteness. Instead, their eyes were glued to the television screen, which had just announced that the "battle of the titans" was just about to begin, followed by a large explosion that faded into the oversize letters of the WWF—the World Wrestling Federation. Yes, I was about to enjoy an hour of American professional wrestling with my fifteen fellow diners, who stared at the screen with rapt attention.

The wrestling program was what one would expect: lots of hyperbolic posturing and shouting; the coming and going of wrestlers and their entourages, accompanied by loud rock music, spectacular pyrotechnics, and glistening sweat; the parading of bikini-clad women in high-heels, who announced the beginning of each round with a placard held high above their heads; and, of course, the wrestling itself, which consisted of move after carefully choreographed move that seemed to increase in ferocity with each painful chokehold or crushing bodyblow. As usual, there were the series of interlocking dramatic storylines, which were difficult to follow completely, but which led various people to suddenly burst upon the arena and disrupt the match, even if temporarily, by throwing chairs, cursing, grabbing the microphone, or even entering the ring themselves in street clothes to deliver cheap shots before fleeing as quickly as they had appeared.

At one point, late in the match, a chair was broken over the top of a wrestler's head, after which what must have been fake blood began to flow in rivulets down his face, covering his shoulders and back in red streaks. This was the first time in my life I had ever actually watched such a spectacle from beginning to end, and there is no question that it was the first time for everyone else present in the room. Indeed, for at least some of the hamlet authorities, this was likely the first time they had ever watched *anything* on television. So there we were: I was watching the screen at the same time I tried to watch the men watching the screen; they watched me watching them at the same time they tried to watch the screen; and we all, for the most part, stared agape at the postmodern Roman carnival unfolding in—if I am not mistaken—Memphis, Tennessee, all the while the dilemmas of modernity swirled around us so thick that you could cut them with a knife.

The men from Canton Iturata had come to Sacaca to meet with representatives of transnational development NGOs, many of which were pushing their agendas now as part of a wider, more fundamental, human rights framework. They had spent the day—as had I—listening to speeches about the relationship between *desarrollo sostenible* (sustainable development) and *derechos humanos* (human rights) and the value of using science in order to improve crop yields, all of which was presented as part of an even larger moral-political transformation of rural Bolivia, one in which "*los indígenas*" would play a fundamental role in creating a "new Bolivia." Even though these were the heady days of late 2005, in which a public discourse of transformation had risen to a fever pitch throughout Bolivia, the context of this particular meeting of transnationals and local leaders was one that had much deeper historical and ideological roots. As I have argued throughout this book, the last twenty years in Bolivia have been more of a return than anything else, a reaffirmation of the patterns of intention that have structured postcolonial Bolivia since the first part of the nineteenth century, even if these patterns of intention—such as liberalism expressed through law—have only played a role as a kind of negative key, or as a submerged discursive presence destabilizing a long history of oligarchic rule, dictatorship, nationalism, and the political exclusion of large swaths of the Bolivian citizenry.

So after soaking in the message of progress and envisioning themselves as part of a different universe, one constituted by technocratic knowledge and expressed through the normative language of rights, these peasant agropastoralists from Bolivia's cultural and geographical extremity were confronted with yet another of modernity's many faces. If people want—or think they want—to see large, synthetically enhanced men and svelte, synthetically enhanced women parade in front of them in an orgy of violence, melodrama, and torrents of perspiration, then an entire market will emerge to satisfy these desires. And why will this market emerge? Because both the spectators and the marketers act to rationally maximize their position on the basis of self (or collective-self) interest. How do we know this to be true? Because the political and economic systems of both the place where this spectacle was produced and watched are based on a set of moral and ontological assumptions that tells us it is.

In a bizarre way, the presence of John Locke could be felt—by me, at least—lurking above the wrestling ring in Memphis, although we can be sure he would not recognize his discursive handiwork there among the double axe handles, cleavage chokes, and knee drops. The rational individual is ultimately autonomous and endowed with a set of rights that function (ideally) to protect this autonomy. If the individual freely chooses to "mix his labor"—in Locke's indelible and profoundly consequential phrasing—with that which nature has provided, he creates private property, something he is both morally and legally entitled to at the expense of all other rational individuals. And if he freely demands a venue in which other rational beings have agreed to beat and humiliate each other for his benefit? This is not a part of the worldview described by transnational development NGOs in Sacaca, but it is as much a consequence of it as genetically modified potato seeds, potable water, and the Indigenous and Tribal Peoples Convention.

It is for these reasons, among others, that it is appropriate that I end this study of Bolivia's complicated modern trajectory with an examination of development and its discontents. In many ways, the encounter with development encapsulates (and restates) most of the book's themes: the way different moments in Bolivian history come to define—even if paradoxically—the constitution of the Bolivian modern; the ambiguous role of the peasant in the country's different postcolonial narratives; and the way development engenders highly ambivalent responses from those it would putatively benefit, the states in which it is done, and critics whose job it is to locate it in relation to much longer processes of colonialism, neocolonialism, and the consolidation of a particular transnational mode of production. This penultimate chapter will examine these connections and ramifications by focusing, as I have done throughout this book, on one region of rural Bolivia. But the story of development, in Bolivia or elsewhere, is a quintessentially transnational one—a story of the circulation of values within one of the most emblematic of contemporary moral economies. As we will see, development in rural Bolivia unfolds through a process of discursive projection, through the imaginings of people who—so the narrative goes—want to be anywhere else but here.

Development and the Phenomenology of Modernity

In his 1995 masterwork, Arturo Escobar dismantles the entire postwar development project top to bottom, that constellation of ideas and practices that the critical geographer Gillian Hart has described as "big D Development" (2001).

Escobar shows, among other things, how what he calls the making (and un-making) of the Third World by the United States—and later its western European allies—was part of a concerted political-economic strategy to find and develop both potential markets and sources of raw materials at a time when the United States was in a period of rapid economic and demographic expansion. Although "Third World" originally had a more benign meaning—it was introduced by the French scholar Alfred Sauvy in 1952 to describe those countries that fell outside the First and Second Worlds of NATO and the Warsaw Pact—its connotations were soon after transformed as part of a wider process of political-economic consolidation. But even though the need for markets and raw materials had existed for at least 400 years (indeed, Bolivia's raison d'être can be traced to these socioeconomic imperatives), the ideological climate had shifted dramatically after the end of the second world war. Although the system of colonialism continued for another twenty years, it was no longer possible within the international legal and political system that was created after the war for nation-states to simply acquire territory or markets by naked force, or out of a commitment to some dubious theory of history, or through a mandate of racial superiority (whether understood as a burden or not).

Instead, what was needed was an entirely altruistic framework in which what theorists in the 1960s and 1970s described as the dependency of poorer (but natural resource–rich) countries would be the necessary result of their need for technological, economic, and military assistance from core countries and the international institutions that served as their proxies (see Cardoso and Faletto 1979; Frank 1967, 1972; Wallerstein 1974). This framework came in the form of "development," a discursively rich concept that, as Escobar documents in great detail, embodied centuries of western desire, fear, guilt, and orientalism. For Escobar, it was crucial to understand both the economic interconnections between the First and Third Worlds and the discursive framework in which these interconnections were both made and justified. This dialectic can be seen in the way Escobar contrasts the assistance that was given to western European countries as part of the Marshall Plan with that given to Third World countries; the former was part of a program of massive grants, the latter was rendered through loans, which bound countries like Bolivia to international financial institutions and their main donors for decades.

To encounter development at this late stage is necessarily to experience it in this way, to see the continual unfolding of the "big D Development" project through a glass darkly. Escobar's theoretical toolkit was the product of a synthesis. He took the assumptions of the kind of neo-Marxist political economy that had emerged within anthropology during the 1960s and 1970s and combined them with the radically destabilizing currents from continental poststructuralism, which provided anthropologists of Escobar's generation with a seemingly endless supply of ideas about how the world and its meanings were constructed (and misconstructed). The first set of tools gave Escobar the ability to place the development encounter within a broader historical and processual context; the second allowed him to examine development at its most intimate scales, which were not, somewhat surprisingly, those in which actual people in different parts of the world either introduce the technocratic apparatuses of development, or receive their fruits, but rather those in which such apparatuses are envisioned, named, and justified.

This detour into what might be called the encountering development thesis at this point is necessary because this is the orientation that has dominated the critical literature—in anthropology and beyond—for at least the last ten years, and it was without question the one that shaped a good portion of my own thinking about the meanings of development in Bolivia since I first began my own encounters with both development and Escobar's analysis of it. As it turned out, however, this thesis was only able to provide a partial framework for understanding the complicated interconnections between development, human rights, and Bolivia's contemporary liberal renaissance.

To show that the development emperor has no clothes is to make a series of claims that are themselves riven with contradictions. Further, the dismantling of "development" created—likely unintentionally—a replacement paradigm that, from a certain perspective, obscures more than it continues to reveal. In saying this I do not mean to deny the force of the critique itself; as I have said, it remains an essential tool for understanding the broader political-economic currents that bring NGOs to rural Bolivia and other discursive flashpoints in the Global South. But this mode of engagement is perhaps a bit too structural: it uncovers connections and imperatives behind what appear to be well-intentioned efforts on the part of governments, international institutions, and transnationals to bring the fruits of science to those most in need, to work for the protection of human rights among vulnerable populations, and otherwise advance the cause of economic and social justice around the world. Indeed, the critique of development goes some way toward explaining why benevolent intentions of this kind can be both inevitable and deeply misplaced at the same time. Yet should development be understood primarily through what lies beneath its benevolent rhetoric? Is this, in other words, where development *is*?

I would argue that we must also seek to understand the phenomenological dimensions of the development dialectic, those actual encounters that take the form of meetings and ferias in places like Sacaca, when those structural conditions that have made meetings and ferias like this possible are actualized, given meaning, and thus transformed into something that is very difficult to define simply *in terms of* these conditions. And there is yet another aspect to the phenomenological encounter with development: the way in which people in different places and times come to see development as part of a new moral economy, one whose circulation has *finally* swept through their provincial town or village or hamlet. This is the moral-psychical dimension of development that is, in a sense, a self-encounter with its meanings, the most intimate level at which development can, and must, be understood.

The reason a phenomenological approach is so critical for my purposes here is because the ambiguities of development reflect so much of what we want to know about those patterns of intention that continue to shape Bolivia's contested present. It also is essential to turn the gaze *away* from these broader frames of meaning in order to come to terms with the hamlet *corregidor auxiliar* who sees his work with NGOs as part of a mission to bring "civilization" to rural Bolivia, or the local rural-legal intellectual who sees in human rights the means through which people in the province will discover a new sense of dignity and moral worth.

How can the multiple encounters embedded in the coming of WWF to Alonso de Ibañez be understood as a function of modernity-as-moral (or political or economic or legal) imperialism? Where were the obvious power imbalances there? I, a conventional transnational elite, was as confused, shocked, and oddly compelled as anyone else present there in that cold pensión. And how can something like a professional wrestling program be seen as just one more expression of a set of homogeneous modern imperatives—an example of something also described as "globalization"—when it is more than anything else a kind of liberal morality play that manages to be both absurd and essentially conservative at the same time? To understand development as a phenomenological problem is to come some way toward resolving these dilemmas—and the others that have hovered over this book—without losing sight of either the finely grained contours of everyday life or the patterns of intention that shape the experiential spaces in which expectations of modernity bloom like 1,000 quinoa plants.

An Ethnography of Grandeur in the Norte de Potosí

To encounter development in rural Bolivia is also to experience something else. In his critical meditation on the practices of everyday life on the Zambian copper belt, James Ferguson (1999) describes the destabilizing and disorienting effects of what he calls an "ethnography of decline." As he documented life in the "difficult and disorderly social environment" of urban Zambia, Ferguson came to be overwhelmed with an almost paralyzing sense of despair. As he explains:

> Despair, fear, panic; broken lives and shattered expectations; this was not what I had set out to look for, but it was, like it or not, what I found. The tragic course that so many people's lives were taking was not only an anthropological fact of some theoretical interest; it raised ethical and methodological difficulties of a sort that I was not well prepared to deal with. My fieldwork left me with a terrible sense of sadness, and a recognition of the profound inability of scholarship to address the sorts of demands that people brought to me every day in my research, as they asked me to help them with their pressing and sometimes overwhelming personal problems and material needs. I could proceed . . . only after arriving at the realization that decline, confusion, fear, and suffering were central subjects. . . . (1999: 18)

Some subtle equivalencies are being made here that need to be underscored. First, Ferguson comes to see the social and economic disorder of urban Zambia as symptomatic of the *experienced* disorder of modernity itself, the way in which "modernity" becomes for people a discursive means through which they attempt to make sense of their everyday lives. This is not "modernity" as a simple analytical or historical category, but one that exists on at least two levels. It exists at the more observable level of economic immiseration, in which changes in the global economy reverberate down to the most local of levels, displacing lives and confounding expectations. But it is also a kind of epistemic disorder, in which "stable, systemic order[s] of knowledge" are replaced by a "tangle of confusion, chaos, and fear" (Ferguson 1999: 19). And if the chaos of urban Zambia can also, to a certain extent, be seen as the chaos of late modernity itself, then the sympathetic encounter with it, the critical engagement of a researcher like Ferguson, can only be an ethnography of decline.[1] This is a methodology for the downward side of a parabolic arc of history, that sloping drop from the heights of early modern optimism to the rapidly declining plunge into late-modern despair. To make this point another way: If there is any understanding to be had from an experience like Ferguson's, it is a *self*-understanding of modernity's essential translucency, the realization that to live in the late-modern world is to view its meanings and implications only diffusely, whether one is an out-of-work Zambian miner or a cosmopolitan anthropologist on the job.

Yet if my own encounters with development in Bolivia seem to suggest a framework of understanding that in many ways differs from those that structure debate both within Bolivia and across the critical discursive universe of the academy, so too the encounter with what Ferguson calls the "underlying metanarrative of modernization" (1999: 20). Although I entirely agree that the trajectory of this metanarrative can appear nonlinear and nonteleological at any point in time from an ever-shifting ground zero within the Malinowskian horizontal slice, I take this disrupture between narrative and practice to be a point of departure, rather than something that should be used to reinterpret the narrative (of modernity/modernization) itself. As we will see below, to study development (or law or liberalism) in rural Bolivia with that kind of persistent presence we mean to invoke by "ethnography"—what Ferguson more modestly calls the "ethnographic aspect" (1999: 21)—is not to study an essential and irreversible decline at all; rather, it is to study something that is not quite decline's opposite, but certainly something that must be located at a stark tangent from it—grandeur.

The realization that the empirical encounter with development, liberal legality, human rights, and those other discursive vanguards is the ethnography of grandeur helps to explain one of the most troubling dilemmas: The fact that the most (structurally) marginalized campesinos in rural Bolivia also can be among the most fervent advocates for the very discursive regimes that shape—and, at times, produce—their marginalization. And as I have said, this is not a case of simple alienation; people find a way to be both committed vernacular liberals (in their dedication to human rights, for example) and sophisticated opponents of something like the capitalization or privatization of land. That is to say, Bolivian peasants have grasped something about the late-modern moment that many of its critics seem to have missed: that its radicalism comes not from promises of economic or more broadly material progress, but in the way it promises membership in an alternative moral universe, one in which both human values and assumptions about the nature of being itself circulate within a radically different transnational body politic.

This means that marginalization must be understood in new ways, again, without having to labor under the heavy burden of macrostructural analysis, because the coming of the idea of human rights to the norte de Potosí has not improved people's lives by any observable degree, at least if we measure improvement by those dominant international metrics like the U.N. Human Development Index. The spreading of human rights discourse over the province in the form of transnational NGO rhetoric, the presence of the SLI and Lucio Montesinos's later human rights activism, and, more recently, through the platforms of new political parties, has not led to an increase in literacy rates, a decrease in infant mortality, an extension of life spans, or anything else that would demonstrate if not a reversal in what Ferguson (1999) would call a "decline," than at least a movement in the right direction.

But the idea of human rights does not depend—despite its historical and political associations with brutality, mass murder, genocide, and other dark moments in the human experience—on its pragmatic usefulness, or on its instrumental effectiveness in *improving* people's lives, or establishing a framework in which *actual* development can take place, or even in preventing those unspeakably dark moments from repeating themselves. Rather, the idea of human rights, whose power comes from the way it *connotes* certain (new or renewed) things about the relationship between individual and community, the transcultural sameness of human beings, the duty of the collective to guarantee at least some spaces of inviolable individual liberty, and so on, takes root at much more intangible levels: those of the moral and social imaginary, those intellectual and affective spaces from which the norms that shape both self-understanding and human action are derived.

To understand the expectations (and dilemmas) of modernity in this way is not to deny the mundane but profound material and social facts that burden the lives of rural Bolivians as much as they do—in different ways, with different cultural meanings—the lives of disaffected urban Zambians. But it *is*, however, to recognize that the often crushing circumstances of everyday life, those observable and undeniable crises that seem to haunt scholars like Ferguson as much as they burden the people at what David Nugent (1997) has called the "edge of empire," are, in a sense, immune to modernity's claims, and vice versa. The idea of human rights, (again) for example, promises nothing less than a new social ontology, one that compels a new set of values, even if, in embracing human rights, rural Bolivians merely appropriate a discursive framework that had always been present in postcolonial Bolivia (though denied to them).

This is why the encounter with development in the norte de Potosí is the ethnography of what I like to think of as *grandeur*, even though the exaltation and sense of utopian liberal optimism that encapsulates the encounter is so jarringly at odds with the realities of life at the ragged edge. The list of social, medical, and economic problems that beset many of the 25,000 people in Alonso de Ibañez is a long and familiar one: chronic alcoholism and alcohol abuse; lack of widely available potable water; chronic violence against both women and children by men (with alcohol playing a key role); economic insecurity and persistent malnutrition (though not outright starvation); almost no standardized prepartum health care; high rates of infant mortality due to easily treatable conditions such as diarrhea; very little access to the wider national cash economy through either labor or consumption; and a location in a dominant historical ethno-class system that is marginal in the extreme (something that makes the ascendancy of Evo Morales, who emerged from such a location, all the more remarkable).

Beyond these familiar burdens, there are others that are perhaps not so despairingly common. For example, the province has had a consistently high murder rate since at least the last quarter of the nineteenth century: roughly two per year, which translates—within the coldly sterilizing language of the standard crime index—into about nine murders per 100,000 people. This rate would be expected for relatively violent urban areas, rather than a level of violence in one of the least densely populated areas of the world not in the middle of civil war or other armed conflict.[2]

Yet despite all of this hardship, violence, and what the international community considers "medium human development,"[3] the return of liberalism's promises—via transnational development—has provided a means through which people in Alonso de Ibañez are able to plunge into the waters of an alternative moral universe, one that celebrates both the development of a particular subjectivity and the ability to "think and feel beyond the nation-state" (Cheah and Robbins 1998). Men in Alonso de Ibañez (as elsewhere in rural Bolivia) die in astonishingly high numbers of cirrhosis of the liver, and women face the complications of childbirth with courage but with the very real likelihood that they will not survive them.[4] But with the transformation of development within a human rights framework, a concern for these (and other) grave physical and social problems has been replaced with a concern for the province's *moral* well-being, even as the signs of moral progress continue to be measured symbolically through the misleading indicators of the modern technocratic state.

Bart Simpson on the Altiplano

The social geometry of the capital of Alonso de Ibañez is the same one found throughout the norte de Potosí, other regions of highland Bolivia, and indeed most of the Andean countries. Sacaca was one of the hundreds of Viceroy Toledo's *reducciones*, those late-sixteenth century towns that were created in order to both control the restless native populations of the colonial Andes, and accelerate the civilizing process by forcing this population to reimagine itself in the shadow of all those administrative and architectural symbols of colonial Spanish rule: the church, the court, the alcaldía, the police station, and the different houses of commerce (see Abercrombie 1998a). These different buildings face each other without noticeable hierarchy across the town's one formal public space: the *plaza*, the village green, a place where tightly circumscribed leisure and spontaneous discussion take place under the gaze of the instruments of spiritual, political, and legal power.

But something else also takes place in Sacaca's plaza, something that could hardly have been anticipated by the architects of Spain's early-modern colonial empire. On most evenings of the week, as the sun is setting and darkness settles over this urban outpost on the altiplano, clusters of young schoolchildren gather on the sidewalks that run in front of Sacaca's general stores. These are the all-purpose *tiendas* that are ubiquitous throughout rural Bolivia. They sell everything from coca leaves and popcorn in large cloth sacks to batteries, candy, vegetables, writing paper and utensils, and blank legal documents, among the many other odds and ends necessary for life in small provincial towns. The owners of the stores live either above, or behind them, and they are staffed by husband and wife, school-age children, and relatives back for extended visits from their new homes in Bolivia's cities. Most of the stores also double as modest drinking establishments. One corner is denoted, in a sense, for this purpose by a small table surrounded by benches at which patrons can quaff large bottles of Huari, Oruro's brew, or, much more rarely, smaller glasses of the insidious fire-liquid known locally as simply *alcohol*, the pure grain alcohol imported from Brazil in oversized tin oil cans.

These little stores don't exactly turn into wild saloons, but it is true that they can become raucous places where NGO workers, members of the hospital staff, people (usually men) from the hamlets, *sacaqueños*, and others (including resident anthropologists) come together to enjoy some good cheer after a long day's work. The stores typically only sell beer and alcohol to patrons in search of a drink. Sacaca also is filled with *chicherías*, which are houses outside of the central plaza where women—always women—sell *chicha* (Quechua *aqha*, Ayua *k'usa*), the fermented corn beer that has been a staple of social life in the Andes for hundreds, if not thousands, of years. These establishments operate according to a completely different social and ritual calendar, and the chicha is only available a few times a year. When it is, however, the chicherías of Sacaca can become liminal social spaces; it's not unusual to find someone like the *actuario* of the *juzgado de instrucción*, for example, *ch'allando*, or ritually toasting, a runa woman with baby at breast.

Like Sacaca's pensiones, most of the plaza's stores also have televisions. Because the few benches in the crowded internal area are reserved for drinking parties, the owners turn the televisions so that they face out the open storefront onto the plaza itself. For about one hour after sundown, the programs are always the same, and they are directed toward the groups of children who sit on the ground in a tight bunch, huddled against the coming night chill. Over several years of observing this consequence of development in Alonso de Ibañez, the programs have not changed very much; indeed, there have been intense loyalties to two television shows in particular, which says much about both the slippery means through which modern values continue to express themselves in new ways in rural Bolivia, and the way the imagination plays a key role in shaping subjectivity in the frontier outposts of the modern project.

The usual sequence is as follows: *The Simpsons* (in Spanish, of course), followed by *Dragon Ball Z*, the crazily popular Japanese anime that follows the exploits of Son Goku and his son Gohan as they defend Earth against a confusing parade of odd villains. The children usually come from hamlets within 30 minutes from Sacaca, places like Totoroqo, Chungara, and Kamacachi, and they return together in groups after the shows are over, usually without adults. This is not actually a problem, in most cases, because many of the children in the closest hamlets make two trips a day anyway in order to attend a special town school—the *Internado*—established by the Claretians in collaboration with their counterparts in the order of the *Hermanas de la Providencia*. Most children who come and go regularly to Sacaca could probably make the journey with their eyes closed.

So there they are each night, three or four groups of children, scattered around the plaza, intensely following the trials and tribulations of Bart Simpson, a boy with his own peculiar problems. It is not clear how much of the actual dialogue these children understand; most of them are Quechua (more rarely Aymara) first-language speakers who are only beginning to hear and study Spanish. The children never laugh at the jokes, although on occasion they trade nervous glances during Bart's sight-gags or during instances of what pass in the world of animation for physical comedy. The action is more nonverbal in *Dragon Ball Z*, in which characters hurl through the sky for seconds on end and spend much of the time using special powers to dispatch their enemies or to prevent one calamity or another from unfolding. Even here, however, the dialogue can be thick and fast; it is the complicated storylines, after all, that partly attract such devoted followers to the (now transnational) world of Japanese manga/anime. Nevertheless, there they sit, night after night, the youngest members of this rural Bolivian province, moving between the animated anomie of the postindustrial United States and the fevered world of Japan's own troubled youth imaginary. And on one occasion, in what I can only imagine was a completely coincidental epistemic moment, these two quintessentially late-modern worlds came together. As I looked on in late 1999, *The Simpsons* episode was set in contemporary Japan itself.

It is not difficult to understand the multiple attractions of these animated television programs for the campesino children who come to Sacaca rain or shine to devote themselves to them. They represent a visual and social experience totally unlike anything else they get in the rest of their daily lives. Like all children, their developing minds demand the nourishment of play, and runa children find ways to exercise their imaginations just like children everywhere. But without sounding artificially clinical (or even sociological), it is not unfair to their parents to say that the children of this part of rural Bolivia are not the center of the kind of obsessive attention to their intellectual and psychological needs that characterizes other locations, places where caretakers do not have to perform enervating labor—sometimes far from home—from early in the morning until sundown just to survive. So for at least a percentage of the runa children in Alonso de Ibañez, those who live in what might only partly ironically be described as the suburbs of Sacaca, the creative brainchild of the same person who gave us the underground rag staple *Life in Hell* provides a primary means through which they are able to imagine a different universe, to transport themselves beyond what is by any measure a difficult life-world.

And there is a curious disrupture here in what might be called the space-time continuum of modernity. Through their consumption of late-twentieth century popular culture, these children project themselves, and shape their identities, in terms of a modern moment that has matured, ripened, and is beginning to deteriorate. Indeed, in its self-referentiality, celebration of parody, and sense of ironic nostalgia, *The Simpsons* is arguably the product of a moment in discursive space-time beyond modernity, what has been described within the cultural milieu from which it emerged as the expression of a post-modernity (although, looking out from Sacaca's plaza, a chronology like this appears unconvincing at best).

Still, there is another way to see something like the coming of *The Simpsons* or professional wrestling not as symbols of the unintended consequences of development or as reflections of what is most expected or desired about "modernity," but rather as a window into how the imperatives (or values) of the development—liberalism—modernity nexus are actualized in social practice. Just as those children in Sacaca's plaza enter the dysfunctional world—such as they can understand it—of post–Cold War Middle America, or the hyperreal fantasy universe of Japanese comic book writers, through the projection of an imaginary that is as much moral as it is anything else, so too their parents' real encounter with the idea of derechos humanos takes place not in meetings with development workers, or when they are given "food for work,"[5] but when they *imagine* themselves as social beings who live in a world in which they are entitled to human rights and miracle seeds and "human dignity."[6]

Envisioning the Bolivian Modern, or, the Parable of the Latrine

In the norte de Potosí, the signposts of modernity are literal. If development has functioned as a kind of summarizing key symbol for the most recent period in the continuing emergence of the Bolivian modern, its presence, and meaning, is marked—or, we might say, indexed—in cement, wood, and metal. When NGOs finish their work in Alonso de Ibáñez, they want to make sure their mission is understood. The signs they leave behind are like fingerposts that say "modernity—this way." All along footpaths, roads, at the top of mountain passes, and in the middle of hamlets and towns, one comes across signage. The signs can clutter up so thickly in some places that some stretches of interdepartmental highway, or entrances to larger hamlets, can come to look like a Las Vegas strip of transnational development. These monuments make sure to announce the major players, of course, and what they either intend to do—yes, sometimes these memorials are erected *before* anything happens—or what they have done (see Figures 6.1 and 6.2).

Figure 6.1. Bolivia's liberal renaissance promises more than anything else a *mosoj causay*, a new life

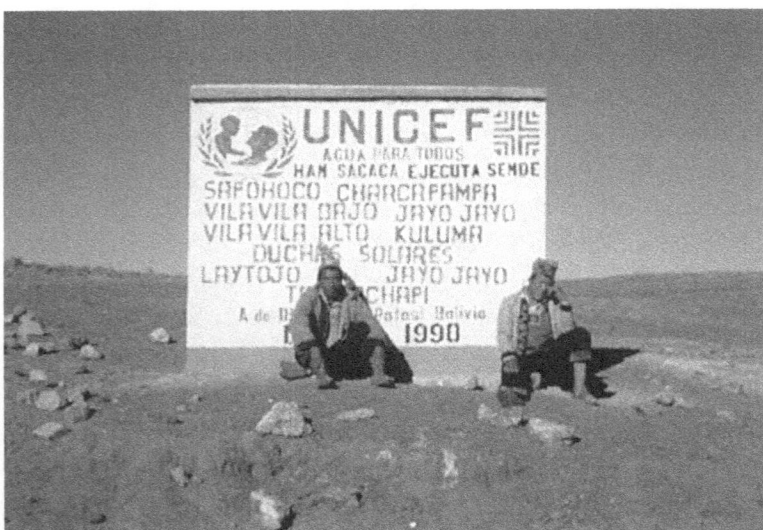

Figure 6.2. Fingerpost in Alonso de Ibáñez that says: "modernity—this way"

But the monuments to Bolivia's expectations of modernity go beyond mere cement or (less commonly) wooden signs; they also are present in the wash basins, solar showers, micro-forests, and, above all, the latrines that stand as both visual and moral cues for the people who remain long after the late-model Toyota Land Cruisers have moved to different places and projects. If the ancestors would have the people of Alonso de Ibáñez look upward to the *apus*, those spirit-beings who inhabit the high places, their cultural gaze now is blocked by news of Bolivia's liberal renaissance—the Dutch and Americans and Swiss are here, and the clean water, sanitary places in which to defecate, and stands of (theoretically) commercially viable eucalyptus saplings are reminders of the moral, political, and economic salvation to be found in this discursive renewal.

It is perhaps odd to end this narrative of development and its discontents with an argument about the discursive implications of outhouses. And I do not want to give the wrong impression. The visual symbolization of development in Alonso de Ibáñez is not some kind of neoimperial project, in which the men and women of the province's hamlets sit idly by as the various transnational armies pour their concrete and deliver cheap copies of the

Figure 6.3. Transnational signage in a field of quinoa: the hamlet whipping post

UDHR. Rather, like Lucio Montesinos's embrace of the idea of human rights, or the calls for social justice by the corregidor auxiliar of Molino T'ikanoma, the men and women of the norte de Potosí are eager to receive and incorporate these symbols, but not primarily because of how they will change the practice of everyday life.

Despite the hazards to health, people still defecate in their potato fields and urinate in streams—and there is nothing less appealing on a frigid morning or evening (when else would they do it?) than the prospect of stripping naked and standing under the dribble of a luke-cold shower, one supposedly heated by the ever-giving sunlight to be found at 4,000 meters. The wooden latrine stands there instead, largely unused, smelling of fresh lumber, as the sanitary equivalent of ILO 169, or the UDHR, or the evening's *Simpsons* episode. It is a visual means through which people can project a different universe, one whose utopianism resonates with a long line of other moral projects that have come to this part of the Bolivian altiplano.

But if the unfolding of the Bolivian modern in Alonso de Ibañez is, in this sense, intersubjective—something whose implications are difficult for many critical scholars, in particular, to come to terms with—it is also, as we have seen throughout this book, shot through with dilemmas. Although the discursive signposts in the norte de Potosí provide a means for people to project themselves, to leave, in a sense, to think of themselves through a different moral, legal, and political language, they also serve the reverse function: They allow people in the province to bring "modernity" to them, to change its meanings, and to render it in terms that are anything but utopian (see Figure 6.3).

Conclusion

New Revolutionary Moves

TO WRITE *ANY* BOOK about *any* aspect of contemporary Bolivia these days is, of course, to undertake a project fraught with a considerable amount of uncertainty. As James Dunkerley has argued (2006), Bolivia is in the midst of an unfolding "third revolution," one whose meanings and implications have so far resisted easy parsing into existing theoretical and historical categories. The stirrings of this emergent revolution were documented with skill and insight from scholars and activists across a wide range, from Nancy Postero's examination of the social and political transition to a "postmulticultural" Bolivia (2007a), to the first-person account and analysis of the 1999–2000 Bolivian Water War by Oscar Olivera (2004), the machinist who emerged as the leader of Cochabamba's *Coordinadora de Defensa del Agua y la Vida*. But even Postero's 2007 account, which provides perhaps the most in-depth recent analysis we have in any language of what she calls the "popular protagonism" that led up to the epochal election of Evo Morales in December of 2005, is marked by a certain amount of tentativeness. As she pierces through the political and cultural rhetoric of the election:

> [t]his will be the real challenge . . . to produce more than talk, to get to some real answers that change the material conditions for the poor and indigenous peoples of the country. Is this possible? . . . What new model of a multiethnic state might emerge that balances the need for recognition and equitable distribution? . . . Bolivia's postmulticultural citizens hope they can provide another option [to the policies of the 1990s and early 2000s]. The rest of Latin America, and perhaps beyond, will be watching their efforts. (2007a: 232)

There is, in other words, much that remains to be seen about both what *kind* of revolution has been unleashed in Bolivia, and, even more important, what the *effects* of this revolution will be for those categories of citizens that had been systematically marginalized within dominant discourses since the first part of the nineteenth century. As Postero rightly observes, Bolivia's contested and ambiguous present is nevertheless significant well beyond Latin America itself, even if the details of this significance are difficult to articulate (see also Postero 2007b). As a follow-up to his 1999 masterwork *Expectations of Modernity*, James Ferguson has written a new critical study of Africa in what he calls the "neoliberal world order" (2006). But if Postero is right, and contemporary Bolivia represents one moment in a broader movement away from the demands of this neoliberal world order, then it remains to be seen if the development of the kind of globalized framework Ferguson describes has not already passed the midpoint in its parabolic arc. And if it has, then how are we to understand the downward slope? This kind of pell-mell uncertainty, the pregnant franticness of which in Bolivia Postero captures so well, brings to mind Gogol's epigrammatic lines about the headlong rush into uncertainty of a different time and place: "Russia, where are you flying to? Answer!"[1]

So it is within this period of ambiguity and desperate hopefulness that this book must make its claims. In part as a response, I have developed a framework of the *longue durée* through which the meanings and implications of Bolivia's modern trajectory can, in part, be understood, by focusing on the emergence and historical transformation of particular social, legal, and discursive patterns. In engaging in an ethnography and critical history of key ideas as much as the social practices through which they are made concrete in particular places and times, I was able to show how postcolonial Bolivia has been marked by a counterintuitive—if not counterfactual—kind of stability, one in which a set of framing discourses has shaped events at the national level as much as it has events in supposedly isolated regions like the norte de Potosí, where encounters with law and liberalism must to a certain extent be observed like the shadows on Plato's cave, or as practices that serve as a negative key to the persistence and meaning of these framing discourses.

This is not to say that these encounters encompass everything important about the practice of everyday life in the norte de Potosí, any more than they do in places like La Paz and Sucre; indeed, these moments merely intrude on what are otherwise the daily rituals of economic production, religious practice, lifecycle rites of passage, music and other art-making, and so on. These varied and rich dimensions of what we can without any irony think of as culture in rural Bolivia have been documented at great and insightful length in ways that demonstrate that it is entirely possible to observe and participate in life in rural Bolivia without having to account for the presence of wider patterns of intention at all. Indeed, there are many good reasons for not *seeing* in this way, not the least of which is that the kind of ethnographic and critical perspective that it requires necessarily obscures many of those mundane facts of culture that constitute the sinew of social life. Moreover, to argue that broader discursive imperatives have shaped the unfolding of modern Bolivia—as much, if not more so, in places like the norte de Potosí as in the centers of national life—is not to argue that these imperatives are ever-present, or that, when present, their influence *determines* social, political, and legal relations. In other words, it is not my intention here to offer up yet another theory of what the intellectual historian Isaiah Berlin (1959) called "historical inevitability." However, as I have tried to show—through the examination of courts, conflict resolution, human rights, gender relations, and development—on the relatively infrequent occasions when Bolivians *are* confronted with these discursive imperatives, their shaping influence is both profound and riddled with dilemmas.

This still brings me back to the current moment. How does the theoretical framework I develop in different ways explain, if at all, Bolivia's emergent revolution? Do the events of the last years signal a rupture in the patterns of intention that have shaped the unfolding of modern Bolivia since the early nineteenth century? Or do they actually demonstrate the continuing influence of these patterns? Before I can answer these questions, it is necessary to bring together and briefly recapitulate the different strands that have been interwoven through the preceding chapters.

The Centrality and Discursive Power of Law

This book has interrogated the ways and means of law in Bolivia. Law and legal forms of knowledge serve complicated functions, from the *juzgado de instrucción* in the capital of the province Alonso de Ibañez, to the highly charged national *Asamblea Constituyente* in Sucre (see below). Law is an important means through which broader social, political, and ideological categories are structured and invested with meaning. At the same time, *the law* is more than simply a key instrumentality in this sense; it is also often the source of these broader categories, and the purpose to which they are directed. As I explained in Chapter 2, the centrality of law has been a dominant feature of public life in postcolonial Bolivia, and the categories of law have provided an important part of the foundation on which modern Bolivia has been built—and rebuilt.

To recognize the centrality of law is to both acknowledge its particular logics and at the same time to see these logics at work well beyond the conventional boundaries of courtrooms, law books, legal decisions, constitutions, and struggles for legal reform. As E. P. Thompson (1975), among others, has taught us, the law is constituted by a discrete set of knowledge practices that are interwoven into the very fabric of society. This means that sites like the SLI, the juzgado de instrucción, and conflict resolution sessions of hamlet authorities in Alonso de Ibañez deserve to be privileged; they are without question the workshops where the logics of law are forged. At the same time, however, these logics are never limited to these sites. This is one of the reasons why the broader implications of law in Bolivia have been largely unacknowledged, especially outside of the main centers of urban lawmaking.

As in other Latin American countries, it is a key principle of official jurisprudence in Bolivia that *the* law is a self-contained and closed system of highly specialized rules and counterrules, whose ultimate purposes, while important, are nevertheless circumscribed and prespecified. These arcane rules must be mastered by a class of professionals; their interpretation is overseen by yet other specialists; and their enforcement and eventual administration take place at symbolically charged times and places. On this view, social actors are either inside or outside the law, and since most are necessarily outside the law, it is not the place to look for broader social, political, or ideological meanings. However, as I have shown at different points throughout this book, there is actually no place outside the law in this sense, because the law is located, as it were, as much in people's consciousness as it is in the rules that constrain or enable their actions. This is what Boaventura de Sousa Santos means when he argues that the law must be located in the "spaces [that are] superimposed, interpenetrated and mixed in our minds, as much as in our actions, either on occasions of qualitative leaps or sweeping crises in our life trajectories, or in the dull routine of eventless everyday life" (1995: 473).

If the legal has played a central role in these multiple and complicated ways, its centrality has been closely associated with its discursive power. This again is partly the result of an apparent paradox. The law is supposedly nonideological, closed, isolated from broader social, political, and economic imperatives, and relevant for people only in those rare and usually unhappy moments of transgression and redress. Yet it is precisely its supposed isolation and nonrelevance that invests the law in Bolivia with such power, *not* as a closed system of rules, but as a kind of pervasive frame of reference through which people understand and challenge identity itself. In contrast with religious, political, or, more broadly, cultural categories of meaning in Bolivia, whose claims on subjectivity are more overt, the law insinuates itself into the "dull routine of eventless everyday life" by confronting people at every turn with the sheer mundaneness of its demands.

Patterns of Intention

If the law has confounded expectations by shaping identity in Bolivia well beyond its orthodox normative and institutional boundaries, the relationship between the law and subject-making must be understood in part through the way it has both reflected, and contributed to, the persistence of broader discursive frameworks. I described one of these dominant frameworks, or patterns of intention, as liberalism expressed through law, or liberal legality, which is a way of understanding the foundational form of legal knowledge through which the Bolivian nation emerged in the early nineteenth century and which has since then continued to serve as a constant, if contested, discursive backdrop against which the claims and counterclaims of Bolivian history have been articulated. I traced the contours of this particular pattern of intention by showing its influence within key moments in Bolivian history.

Equally important, however, I focused on contemporary social practices in one particular region of rural Bolivia to show how the coming of human rights, transnational development, national campaigns against gender violence, and even the interconnection with global mass culture can be understood as part of a broader historical process of liberal subject-making. I have used the image of the encounter in order to emphasize the agency of social actors in the norte de Potosí, whose confrontations with law and liberalism—and with liberalism expressed *through* law—are both intentional and circumscribed at the same time. In other words, in developing a framework of the longue durée in order to understand at least some contemporary social practices in Bolivia—in the norte de Potosí or elsewhere—I have acknowledged the richness and meaning in what the philosophical novelist Walker Percy (1961) called "the little way," while at the same time showing how even those moments of "sad little happiness" (again, Percy) in Alonso de Ibañez are bound up with what is most consequential about modern Bolivia itself.

To locate legal and political practices in rural Bolivia in relation to broader patterns of intention is not to diminish their concreteness and contingency;

there is obviously much about the practice of everyday life in the norte de Potosí that cannot be understood merely as a reflection of wider currents. But this book has not been a study of these centripetal cultural forces, as important as they are; rather, I tracked those *centrifugal* processes through which a place like Alonso de Ibañez in the *extremo* norte de Potosí becomes generatively interconnected with both centers of national power like La Paz and Sucre and broader transnational networks.

To this extent, this effort complements a long tradition within Bolivian and Latin American studies more generally that has described the wider systems that have shaped and at times constrained social life for people. However, where my study of the relationship between local encounters with law and liberalism in the norte de Potosí and broader networks makes its contribution is in the way it looks behind the concrete economic, political, and legal institutions and actors that have symbolized a kind of permanent and essential interconnection in Bolivia. It has been a basic argument of this book that networks such as these are expressions of a set of more fundamental, discursive imperatives, which have played a shaping role in Bolivian history even as political regimes have come and gone, a wide range of economic policies have been implemented and have failed, and the position of the nation-state itself in relation to its regional neighbors has been transformed.[2]

To see patterns of intention shaping the unfolding of modern Bolivia as much in places like the norte de Potosí as elsewhere is not—to risk belaboring the point—to ignore the dynamics of social change, or (again) the richness of all those little moments that, taken together, constitute everyday life for people from Molino T'ikanoma to the wind-swept and politically explosive barrios of El Alto. It is, however, to recognize the presence of a set of pervasive and dilemma-ridden logics that have at each moment in Bolivian history created both constraints and possibilities for those engaged in public life, from negotiations over development projects in rural hamlets to current debates over the form and content of a new national constitution.

Subject-Making in the Norte de Potosí

Recall that in Chapter 1 I struggled with a set of epistemological, ethical, and political concerns, one of which was the question of how my sustained engagement with one region of rural Bolivia could be justified—and, of course, it very much was an assumption that the kinds of research and critical analysis that form the backbone of this book are not, somehow, self-justifying. Concerns like these have become part and parcel of the reflexive anthropologist's existential condition. And they frustratingly enter into the practice of research itself, because the contested status of the researcher becomes a local cultural category, a problem that demands a solution.

In grappling with the ambiguity and shifting grounds of legitimacy of my long-term engagement with Bolivia, it has never been enough to simply carve out spheres of inquiry, define questions that need answering (usually with much toil of different kinds), and then emerge from the mysterious process with the kind of talismanic clarity that has traditionally rendered anthropological accounts inimitable and authoritative at the same time. But neither is an easy solipsism an acceptable response to these concerns, the kind of self-regard in which the very real and often useful insights that emerge from social research and critique are elided or treated suspiciously. Instead, in the course of considering what specific and historically grounded encounters with law and liberalism in Bolivia tell us about broader frames of meaning, I have tried to strike something of a middle ground, one in which the fraught nature of the research experience is seen as yet one more dilemma of modernity itself.

Of course I am not the only anthropologist to formalize meta-reflections of this kind, to cope with the problematic nature of ethnographic research in part by simply acknowledging its essential ambiguity. Yet after grappling with these different problems, I nevertheless felt compelled to justify my continuing and critical presence in Bolivia on epistemological grounds. I argued that even though the social researcher has been dramatically and perhaps permanently dethroned in Bolivia as political activists, amateur philosophers, journalists, and others have stepped in to provide cultural analysis, frameworks for social action, and critical perspectives on contemporary realities, there remained several ways in which the voice of the critical ethnographer remained vital.

One of these was the extent to which the study of particularized moments in contemporary Bolivia could be shown to resonate well beyond themselves as reflections of wider—if not necessarily more profound—discursive trajectories. But I also argued that to anchor illustrations of these kinds in a region of rural Bolivia that has long been constructed and marginalized in certain ways was also to show how conventional accounts of power relations were not what they seemed. This is because the same set of social, economic, and material circumstances that makes a place like the norte de Potosí an object of international and transnational empathy also converts it into a key location in which the constraints and possibilities of late modernity are intensified in powerful and potentially explosive ways. Thus, even more than in the halls of university faculties in Bolivia's cities, or in front of televisions in middle-class homes where a culture of consumption is being cultivated, it is during reunions with NGO officials, or highly charged court sessions, or through ferias *de salud* (or "health fairs") on lazy Sundays in the plazas of provincial towns that what Gilles Lipovetsky (2005) called a "hypermodernity" is emerging in contemporary Bolivia.

This explanation parallels what Hardt and Negri (2000, 2004) have written about the differentiation of power within the global configuration they call "Empire." They argue that power can be best detected at the capillary ends, at those places at which the imperatives of the neoliberal world order are at their most urgent and least obscured. Further, Hardt and Negri claim that those actors who find themselves at those precise points at which power is transfused from Empire into the body politic are those most likely to resist the operation. This is where the usefulness of their framework for understanding subjectivity in the norte de Potosí ends. As I have shown at different points throughout this book, social actors in Alonso de Ibañez are as likely to embrace the expectations of modernity as resist them. But in appropriating and then vernacularizing these expectations, people like Lucio Montesinos or the *corregidor auxiliar* of Molino T'ikanoma do not simply constitute themselves as liberal subjects ready to reinforce the dominant structures of political and economic power that have historically marginalized or exploited them.

Rather, they *reclaim* these expectations (see also Goodale 2006b), those frames of reference that are derived from the interlocking set of ideas about human nature, the operation of natural laws in the social world, the proper ends of life, the relationship between the individual and community, and so on. It is *this* that is the real act of subversion, the place where the real hope for social transformation lies. It is not by imagining a utopia—Marxist or otherwise—in which everything is different, and more perfect, than it really is. And nor is it in enacting what anthropologists describe as a "world-reversal"—the complete inversion of existing relations in the here and now—even if categorical transgression remains an important part of cultural life throughout the rural Andes (see Butler 2006). Instead, by first meeting *modernidad* on its own terms, and then reclaiming it, people in the norte de Potosí—as elsewhere in Bolivia—assert for themselves the right to shade its meanings ever so slightly, not by way of making it into something else, but in order to enlarge its actual (if ambiguous) possibilities.

Modernity in a Minor Key

It is very difficult indeed for the embedded social researcher and critic to fully understand this unlikely result; this is in part why the emergent revolution in Bolivia has proven so confounding for even the most perceptive observers. This is also why commentators—both national and international—have been so quick to describe Evo Morales as a "new leftist" and then link him so closely with Hugo Chávez, the president of Venezuela, as if they shared the same political and moral DNA. No one was prepared for the kind of revolution that is in fact unfolding in Bolivia, one in which newly enfranchised subjects are appropriating the modern project by intensifying it. This gap between the expectations of—and against—modernity and what we might call Bolivia's "actually existing" modernity also helps explain the confusion and contestation that surround institutions like the SLI, the different organizations in the norte de Potosí committed to implementing national women's rights legislation, and the continuing negotiations over development in provinces like Alonso de Ibañez. It is not that there is local resistance to these initiatives, whether anchored in culture, nationalism, or a resurgent and militant indigeneity; rather, the confusion comes from the fact that these heralds of late modernity are *valued* differently and unexpectedly. The Peace Corps volunteer or the NGO worker or the medical doctor on rural service are skeptical about their own modernizing presence, while ordinary social actors who are expected to be the *objects* of their ironic benevolence express impatience that the fruits of modernity are not coming fast enough.

This wasn't the only dilemma that could be seen complicating the study of encounters with law and liberalism. I also examined the ways in which the coming of human rights discourse to the norte de Potosí set up a conflict between the heightened rights consciousness it fostered and the other, especially economic, aspects of Bolivia's liberal renaissance. This is yet another reason why the current moment in Bolivian history is particular susceptible to misinterpretation. The discursive use of "neoliberalism" to describe the period after the restoration of civilian government in the 1980s up to the election of Evo Morales in 2005 both reflected, and reified, the tendency to treat economic, political, social, and legal developments as pieces of an internally coherent puzzle, one that was to a large extent put in place—or, at the least, directed by—a small group of international political and economic institutions. It is true that everything from the New Economic Policy of Víctor Paz Estenssoro (see Decree 21060, 1985) to the specific mechanisms of economic decentralization within the Law of Popular Participation from Goni's first government in the mid-1990s, were largely "new" economic initiatives that reflected the influence of external actors committed to a broader, perhaps global, socioeconomic restructuring in those fin de siècle times.

But underlying—and, to a certain extent, undermining—these economic symbols of neoliberalism were the political, legal, and—we might say—moral shifts that were occurring at the same time, shifts that were then—and still are—best symbolized by the relentless presence of human rights discourse. The conception of the person that is embedded in the idea of human rights is one that both monadically encapsulates the subject and exalts him at the same time. Among other complications, this form of subjectivity can only with much discursive violence be shaped into a basis for collective identity and political action, as scholars like Postero (2007a) have demonstrated so convincingly. To foreground the importance of a reborn rights consciousness in Bolivia—whether in the norte de Potosí or elsewhere—is to show how human rights, economic privatization, market democratization, and other markers of "neoliberalism" do not simply constitute coequal pillars in a broader, and discursively consistent, project. Instead, the transformation in subjectivity that is required by human rights discourse is both the means and the end of a more fundamental trajectory, which explains why political leaders in contemporary Bolivia can adopt a rhetoric of anticapitalism at the same time they articulate a vision of the subject that is almost "hyperliberal" (Brown 2006) in its commitment to human rights.

This does not mean, however, that by intensifying and appropriating the expectations of modernity in this way that Bolivia's current revolutionaries have become "conscripts" of the very episteme that would apparently liberate them (Scott 2004). Rather, they are more like modernity's alchemists. In combining the grandeur of human rights discourse, indigenist imagery from selected moments in Bolivian history, gestures toward redistributive modes of production, and direct democracy, they are creating a powerful discursive mix with uncertain properties. The question remains whether a blending of this kind, which Bruce Knauft (e.g., 2002) and others have described as a modernity in the vernacular, will produce the transmutation that is the purpose of all alchemy. Will it lead to "another option" (Postero 2007a: 232), one that establishes the foundation for a new Bolivian century? Or, like the quest to transmute lead into gold, will the effort prove in the end to be futile? What can be said is that despite the boldly idealistic rhetoric surrounding its emergent revolution, Bolivia's actually existing modernity, that ambiguous blending that looks back as much as it looks forward, has a certain nostalgic solemnness about it—it is a modernity in a minor key. In what remains I examine the future implications of what can be heard behind the siren song of Bolivia's "third revolution."

Revolutions, New and Old

On December 18, 2005, Juan Evo Morales Ayma, the former leader of Bolivia's coca growers movement, became the Republic of Bolivia's eightieth president. Morales and the *Movimiento al Socialismo* (MAS) party won with 54 percent of the vote and his share of the total—in which 84.5 percent of eligible voters participated—was almost double that of Jorge Fernando "Tuto" Quiroga Ramírez (29 percent), his closest challenger, who went down in a crushing defeat. The rise of Morales must be seen as part of a broader shift in Bolivia's modern trajectory, in which the nation's historically disenfranchised and marginalized majorities appropriated dominant national discourses in order to claim their patrimony—not a patrimony of land, control over resources, or political participation, but a patrimony of personhood, in which the conception of the subject that fueled the birth of the nation itself was opened to the large swaths of the populations that had always been excluded from it.

The basic historical and political outline of the immediate events that culminated in Morales's election has been developed at some length in different forms by academics, journalists, and others, and does not need to be rehearsed in any detail here (see, e.g., Albro 2006, Gordillo 2000; Kohl and Farthing 2006; Olivera 2004; Postero 2007a; see also Goodale 2006b). The conventional account, which I have alluded to at different points in discussing the multiple problems of "neoliberalism," has Bolivia entering a qualitatively distinct period in its political, economic, and social history with the restoration of civilian rule in the 1980s. Under pressure from international institutions and members of certain segments of Bolivia's tiny elite that had most to gain from policies like structural adjustment, the accelerated privatization and capitalization of land, the "rationalization" (read: contraction) of historically and culturally important sectors like mining, and the willingness to cooperate with the United States in its hemispheric drug war campaigns, a succession of administrations from Víctor Paz Estenssoro (1985–89) to Gonzalo Sánchez de Lozada (1993–97; 2002–3) laid the groundwork for the epochal rupture of December 2005. Even as indigenousness took on new and powerful meanings—from the 1990 March for Territory and Dignity (see Healy 2001, Yashar 2005) to the collectivist and nostalgic aspirations of the *Federación de Juntas Vecinales de la Ciudad de El Alto* (Lazar 2006)—the government continued to defy what eventually became an inexorable process through which resistance to inequality and structural violence was reinterpreted within a subtly, but profoundly, different discursive framework.

I want to focus here on two key markers of this post-2005 revolutionary moment: the discursive universe of MAS and the unfolding (as of July 2007) *Asamblea Constituyente* in Sucre. Both the radical hybridity and essentially conservative nature of MAS are arguably best revealed through codifications of its aspirations rather than through an analysis of the inevitable contradictions in its post-December 2005 political practice. The clearest statement of these aspirations can be found in MAS's declaration of ideological principles, which was revised and finalized in December of 2003 at the party's Fifth National Congress in Oruro.[3] The declaration begins with an extended analysis of how Bolivia emerged as a modern nation-state. The focus is on the negative impact of the industrial revolution and the incorporation of a set of basic beliefs that treat the individual as simply a cog in a larger socioeconomic machine. All of this reemploys a rhetoric that has changed very little from at least the early twentieth century, but here it serves as a discursive mask behind which lies something quite different. Instead of locating the impulse for change, and the source of alternative strategies, within the inevitability of history, MAS's statement of principles develops what we might call a "moral cosmology," one that reflects both more, and less, difference to what is purports to replace than it realizes.

This new moral cosmology of MAS—and thus, to a certain extent, of contemporary Bolivia—is one that is supposedly neither "atomistic" nor "industrialist." That is to say, the replacement paradigm that MAS represents does not treat the individual as ontologically or socially isolated from "the community, the union, [or] the family" (MAS-Bolivia 2007) and it rejects industrialism as the engine of Bolivia's future economic and social development. Instead, the individual is reinscribed back into a cosmos that is governed by both the laws of nature and the laws of a well-functioning government, the latter of which should ideally both mirror and actualize the former. The emphasis is on symbiosis: between the individual and the collective, between men and women, and between rights and obligations. The reason that industrial capitalism is rejected as a dominant mode of production has nothing to do with the ideology that underpins it. Rather, it is because the extractive capitalism that shaped much of Bolivia's pre- and postcolonial history led to dramatic imbalances that made the kind of symbiosis exalted by MAS impossible. This does not mean that the rise of industrial capitalism was always inconsistent with the key assumptions of liberalism or modernity more generally. But it does remind us that it is essential to retain a focus on a more basic set of principles, those that define the nature of the subject, the relationship between the individual and the collective, and the proper means through which justice can be achieved.

The moral cosmology of MAS is one that would fit very comfortably beside those developed by modernity's intellectual avatars, many of whom actually—and importantly—make an appearance within MAS's statement of principles itself. So even though MAS opposes the "Newtonian paradigm in which the world is an inanimate machine governed by eternal mathematical laws," and even if MAS also declares itself opposed to "the century of Enlightenment, embodied by Jhon [sic] Locke,[4] Thomas Hobbes . . . [and other] philosophers and English economists . . . , all those ideologues of the present industrial society" (Part 3.1), its declaration of twenty-one principles develops a vision for a new Bolivia that could have been titled "On (Bolivian) Liberty."

This is a Bolivian society built on social justice (Art. 1), universal human rights (Art. 2), participatory democracy (Art. 3), liberty and liberation (Art. 5, 9), tolerance (Art. 6), humanism (Art. 10), a government that derives its legitimacy from the people (Art. 15), moral and political autonomy (Art. 18), and the obligation by the government to give political and social policies a firm scientific basis (Art. 21). Despite its unsurprising rhetorical thrusts at "modernity" and "modern society," in other words, MAS's statement of ideological principles envisions a "critically modern" Bolivia (Knauft 2002), one that to a certain extent—as the different points of internal contradiction within its statement indicate—"unwittingly recapitulat[es]" (Knauft 2002: 3) key features of "older views" at the same time it alternatively appropriates and vernacularizes them.

It is a curious fact that the only thinker from western intellectual history who is invoked approvingly by MAS is Hegel, who is cited for the proposition that the world is necessarily comprised of slaves and masters. This is a revealing discursive gesture by MAS and one that reinforces my argument that it is wrong to focus on second-order economic effects within particular moments in Bolivia history (even if MAS also does this). Hegel uses the *Herrschaft und Knechtschaft* dialectic, from *The Phenomenology of the Spirit*, to develop the idea that self-consciousness is forged through a dialectical struggle between two preexisting versions of the self, neither of which (here master or servant), taken alone, is sufficient for self-realization. Bolivia's emergent revolution is also one that must be understood primarily as a revolution of (self-)consciousness, a movement that is searching for new grounds on which to appropriate and expand old discursive categories.

The *Asamblea Constituyente*, or Constituent Assembly, has emerged as another key symbol that provides clues for how to interpret the meaning and implications of post-2005 Bolivia. The assembly was an initiative that became a main part of MAS's political platform from its first years of national prominence. During the election campaign Morales used the prospect of a fully empowered constituent assembly to mobilize support for his other policies, especially the promise to nationalize the major resource industries. In invoking the prospect of a constituent assembly, Morales was drawing both on what Postero describes as a "long-held demand of indigenous and labor sectors" (2007a: 2), and firmly locating Bolivia's emergent revolution within a particular discursive context. Although the short-term objective of the assembly—the last was held in 1967, during the regime of the military dictator René Barrientos Ortuño—is to debate and then draft a new national constitution, its social function is much broader: It is to be "the scene of encounter and public debate between the members of the community with the objective to reform and/or recast the political-institutional bases of social coexistence, that is to say, the rules, conditions, processes, and procedures of social life itself" (República de Bolivia 2007).[5]

There are three main historical and ideological components of Bolivia's Assembly, all of which point in the same analytical and interpretive direction. First, a "constituent" or "constitutional" assembly is a forum with deep historical roots, through which the bases for social, legal, and political organization were radically "recast"—as the multiple means for protecting, enabling, and perpetuating a collectivity of subjects *defined as* the bearers of natural rights (Alexander 1998; Bobbit 1982; Marshall 1984; McIlwain 1947). Assemblies of this kind were first realized in practice most importantly during the socio-political movements of the Enlightenment and early post-Enlightenment: think of the French *Assemblée nationale constituante*, or National Constituent Assembly (1798), the U.S. Constitutional Convention (1787), and of course the constituent assembly that created the Republic of Bolivia itself, the 1825 *Congreso de Chuquisaca*.[6] Although Bolivia's current constituent assembly is formally characterized by a kind of discursive openness and the possibility of multiple outcomes—it is a scene of "encounter and public debate"—in fact the nature of the forum itself prefigures both its "real" (rather than its "intended") purpose and the likely outcomes, because it exists to develop structures within which the (human) rights of citizens will be recognized and collectively enforced.

Second, Bolivia's Constituent Assembly, like all such assemblies, is a vehicle for both establishing and institutionalizing legitimacy, but a legitimacy of a very particular kind. This is not primarily a form of political legitimacy, because membership in the assembly is necessarily both limited in number and circumscribed in representation; in other words, the establishment and functioning of Bolivia's assembly are not meant to be a substitute for larger-scale democratic processes. Rather, the assembly is a forum for legitimating a particular ideological worldview through normative and rhetorical gestures that are largely symbolic. And if part of what is being symbolically legitimated in the case of Bolivia's assembly is a paradigm shift, it is a movement not toward something radically new, but the extension in radically new ways of a conventional, indeed dominant, ideological orientation.

It is no coincidence that the quintessential symbol of this orientation is a constitution: the normative framework through which the relationship between citizens and the state is recognized and elaborated, a relationship—in this case, as with Bolivia's first and subsequent constitutions—fundamentally structured by the imperatives of preexisting human/natural rights. So if the "Constituent Assembly will reestablish the political-institutional bases [of society] beginning with a wider diversity of perspectives and visions of all Bolivians" (República de Bolivia 2007), this wider diversity most importantly refers to the category of liberal citizenship, the universe of Bolivians whose political, social, and moral lives are grounded in the assumptions of which human rights form the cornerstone.

Finally, the assembly in Sucre is a site of performance, a place where Bolivia's emergent revolution can be given form and substance in a dramatic public sphere. Daniel Goldstein has been tracking the relationship between performance and different forms of subjectivity in Bolivia since the mid-1990s (see especially Goldstein 2004; see also 2007). His research has shown how Bolivia's historically marginalized citizens enact dramatic spectacles as a form of resistance, a way of creating alternative spaces in which dystopian mirror images of justice, law, and dignity shimmer in the form of lynchings, corporal punishment of suspected thieves, and other moments in what Goldstein calls Bolivia's "carnival of violence" (2004: 182).

With the establishment of the assembly, the essential link between performance and subjectivity remains exactly the same. But much has changed: the dystopian has been replaced with the utopian; performance does not function as a form of resistance to exclusion, but as the celebration of new categories of *inclusion*; and the whip and the noose have given way to the gavel, the pen, and copies of the *Declaración Universal de Derechos Humanos*. And if the assembly is a site in which new variations on liberal subjectivity are being performed, then it differs from the *Congreso de Chuquisaca* only in the categories of actors legitimately present, which is a small, but obviously profound, difference. Indeed, we might say that it is within *this* difference that the heart of Bolivia's revolution is to be found, the aspect of the current moment in Bolivia that is, in fact, *revolutionary*, which brings me back to the broader question with which I began this final chapter: How do the analytical frameworks that I have developed through the examination of different encounters with law and liberalism contribute to an understanding of this current moment?

A counterdiscursive thread that runs through each chapter of this book, to greater or lesser degrees, has been the argument that law and liberalism, and liberalism expressed *through* law, have indelibly shaped the twists and turns of Bolivia's modern trajectory. I tracked the presence of this shaping influence through its different instantiations and I used one important region of rural Bolivia to illustrate the point that law and liberalism are dominant ordering principles as much, if not more so, in the dusty and ignored corners of rural Bolivia as in the urban centers of the nation's legal and political life.

Although the contours of these patterns of intention must appear, at one level, to be historical (that is, abstracted from the quotidian concerns of ordinary social actors), in fact a guiding principle throughout has been that these patterns have meaning *only* as they provide a rough framework for the practice of everyday life, even—or, *especially*—when such practice is oppositional, contestatory, or cloaked in the language of epochal rupture. In other words, we can only really understand the shaping presence of law and liberalism in Bolivia through the experiences of the women who made their way to the SLI, or by empathizing with Lucio Montesinos as he describes his journey of moral transformation that accompanied his exposure to the idea of universal human rights, or at the interface between transnational development organizations, local political and ethnic leaders, and the (often bizarre) imperatives of global mass culture. And, I would suggest, we can understand it in the rise and eventual apotheosis of Evo Morales and the fragile sociopolitical triumph of MAS.

This thread is counterdiscursive because it moves somewhat—and reluctantly—against conventional historical accounts of modern Bolivia, which is not to say that in its particulars it does not resonate with them. But it is not a linear approach to understanding either the details or the broad sweep of Bolivian history; it is not episodic or dependent on narratives that jump from one military coup or one economic recession or one interregional war or one massacre of miners or one incident of American interference to another; and, perhaps most controversially, it does not adopt one of several competing versions of power relations in Bolivia, in which urbanities and provincial mestizos ride roughshod over indigenous peoples and campesinos, Bolivia's "open veins" bleed away the country's life energy, and the forces of globalization lay the groundwork for a nation of consumers ready and willing to be supersized.

Instead, I have pointed to a counterintuitive kind of stability within Bolivia, one that can be visualized, if not cyclically, then as a discursive double helix in which law and liberalism twine around both a common axis and each other, and the common axis is the chronology of modern Bolivia itself. This interpretive framework can help us understand the meaning and implications of all those little encounters with human rights discourse over time in places like Alonso de Ibañez at the same time it helps explain why it is that Bolivia's emergent revolution is essentially liberal, even if the version of liberalism expressed through MAS's statement of ideological principles, or in the objectives behind the Constituent Assembly's twenty-one commissions, or in the invocation of Pachamama as an alternative source of human rights, vernacularizes those "older views" of liberalism through which the nation emerged in the nineteenth century. The Constituent Assembly of Evo Morales, that is to say, is not a twenty-first century Bolivian International (or the Sucre Commune), a forum for connecting these new revolutionary Bolivians with their proletarian comrades in other hotspots in postneoliberal Latin America (or elsewhere). Instead, the assembly is the Congreso de Chuquisaca in the mirror, in which a similar set of ontological, moral, and political assumptions are reflected onto radically different categories of Bolivians.

Despite the ways in which the rhetoric of Bolivia's liberal revolutionaries invokes images that have led commentators to lump Morales and MAS into Latin America's *nueva izquierda* (or New Left), Morales is no Che Guevara with an interactive website.[7] A more useful, and even uncanny, historical comparison is with Benito Pablo Juárez García, who served five terms as president of Mexico between 1858 and 1872. The resemblance is not on account of the fact that they were the first, and second, indigenous presidents respectively of Latin American nation-states, which is way of locating them that perhaps unintentionally draws on several interconnected racial, colonial, and orientalist discourses.

Rather, Morales and MAS have implemented a series of reforms that are an ideological resurrection of those of Juárez's *La Reforma*, which was also a liberal revolution committed to participatory democracy, the extension of rights in Mexico to include the poor and especially the indigenous, and, above all, the drafting of a constitution that would symbolize the nation's commitment to equality for all Mexicans (Meyer, Sherman, and Deeds 2006). It would be absurd to push a comparison like this too far, and not only because *La Reforma* of mid-nineteenth century Mexico collapsed under the weight of its own utopianism, a process of despair and disillusionment that paved the way for the incompetence and brutality of that period in Mexican history known as the *porfiriato*. But associating Morales and MAS with a figure like Juárez is yet another way to make an important point about Bolivia's emergent revolution: In both its form and content, it is as much a discursive return as it is a break with the past. It is a revolution, that is to say, that is both regressive and progressive at the same time.

To describe Morales and MAS as twenty-first century liberal revolutionaries is also in part a way to explain their rise and sociopolitical accomplishments, the most important of which, obviously, was the margin of victory in the 2005 national elections, which demonstrated political support that transcended ethnic, class, and regional divisions in Bolivia.[8] However, the watershed moment was the late 1980s and early 1990s, when new political and social movements rearticulated a long list of grievances—ethnic discrimination, political marginalization or exclusion, lack of control over local resources, excessive obedience to international financial institutions, among others—within the discursive frameworks of human rights. By the time the thousands of spontaneous participants in the 1990 March for Territory and Dignity reached La Paz from Trinidad, in the Beni, the seeds of Morales's 2005 victory had been planted. The national media covered the march in both print and on television and they served as the conduit through which demands over social problems faced by several lowland indigenous groups grew into a debate over the extent to which Bolivia itself would recognize and protect the human rights of all its citizens.

When derechos humanos became a mantra for enough Bolivians outside of the indigenous movements themselves, and, even more, when enough Bolivians were willing to concede the fact that the country's many social problems could be addressed in new ways through human rights, the revolution had begun. How else to explain the seemingly sudden willingness of Bolivia's non-indigenous, urban, and petit bourgeoisie to accede to the dramatic categorical expansion that MAS represents? It was always much easier to resist what were similar proposals for social change motivated by similar historical and political conditions when the discursive framework within which they were embedded demanded an ideological and historical world reversal. Morales and MAS do not promise to turn the world upside down; they do not demand that Bolivians think and act in terms of a set of assumptions about a world that exists in a kind of parallel universe to the one that gave birth to Bolivia itself. Rather, they simply demand an expansion of the categories of modern Bolivia, the universalization of the liberal subject, and a commitment to equality of rights.

Reference Matter

Notes

Chapter 1

1. Flotas are the buses (and bus companies, or "fleets") that service transportation routes of all kinds in Bolivia. They are relatively new full-service buses with assigned seating, cargo bins overhead, stereo systems, one or more television monitors for in-trip movies, and restrooms, although restroom doors almost always are locked. Flotas service all of the longer inter-city routes throughout Bolivia, and many of the provincial routes, depending on the condition of roads and other factors.

Camiones, by contrast, are open, flatbed trucks that are loaded with people, small animals, and cargo, often so tightly that people must stand on their cargo for what can be trips of eight hours or more. During the rainy season, as the rain begins, passengers will yell "*¡carpa pues! . . . ¡carpa maestro!*" ("well, cover us! . . . cover us driver!") until the driver and his assistant decide to pull over and stretch a tarp over the top of every-one and everything, which can create the feeling of being suffocated. Depending on road conditions, camiones typically can move faster than flotas, and *camión* drivers have a reputation for being younger and more daring, a reputation that they justify in many instances by passing on blind uphill corners, or out-racing other flotas or camiones. This daring has its price, of course, and camiones in different parts of Bo-livia regularly plunge over the side of cliffs with fifty or more people aboard. One in-ternational agency (the Inter-American Development Bank) rated one stretch of Bo-livian road, between La Cumbre and Coroico, the most dangerous in the world. In different years, it is not uncommon for twenty or more passenger vehicles to go over the side on this road, one almost every two weeks.

2. This point also must be understood in light of the fact that Bolivia is one of the least densely populated countries in the world, with about eight people per square kilo-meter, which places it at rank 210 out of 230 countries, according to the United Nations Population Division (2003).

3. For a discussion of the use of "puna" as a topographic category in the Andes, see Flores Ochoa (1977); Murra (1972, 1978); Zorn (1997: 99–101). For a discussion of its use as a social category, see Angelis-Harmening (2000); Bernal (1984); Godoy (1983).

4. A farmer described to me the process of selecting potatoes for ch'uño. Potatoes are grouped into classes. The first class of potatoes are always the ones considered the healthiest and the ones that are fairly large ("about the size of an egg"). These go for seed. Depending on the size of the harvest, the next class of potatoes is used either for sale, if there are enough to justify the trip to market, or for the family's food. Thus, this second class would actually be broken down into two classes if there are enough for market, with the best half going to market and the other half being used for personal consumption. The third (or fourth) class is comprised of the potatoes that are small ("the size of marbles") and "ugly" in some way. These are used to make ch'uño. Ch'uño is made by taking the batch of potatoes and crushing them, usually underfoot, until they are like discs. They are freeze-dried at night in the upper puna and stored in people's houses in the rafters. They then can be taken down and cooked in soups or used as a main course for months afterwards. Popular ways to prepare ch'uño as a main course in Alonso de Ibañez include serving them with eggs, cheese (very rarely), or with puree of peanuts (the most common) spread over the top.

5. Zorn (1997: 81–83; and fns. 40–42) has a detailed discussion of language use in Alonso de Ibañez compared with language use in Taquile, Peru, where she also did research. As she rightly notes, as elsewhere in Bolivia, the social, legal, and ethnic complexities of language use in the norte de Potosí is an area that is ripe for more detailed study.

6. On the topic of multiculturalism and identity in Bolivia, see especially Nancy Postero's excellent book (2007a).

7. For an excellent account of the political, legal, and cultural contexts of lynchings in Bolivia, see Daniel Goldstein's study (2004), which employs a series of innovative arguments in order to locate the spectacle of public lynchings—or attempted lynchings—in the same discursive and performative space as an annual street carnival and festival in one of Cochabamba's marginal barrios.

8. Abstract and putative because "indigenous customary law" is not defined either within Bolivia's revised Code of Criminal Procedure, or at other places where the content of basic Bolivian legal categories is delineated, such as the National Constitution or the Civil Code (although this might change through the work of the current Constituent Assembly in Sucre; see Conclusion). Although I go into this topic in greater detail in Chapter 2, it is enough to note here that "indigenous customary law" was never intended to describe a set of substantive principles, but represents rather the culmination of a process of liberal (or "neoliberal") consolidation in Bolivia, which has required the employment of a discourse of collective rights, of which "customary law" is one example. At the time the National Constitution was amended in 1995, this

same discourse found expression through another set of jurisprudential signifiers in new Article 171: "social, economic, and cultural rights."

9. For good discussions of this march, see Healy 2001; Yashar 2005.

10. In their 2000 book *Empire*, Michael Hardt and Antonio Negri make the entirely plausible claim that what has characterized the postwar era has been the effort by Third World countries—primarily through their national elites—to escape from the "exploitation and domination" of modern forms of legal, social, and political organization. As they say, these postcolonial elites "recognized *that the primary task is not getting into but getting out of modernity*" (2000: 251). But as Bolivia's recent history shows, the task for many early twenty-first century social reformers and revolutionaries is not getting out of modernity, but getting into it—and fast!

11. In the Conclusion, I analyze the relationship between the 2005 election of Evo Morales and the rise of the *Movimiento al Socialismo* (MAS) party, and the process of renewed liberal subject-making that began in the early 1990s.

12. For a good discussion of the relationship between liberalism and Bolivian political culture (between 1899–1934), see Vila De Prado 2003.

13. In his twenty-five page bibliographic essay on Bolivian studies (1982, updated in 1992 and 2003), Herbert Klein surveys the entire range of scholarship on Bolivia. There is no mention of law, legal institutions, or the importance of legality itself for understanding Bolivia. After referencing works on medicine and the army, Klein remarks that "the important profession of law has not been adequately treated" (1982: 276).

14. This is also the way another transcendent source of truth is signified in Bolivia (as elsewhere): "the word" is also the Word of God.

15. For a typical scientific-bureaucratic account of Bolivia's official misery, see the data produced by the Latin American and Caribbean Bureau of the United States Agency for International Development (USAID), which read like a veritable parade of horribles, a parade in which Bolivia marches in front. For example, in 2003, Bolivia was second (to Haiti) in the number of infant deaths per 1,000 live births; in 2006, it was second (again, to Haiti) in adult mortality rates per 1,000 persons; in 2006, Bolivia had by far the highest ratio of incomes of the wealthiest 20 percent to the poorest 20 percent of the population; and so on (USAID 2007). For a devastating critique of the statistical means through which countries like Bolivia are "made and unmade," see Escobar 1995.

Chapter 2

1. For a remarkable study that links the project of liberal nation-building with cultural practice in Potosí Department, see Platt 1993. See also Platt 1987a.

2. One encounters the entire architecture of the jurisprudential understanding of law in Bolivia through, among other things, an examination of law school curricula. Besides works in jurisprudence and legal theory, students are often assigned more ideological treatises, such as Ángel Osorio y Gallardo's classic *El alma de la toga*, which

makes the practice and understanding of law ideally an expression of a kind of virtue with roots in ancient Rome (see, e.g., the complete curriculum of the law faculty at the Universidad Técnica de Oruro [UTO 2006]).

3. For two excellent recent studies of the cultural and political nuances of human rights in practice, see Englund (2006) and Merry (2006a); see also Goodale and Merry (2007). For a more theoretical treatment of the gap between the rhetoric of international law and the reality of its implementation in the developing world, see Balakrishnan Rajagopal's *International Law from Below* (2003).

4. The following section is indebted to several basic works on Bolivia's early republican history, including Arguedas (1922), de Mesa, Gisbert, and Mesa Gisbert (2003), and Crespo, Crespo Fernández, and Kent Solares (1995). The standard reference for the history of Bolivia in English, Herbert S. Klein's *Bolivia: The Evolution of a Multi-Ethnic Society* (1982/1992/2003), does not describe legal processes or development in any detail. Klein's historical perspective could be described as political-economic, and from 1825 to the end of the twentieth century his account of Bolivian history gives political, and especially economic, developments the lion's share of his attention. Although this is an understandable decision on Klein's part, it is a basic argument of this book that Bolivia's legal trajectory has been more consequential than historians have acknowledged, has served as a source of legitimacy for Bolivia's relations of production over the last 175 years, and, most important, is the place to look in order to understand current efforts to reclaim the promises of revolutionary liberalism and extend them to the country's indigenous and peasant majority.

5. For an excellent study of Arguedas's complicated and pessimistic understanding of Bolivia's modernity, see Oscar Osorio's essay "El dolor de ser boliviano" (2003).

6. In much the same way as Mozart's *Ein musikalischer Spass* was considered the "negative key to Mozart's whole aesthetic," according to Einstein (1945).

7. As should be clear by now, in arguing for the importance of *liberalism* expressed through law, I am drawing a basic distinction between this foundational pattern of intention and any ideas or practices that came and went with the *Partido Liberal* in Bolivia, which was founded by Eliodoro Camacho after Bolivia's involvement in the War of the Pacific (1879–80) and which shaped national politics, to greater or lesser degrees, until the National Revolution in 1952.

8. Gastón Gordillo is perhaps the most recent critical scholar of Latin America to appropriate Adorno's analytical framework. In his study of memory in Argentina, Gordillo argues that memory is intimately linked with the constitution of social spaces through contradictions, and he uses a negative dialectics in order to describe and understand these contradictions (2004). Here I argue that liberalism in its legal expressions operates in much the same way in Bolivian history, as an ever-present negative counterexample to the apparent disorder of military coups, populist reform, economic crisis, and "revolution."

9. An important exception to this was the Santa Cruz region, where haciendas and other preliberal social and legal structures remained in place. This meant, among other things, that Santa Cruz remained a bastion of social conservatism where wealth was concentrated in the hands of a small network of retrograde elites. It also meant that Santa Cruz was to be a breeding ground for a long line of antiliberal conservatives, including Hugo Banzer Suárez (1971–78, 1997–2001).

10. For a more critical account, see Medeiros (2001).

Chapter 3

1. There is also the *Tribunal Constitucional* in Sucre (a product of the judicial reforms of 1994) that provides guidance on the constitutionality of laws and decrees and (ideally) serves as a check on state power. For a study of the 1994 constitutional reforms, see Harb and Moreno 1999.

2. The *corregidor* titular is an authority position with both political and legal functions that dates from the colonial era (see Cole 1985; Zorn 1997). Originally, the corregidor titular was meant to serve as an intermediary between Spanish colonial officials and the native population, and in Alonso de Ibañez the corregidor titular still functions in this capacity, although the Spanish empire has been replaced by the Bolivian state and its representatives: the subprefect, the police, the mayor, and so on. The corregidor titular of Canton Sacaca (there are also *corregidores titulares* of the province's other cantons) is always a *sacaqueño*, but someone with deep family or historical ties to regions outside the capital, and thus someone who is believed to be more sympathetic to campesino problems.

3. An *ayllu* is a macro-regional fictive kinship category that was probably created to deal with the challenges of living in the extreme ecological zones in the Andes (Murra 1972, 1975). The ayllu has been an important unit of Andean social organization since pre-Hispanic times. Particularly in the north of Potosí, ayllus retain many of their historical features, including "an internal organization based on dual and vertically-organized segments, communal distribution of resources, and a 'vertical' land tenure system which includes the use of noncontiguous *puna* (highland) and valley lands" (Rivera Cusicanqui 1991; see also Platt 1982).

4. MAS is the party of Evo Morales, the former head of Bolivia's coca growers movement, who won a stunning electoral victory in December 2005, becoming Bolivia's first self-identifying indigenous president. MAS had been a significant organizing presence during the waves of protests in Bolivia that began in 1999 in the Cochabamba Valley and which culminated, arguably, in Morales's election. During this same period, MIP has been led by Felipe Quispe, El Mallku, a firebrand indigenist politician who also ran during the 2005 elections (he received 2.2 percent of the vote). MOP is a regional political party that dates from the early 2000s. In its use of indigenist symbols and a rhetoric of resistance that draws on (at times romanticized) key moments in Bolivia's

long sweep of pre-Colombian, colonial, and republican history, MOP is much closer to MIP than to MAS. Scholars are just beginning to make sense of the 2005 elections and their aftermath (see, e.g., Albó 2006; Albro 2006; Goodale 2006b; Postero 2007a), although as I argue in the Conclusion, current shifts in Bolivian politics are taking place within—not against, or outside—a much longer trajectory of Bolivian history.

5. Here and elsewhere in the book, I refer to individuals by their official titles, rather than given names, except where people have encouraged me to use their names (or where there was a general understanding that I would do so), or where the individual is a public figure whose anonymity cannot be protected in this way. Although I sit on my own current university's institutional review board (IRB), I believe the problem of "human subjects research protection"—as it is called in the argot of biomedical research that gave rise to the protocols that govern much of the research I draw from in this book—has been very poorly understood. Anthropology provides its own set of guidelines for researchers (see, e.g., the American Anthropological Association's Code of Ethics), which are much more sensitive to the methodological, epistemological, and ethical nuances of deeply engaged qualitative fieldwork. Nevertheless, it seems inevitable that the decision whether to use subjects' names in publications, or the question of how to protect "data" (many IRBs suggest keeping field notebooks under lock and key when not being used, hardly a practical suggestion for many of us), not to mention the even more problematic issue of "informed consent," will continue to be difficult to resolve or convincingly address in advance or in the abstract.

6. The classic account from *Bleak House* shows that the experience of a *juzgado de instrucción* in rural Bolivia is not so different from that of the courts of chancery in Victorian England: "Jarndyce and Jarndyce drones on. This scarecrow of a suit has, in course of time, become so complicated that no man alive knows what it means. The parties to it understand it least, but it has been observed that no . . . lawyers can talk about it for five minutes without coming to a total disagreement as to all the premises. Innumerable children have been born into the cause; innumerable old people have died out of it. Scores of persons have deliriously found themselves made parties in Jarndyce and Jarndyce without knowing how or why; whole families have inherited legendary hatreds with the suit. The little plaintiff or defendant who was promised a new rocking-horse when Jarndyce and Jarndyce should be settled has grown up, possessed himself of a real horse, and trotted away into the other world."

7. *La palabra* is a complicated form of reference. One can describe it in a general way as an invocation of authority or legitimacy, a way of framing more specific arguments by linking them to a higher and more authoritative power, whether this power is derived from the law or more ethereal sources.

8. Multas levied by authorities outside of Sacaca are not symbolic, as they are with the corregidor titular, but rather represent an attempt at actual compensation for damages. If the amount is too high, it will not be paid, as everyone understands, so it is

usually somewhat less than what the authority (and the aggrieved party) determines is the real value of the loss. More often than not, the multa is levied in a form other than cash, such as a promise to repair a damaged wall or provide work of some kind, or to provide a certain amount of future crops, and so on.

9. In Alonso de Ibañez, distance is interestingly measured by the early colonial Spanish unit "leguas," or leagues, a league being understood as the distance that a normal adult can *walk* in one hour. (Not travel on horseback, as would be more typical. On the inherent difficulties of the "the elusive Spanish league," see Chardon 1980). This distance works out to about three miles (about five kilometers) depending on the season—rainy or not—and the direction one is walking—along river valleys or across and over them. Using Sacaca as a starting point, hamlets lie at varying distances ranging from one half to nine or more leagues. If one walks for more than fifteen hours from Sacaca in any direction, one will pass over into either another province in the same department (Potosí) or into a province in another department.

10. In 1990, the Peace Corps returned to Bolivia after having been expelled since 1973. Since then, Sak'ani has been considered *the* most difficult Peace Corps posting in Bolivia; for example, the organization could not find a replacement after one of its more successful volunteers left Sak'ani in 1999. Sak'ani is very remote even by Alonso de Ibañez or north Potosí standards and it is easy to understand how a young American without Quechua or, in some cases, even Spanish, would find it a difficult place to live and work. One man, an ex–U.S. Marine who told Peace Corps officials in La Paz that he wanted a "hard core" assignment, was the first person sent as a replacement to Sak'ani in early 2000, but he "abandoned his post" (as they say in peculiar, quasimilitary Peace Corps jargon) after four weeks.

11. This translation of *qhelqeri* is not without controversy, however. In the third edition of Jesús Lara's standard Qheshwa-Spanish dictionary (1991), he uses *qellqay* for the Quechua infinitive "to write" and derives from this for "scribe" *qellqaykamayuj*, which joins the classical Quechua suffix –kamayuj, meaning "one who gives force" or "one who animates" something, to the verb root. However, he also uses *qellqaj* for a plain "writer," which is also grammatically correct but somewhat artificial, because it is not at all clear that these Quechua words were ever used in practice until quite recently. In the norte de Potosí, the local orthography for this legal actor of historical significance would be qhelqeri, since the first q is aspirated (which is indicated in Bolivian Quechua, or Qheshwa, by "qh"). It is possible that the actual word qhelqeri is a regional or local corruption of the more correct *qellqajkamayoj*, one that combines an Aymara substantive noun form ending –i with the Quechua root, but I cannot be certain of this. What is clear is that the word used in Alonso de Ibañez to describe the person without a license who functions as a lawyer is not to be found in any standard Quechua dictionary.

12. In Alonso de Ibañez, all *defensores* are sacaqueños, although people from the hamlets regularly use their services when they are required to appear as plaintiffs or

defendants in the juzgado de instrucción. The reputation of the defensores in Alonso de Ibáñez varies widely, and over the last ten years there have been on average five working at any one time. Some are believed to be basically corrupt; others are seen as real *compañeros*, advocates for the province's campesino majority, who must travel for many hours at times to face the disciplinary gaze of the state's legal machinery.

Chapter 4

1. Although a book like Simone de Beauvoir's *The Second Sex* (1949) developed the idea that the category of woman is constructed by society, and thus the reflection of existing prejudices about what has been historically seen (at least in Europe and the United States) as the inferior of the two sexes, the political and intellectual historical context in which de Beauvoir was working was dramatically different than it would be for later feminists. It wasn't until the 1960s that feminist theorists were able to link the construction of woman—a process now described with the political-analytical term "gender"—to wider problems, like colonialism and capitalism, which were themselves receiving a totally new kind of critical attention (remember in this context Marx's generally agnostic perspective on the "female question").

2. A woman from the cantonal hamlets outside the provincial capital who actually commits adultery, or who is the subject of an adultery accusation with some basis in fact (or not, as the case may be), can find herself the victim of much more serious treatment. Since 1883, there have been 194 cases of murder or attempted murder filed in the *juzgado de instrucción*. Of these, at least ten involve adultery or accusations of adultery. This is not to mention the other cases of physical violence against women that go beyond what would be considered acceptable—even expected—responses by men for various types of wifely or daughterly negligence. Even mothers-in-law are not immune. In a 1903 case, a son-in-law was charged with attempting to kill his mother-in-law with large stones because she "encouraged adulterous behavior that set a bad example for her daughters," including the man's wife.

3. The Bolivian Penal Code draws a distinction between "violation" and "rape" (in Articles 308–17). Rape is restricted to cases in which the victim has either not "arrived at puberty" (*rapto proprio*), or has but is less than seventeen years old at the time of the crime (*rapto impropio*). Title XI also is preoccupied with sexual crimes that were the result of trickery or dishonesty, including a peculiar crime called "substitution of person" (gaining "carnal access" by pretending to be a different person).

4. The most important of these international instruments was the Convention on the Elimination of All Forms of Discrimination Against Women (CEDAW), which Bolivia ratified in 1990.

5. The literature on gender in Bolivia, the Andes, and Latin America more generally, is obviously a large and dynamic one, and it is not my intention in this chapter to relate my arguments about law and subjectivity directly to it in any detail. I am

primarily interested in the extent to which scholarly work has contributed to the emergence of the broader multiple narratives of gender that shape—and are shaped by—the practice and experience of law in Bolivia. Having said this, I should mention that beyond Harris's many writings, I have benefited greatly from the work on gender in Bolivia by scholars such as Arnold (1997a, 1997b), Barragán (1999), Gotkowitz (1997), and Zorn (1997).

6. In her study of gender in rural Peru, Billie Jean Isbell explains that "the clearest expression of [gender] complementarity is found in the belief that one is not an adult until one marries. Chuschinos say that a male and a female are not complete until they have been united with their 'essential other half' " (1978: 214). For a critical comparison of the work of Harris and Isbell within Andean studies more generally, see Salomon 2001.

7. I think it is intriguing, though not surprising in light of how "gender" has developed over the last thirty years or so, that the concept has *not* come to mean—in Bolivia, if not elsewhere—the coequal analysis of the social construction of both femaleness and maleness, or of the many other alignments that can be (and sometimes are) included within "gender," such as the relationship between different age sets or, even more, the impact of political and ideological campaigns to shift the perceived historical inequalities between women and men. Within Latin American studies, I think of the work of Matthew Gutmann on masculinity and the "meanings of macho" in Mexico City as a necessary corrective to an unfortunate narrowness within much of the gender studies literature (see, e.g., Gutmann 1996, 2003).

8. Different high-profile human rights activists in Bolivia have often described to me the way the Beijing Conference, and the legislative and political shifts in Bolivia that preceded it, was a watershed moment for both human rights consciousness in Bolivia and their own personal journeys as activists and public actors. For example, Jeanette Alfaro, who is the director of the *Servicio Legal Integral Municipal de La Paz*, still proudly displays posters of the 1995 U.N. conference on her office walls and speaks with regret about the fact that so few Bolivian women were able to attend the meetings.

9. Article 10 reads, in part, "States Parties shall take all appropriate measures to eliminate discrimination against women in order to ensure to them equal rights with men in the field of education and in particular to ensure, on a basis of equality of men and women." Throughout the developing world, states parties like Bolivia have relied heavily on collaborations with transnational NGOs for financing and technical assistance in helping to implement provisions like this one.

10. The most well-known of these was called Yuyay Jap'ina.

11. I use hamlet, and not *ayllu*, as the social unit that structures marriage rules because I have not found, across forty hamlets in Alonso de Ibañez, that people follow consistent patterns for marriage restrictions that are based on minor ayllu affiliation. The only clear pattern is one in which men and women of the same hamlet do not

marry. Beyond this, I have found married couples from the same minor ayllu, inter-provincial couples, and interdepartmental couples. I have, so far, never come across a man (or woman) in the hamlets of Alonso de Ibañez married to someone from a differ-ent country, although there is no reason—based in local normative practice—why this couldn't happen.

12. Whether a daughter decides to return regularly to work her future allotment ob-viously depends on things like the distance between the hamlets, the age of her children, the willingness of her husband to agree to her long absences, and so forth. But a woman who does decide to maintain constant contact with her birth hamlet, and who plants and harvests the family's land, faces a very difficult life. Women who choose this path must, in effect, perform two rounds of agricultural work at the same time. Women who work the lands in their birth hamlets do not, of course, become exempt from their work duties in the hamlets of their husbands. Women and men divide all labor during each day, and the labor of both is equally vital to the survival of the family (as the principle of complementary unity suggests). A woman must therefore find a way to perform all of her family, agricultural, and pasturing duties in the hamlet of her husband in addition to the agricultural duties she will likely share with her brothers—and, most likely, her mother—in her birth hamlet.

13. Although it is tempting here to venture into perilous waters and speculate about the reasons for patrilocality in rural Bolivia, this is beyond my competence or immedi-ate interest. Nevertheless, given the sparse population density of places like Alonso de Ibañez, it is clear that exogamy of some type is needed for both social and biological rea-sons. If out-marriage is necessary, then the problem of postmarital residence arises. The married couple has to live *somewhere*. There are four main possibilities according to the standard anthropological literature on the subject: patrilocality (couple lives in hus-band's place), matrilocality (couple lives in wife's place); bilocality (couple can live in ei-ther place), and neolocality (couple does not live in either place, but establishes a new location for the family unit). (I leave out of this list more exotic patterns like "avuncu-locality" and "viril-avunculocality.")

14. Most strikingly, *defensores* are not bound by the various professional codes of ethics because they have not received legal training and are not affiliated with a *colegio de abogados*, an organized association of lawyers that regulates the legal profession.

15. This figure excludes the hundreds of women who came to the SLI during the years of its operation, because only women (and their children) could use its services. The fact that a high percentage of his clients continued to be women even after the SLI was closed in 1998 is obviously related to both his work as its director and his more gen-eral human rights advocacy, in which he focuses on rights related to the *roles de género* (for more on Montesinos and the SLI, see Chapter 5).

16. Because the written records kept by hamlet authorities in Alonso de Ibañez do not include lists of cases or disputes over time, and because politico-legal authority

positions usually change every year or every two years, it is very difficult for even the most sympathetic interlocutor to give accurate information on this point. I usually ask about the gender of legal actors in different ways, and people usually say something like "about half" of all disputes involve women. This, combined with the legal sessions I have observed across the province over the years, leads me to the conclusion that something like 50 percent is the correct figure.

17. This is one of the reasons that the leading cause of death among adult women in Alonso de Ibañez is complications arising from childbirth. The third leading cause of death is what the local clinic describes as "alcohol-related problems," which includes accidents while intoxicated (e.g., falling off a trail at night in the rainy season, something that happens with surprising frequency), deaths related to domestic violence where alcohol was involved, and the commission of suicide while intoxicated (ENDSA-Sacaca 1998). The leading cause of death for adult men in the province is clinical alcoholism and the diseases it causes, such as cirrhosis of the liver.

18. The court is closed for national holidays, departmental holidays, and the local fiestas. All courts in the department, including Sacaca's JDI, take a *vacación judicial* (judicial holiday) between March 1 and March 22. These three weeks, together with the other vacation days, add up to about forty-five days of vacation per year. This does not include times of the year when the court is officially open but closed in practice; during the entire Carnaval season, for example, the court can be closed without notice at any time.

19. I thank Nancy Postero (in personal communication) for reminding me that Santa Cruz is the "beauty pageant capital of Bolivia."

20. The *juzgado* also has two other, nonpublic spaces, one of which is used to store the judicial archives (which I have been organizing and cataloging, off and on, since 1998), and the other which is used to store supplies and where the juzgado's yearly *ch'alla*, or ritual drinking party, is held during the Carnaval season.

21. There is something like a radius of effectiveness in Alonso de Ibañez, within which the police officer will, on occasion, leave the town in order to conduct investigations, arrest suspects in serious crimes, and secure attendance at court sessions, but this radius only extends about half a league from the town's plaza, which means he will walk about thirty minutes from Sacaca in any one direction. This also means that only three to four hamlets are within an acceptable distance out of two hundred in the province. Several hamlets lie along relatively flat axes that follow rivers and are therefore accessible by motorized transport during the dry season. The provincial police officer in Sacaca usually has a motorcycle, which gives him the ability to make longer trips. Nevertheless, the police officers of Alonso de Ibañez who I have known have never been to the vast majority of the province's hamlets and during the periods of their tenure could not identify more than a handful by name.

22. Because defensores are not bound by—or indeed have any knowledge of—the code of ethics that regulates the practice of the legal profession in Bolivia, they would

not agree to take on a client out of respect for a mere abstract principle, like a defendant's right to zealous representation. Defensores are concerned first with whether and how a prospective client will compensate them for their services; and second, they take on cases in which they have a personal interest, one that can be based on things like kinship obligations or the promise of continuing defensor-client relations. However, I have never known a defensor to accept a case, like one that involves the sexual abuse of a child, out of a sense of obligation to an abstract legal or moral norm even though they—like most people—are horrified by the underlying facts of the case.

Chapter 5

1. Bolivian law quite clearly distinguishes between civil and religious weddings (in Articles 41 and 42). As Article 41 insists, the law "only recognizes civil marriage," while at the same time (in Art. 42), it ensures that religious marriages are "independent of the civil [wedding]" and can be "freely celebrated according to the beliefs of the contracting parties." The *Código de Familia* requires the presence of *testigos*, who must be adults of sound mind willing to formally attest to the legal capacity of the contracting parties. However, throughout Bolivia the testigos will usually be *padrinos*, whose presence, duties, and social roles are much more complicated than those of simple witnesses to legal proceedings.

2. From independence in 1825 until 1877, Sacaca was part of Chayanta Province. In 1877, the province was divided into two provinces, North and South Chayanta, and these provinces were renamed in 1880 as Chayanta and Charcas. In 1923, the current province Alonso de Ibañez was created from the second and fourth sections of Charcas Province.

3. The official Claretian website describes their mission in the following way: "The Claretians are committed to seeing the world through the eyes of the poor. We strive to respond to the most urgent and timely needs, using all means possible to care for the spiritual and material needs of others" (Claretian Order 2006).

4. As of 2006, Sacaca was still the only location in the province with twenty-four-hour electricity. Even Caripuyo, the capital of the province's second section, did not have twenty-four-hour electricity. Some hamlets had generators and others were experimenting with solar electricity with the help of transnational NGOs. But even though electricity was seen as a fundamental need for the hamlets, the concern expressed by several officials in Sacaca was that the hamlets would not be able to pay for the electricity if they were connected to the province's transformer, a concern that is well-founded. Electricity is relatively expensive and people in Sacaca use a variety of strategies to reduce their monthly bills, the most common being restricting the use the lights to special occasions or to certain hours of the day. When a *sacaqueño* fails to pay a bill in a timely fashion, the local technician for SEPSA (*Servicios Eléctricos de Potosí S.A*), the Potosí electricity concern that maintains an office in Sacaca's plaza, merely walks to the house

and disconnects its electricity until the bill is paid in full. Many houses in Sacaca will go without electricity because of unpaid bills for months or even years. However, people in the town have still not become fully dependent on the use of electricity. I have observed that many townspeople live much as people in the hamlets do, using candles for light.

5. Paz Estenssoro's political biography almost defies belief. He cofounded the *Movimiento Nacionalista Revolucionario* (MNR) in the early 1940s and led it in the National Revolution of 1952, after which he became Bolivia's first postrevolutionary head of state. He would go on to serve two more full terms as Bolivian president during quite distinct periods over the next three decades, so that *thirty-seven years* separated the beginning of his first presidency (1952) from the end of his last (1989). When he wasn't actually serving as Bolivia's president, Paz Estenssoro was either running for the position (1979), being sent into exile to prevent him from serving as president (1964), or agitating behind the scenes to reinvent the MNR in order to keep it politically and socially relevant.

6. Bolivia ratified ILO 169 in 1991, only two years after it had been adopted by the ILO's general conference. Bolivia was the fourth country in the world to do so (after Norway, Mexico, and Colombia). Some scholars have mistakenly asserted that Bolivia ratified ILO 169 in 1989, the year it was adopted by the general conference, but it was in fact ratified at the very end of 1991 (on December 11; see ILO 2007). www.ilo.ch/ilolex/english/convdisp1.htm, accessed on July 1, 2007

7. Although CEDAW was ratified by Bolivia in 1990, this was a full ten years after it had been signed in May of 1980. This earlier event is of some importance because it occurred during one of the most chaotic periods in Bolivian history. Bolivia's national elections of 1979 led to a tumultuous series of events that saw a woman, Lidia Gueiler Tejada, installed as a caretaker president until new elections could be held in June of 1980. For a brief time, Gueiler Tejada was Bolivia's first—and only—female president and one of the few in Latin American history (*elected* female presidents are even rarer). With only two months to go before she was deposed in a bloody coup by General Luis García Meza, Gueiler Tejada managed to convince the Bolivian congress to sign CEDAW, an act that committed the country to beginning the process of ratification and eventual implmentation. Although it took ten years, Bolviva *did* eventually ratify and implement CEDAW through a series of domestic human rights laws that were the single most important means through which human rights discourse found its way onto what Shannon Speed has called the "local terrain" (Speed 2008).

8. Someone who had also undergone a transformation of sorts, from the Colonel (later General) Banzer Suárez of the notorious *banzerato*, as the period of his dictatorship is called, to the physically and politically enfeebled man who, nevertheless, was democratically elected Bolivia's president in 1997. As we now know, Banzer was already dying of lung cancer by the time he was elected. A chain-smoker for decades, Banzer received treatment at Walter Reed Army Hospital in Washington D.C., but died in May of 2002.

9. For important examples of the antineoliberal critique in Bolivia, see Antezana 1999 and Solón 1997.

10. Others have also made this point. For example, Nikolas Rose has argued that what is known as "neoliberalism" can be better understood as "advanced liberalism" (Rose 1996).

11. Recent anthropology has provided critical insights into the importance of technocratic knowledge practices within contemporary discursive formations. See, for example, the large collection of essays in the volume *Global Assemblages* (Ong and Collier 2005). Other important examples include Tsing 2004, Piot 1999, and a collection of essays on the "new" global economy (Fisher and Downey 2006).

12. Law 1493 (September 17, 1993), a law passed through Bolivia's executive branch, created the Ministry of Human Development. Article 71, No. 5 of Supreme Decree 23660, created the National Secretariat for Ethnic and Gender Issues. Articles 85, 86, and 87 of this same Supreme Decree created the Subsecretariat for Gender Issues responsible for all political matters related to women. The Ministry of Human Development, in Resolution 139/94, adopted the National Plan for the Eradication, Prevention, and Punishment of Violence Against Women. Article 1 of this resolution created the system of Servicios Legales Integrales to carry out the resolution's objectives. Law 1674 (1995), passed by the Bolivian Congress, outlined the nature and function of the SLIs and authorized their establishment. In practice, SLIs can only be established after a formal application is made on behalf of a municipality with the assurance that supplemental funding will be provided.

13. The numbers of new criminal cases opened in the JDI between 1985 and 1994 are as follows: 1985 (38), 1986 (31), 1987 (29), 1988 (25), 1989 (23), 1990 (21), 1991 (30), 1992 (16), 1993 (23), 1994 (27).

14. The SLI did not keep a daily log by name of women who stayed at the center beyond what it took to conduct an intake interview, but Montesinos has confirmed that the center quickly filled to capacity and could not accept new arrivals for longer stays until women already present decided to return to their hamlets.

15. Ñuñumayani is a very small, almost paradigmatic, hamlet in Alonso de Ibañez. Although located within an hour's walk of a major road, it is far from the provincial capital; the capital of its canton (Iturata) is slowing dying; the few people who remain are mostly elderly (including one man who in 2005 claimed to be over ninety years old); and it occupies a relatively insignificant position within its corresponding minor *ayllu* (Minor Ayllu Urinsaya).

Chapter 6

1. In his more recent book (2006), Ferguson shows how expectations of modernity function as a kind of folk narrative embedded in Africa's different national and regional histories, although in making these comparisons one can see how consequential those "global shadows" have become for many different regions and contexts.

2. Compare the murder rate in Alonso de Ibañez with the following: Buenos Aires (6.4), Santiago (8), Mexico City (19.6), Medellín in 1995 (248), New York City (7.3), Los Angeles (17.5), and Montreal (3.4) (Piquet Cameiro 2000; Buvinic and Morrison 1999). The omnipresent historical fact of intentional killing in this part of Bolivia presents any number of interpretive, ethical, and methodological difficulties, which I hope to explore in a future book.

3. The Human Development Index (HDI) uses three distinct indices in order to measure a country's level of human development: life expectancy; education (which is divided into two subindices—adult literacy and gross enrolment); and per capita gross domestic product. Based on outputs, countries are categorized as high development (1.0–.8), medium development (.799–.5), and low development (.499–.281). Bolivia's 2008 HDI was 0.695, which puts it at number 117 in the world, just below Honduras and Kyrgyzstan and just above Guatemala and Gabon. The highest ranked country is Iceland (.968). Twenty-four of the lowest twenty-five are in Africa, including Sierra Leone (the lowest) at 0.336. Zambia, by the way, is ranked 165, just twelve places above Sierra Leone (U.N. Development Programme 2006).

4. Through the assistance of the type of transnational networks described at different places in this book, an ambitious new hospital was opened in the capital of Alonso de Ibañez in 1997. The hospital features a full-service pharmacy, X-ray machine, a laboratory staffed by a full-time technician, and room for approximately forty patients. The hospital is able to provide many types of primary care medicine and, as of 2005, a full-time dentist also has been stationed in Sacaca. The hospital lacks full-time specialists, and the directors of the hospital continually have emphasized to me that the hospital desperately needs a surgeon and an anesthesiologist. Without these, patients must make the six-hour trip to Oruro for surgical emergencies, which is very difficult for sacaqueños and impossible for people in the hamlets, because they must pay for the ambulance. However, the hospital, like any good shepherd of the modern body (see, e.g., Foucault 1973), also is staffed with statisticians, whose job it is to maintain a steady *regard medical* (or "medical gaze") over the people in the province. According to their numbers, the leading cause of death among men in the province is clinical alcoholism. The leading cause among adult women is complications arising from childbirth.

5. One NGO active in Alonso de Ibañez—and indeed throughout the norte de Potosí—is Project Concern International (PCI), an American organization that (at least in this region) specializes in so-called work-for-food projects. PCI enters into contracts that require individual hamlets to perform certain kinds of work in exchange for food. Hamlet authorities must keep detailed records of their work hours and have their work inspected by PCI before food will be distributed. The work to be done is arranged during preliminary negotiations, in which the needs of the community are assessed by hamlet authorities and PCI officials. Not surprisingly, many hamlets suggest that new

roads are their most pressing need, and the work they perform often involves building new roads or improving existing ones. One PCI worker who was nearing the end of his short-term assignment was jaded about the role PCI played in the province. He felt that the real beneficiaries of PCI's work in the province were U.S. farmers, who provided the bulk of the food that PCI distributed. The farmers were under contract with USAID, which served as a guaranteed buyer at prices that were, according to this PCI informant, well above market value.

6. The concept of human dignity has become almost the last discursive stick in the liberal bundle to resist critique, examination, and wonder. While "human rights," "liberty," "possessive individualism," and "moral autonomy" have all come in for critical scrutiny of one kind or another, "dignity" alone has remained in its transcultural, naturalistic bubble. For example, in his 2007 book, Ari Kohen argues that dignity is a universal idea about standards of treatment around which international institutions, nation-states, and individuals can develop consensus. He also argues that this universal sense of right conduct is the source of legitimacy for the major international human rights instruments like the UDHR. But surely "dignity," with its connotations of courtly nobility and intrinsic (if exclusive) value, is as discursively fraught as those other liberal signifiers whose relationship to the social practices they signify is equally ambiguous.

Conclusion

1. This is taken from his "epic poem in prose" *Dead Souls*, in which Gogol uses the metaphor of the troika rushing headlong through the countryside to describe the uncertainties of mid-nineteenth century czarist Russia.

2. I have in mind here everything from the actual loss of territory as a result of war or other regional conflicts (1879–83; 1903; 1932–35), to the shifting alliances between Bolivia and other South American nations during distinct political and historical epochs.

3. This statement can be accessed in different ways, but like most successful twenty-first century social and political movements, MAS maintains a well-designed webpage, at which one may download the party's official platform (www.masbolivia .org; last accessed on May 1, 2007).

4. It is a common practice in Bolivia to adopt English-language given names, but with a slightly modified spelling. The appearance of a "Jhon" Locke in MAS's statement of principles reflects this national practice.

5. The most up-to-date information on Bolivia's *Asamblea Constituyente* can be found at the official government website, www.constituyente.bo, which tracks the assembly's progress, provides a list of elected members (called *constituyentes* or *asambleístas*), and carries links to judicial and legislative databases for researchers and members of the public and press.

6. "Chuquisaca" was the name of the old colonial center in Bolivia that was renamed Sucre in August of 1825, five days after the declaration of independence, in honor

of Antonio José de Sucre. Besides the fact that contemporary Sucre is the legal capital of Bolivia (the country divides its branches of government between Sucre and La Paz), it is certainly not a coincidence that the current constituent assembly is located in the city most closely associated with Bolivia's first liberal revolution.

7. This is how Kevin Healy describes Morales: He "can be viewed as one part Muhammed [*sic*] Ali, one part Geronimo and one part Che Guevara. His defiant attitude toward public authority as a social activist is akin to Ali's, as is his brash, in-your-face personality and bravado. As Geronimo fought for indigenous rights by leading small, armed raids to surprise his foes, Morales mastered nonviolent road-blockade tactics to defend indigenous rights which—although violating the rights of other citizens to transit freely—compelled the Bolivian government to negotiate on agendas that include coca and others of national concern. The Guevara connection comes from Morales' revolutionary commitment to the poor" (2006).

8. The most important exception to this is the case of the Department of Santa Cruz, the largest of Bolivia's nine departments. During the 2005 elections, departmental prefects were elected for the first time by direct vote (they had previously been appointed by the president). Rubén Costas Aguilera was elected prefect of Santa Cruz. Costas is the head of a new political and social organization, *Autonomías Para Bolivia* (APB), and has emerged as one of the fiercest critics of Morales since 2005. APB is not an official political party registered with the National Electoral Court, but is "the people organized," as APB describes itself in a recent filing with the Constituent Assembly (República de Bolivia 2007). Costas is the leader of Bolivia's autonomy movement, which is seeking legal semiautonomy in large part for economic reasons. Santa Cruz is by far the richest of Bolivia's departments. Its *legal* economy is based on agriculture and it contains very large, but unexploited, reserves of iron ore, magnesium, and, most important (and politically sensitive), natural gas. In July 2006 Santa Cruz was one of four departments to vote in favor of increased autonomy in a special national referendum, although the issue of autonomy will ultimately be resolved within the Constituent Assembly. The results of the referendum point to dramatic internal divisions on this issue, as the following yes (for)/no (against) percentages indicate: Chuquisaca (38/62), La Paz (26/74), Cochabamba (37/63), Oruro (25/75), Potosí (27/73), Tarija (61/39), Santa Cruz (71/29), Beni (74/26), Pando (58/42) (CNE Bolivia 2007).

Bibliography

Primary Sources

Archives Consulted

Hamlets

Cuaderno de actas, Janq'o-Jaqe, Minor Ayllu Qollana Cuerpo
Cuaderno de actas, Kamacachi, Minor Ayllu Saqa Cuerpo
Cuaderno de actas, Molino T'ikanoma, Minor Ayllu Jilawi Cuerpo/Mayor
Cuaderno de actas, Sillu Sillu, Minor Ayllu Chaykina Abajo

Potosí

Casa Nacional de la Moneda
 —Corte Suprema de Justicia
 —Escrituras Notariales
 —Prefectura Departamental

Sacaca

Alcaldía de Sacaca
Corregidor titular de Cantón Sacaca (cuaderno de actas), 1996–1999
Director provincial de policía de Sacaca, 1998–1999
Escuela Mixta "Ladislao Cabrera" y Colegio Nacional Mixto "José Alonso de Ibañez"
Fe y Alegría
Hospital San Luis
Juzgado de Instrucción
Notario de Fe Pública
Registro Civil # 409
Registro Civil # 2502

Servicio Legal Integral–Sacaca
Subprefectura de Alonso de Ibañez

Sucre

Archivo Nacional de Bolivia, padrones de indios (revisitas)

Serials Consulted

Comarca/Rich'ariy (Sacaca)
El Comuntario (La Paz)
Desarrollo (VAIPO) (La Paz)
El Diario (La Paz)
Hoy (La Paz)
Jallalla, Boletín Informativo de la Misión "Norte-Potosí" (La Paz)
Mujer Pública (La Paz)
La Patria (Oruro)
Presencia (La Paz)
Pulso (La Paz)
El Tinku (Sacaca)

Bolivian Laws Consulted

Ley No. 696, Orgánica de Municipalidades
Ley No. 1551, Participación Popular
Ley No. 1615 (Art. 171), Constitución Política del Estado
Ley No. 1654, Descentralización Administrativa
Ley No. 1817, Ley del Consejo de la Judicatura
Ley No. 1818, Ley del Defensor del Pueblo
Ley No. 1970 (Art. 28), Código de Procedimiento Penal
Ley de Organización Judicial

Bolivian Legal Codes Consulted

Código civil
Código de ética profesional para el ejercicio de la abogacía
Código de familia
Código de minería
Código de procedimiento civil
Código de procedimiento penal
Código penal

Secondary Sources

Abel, Richard, ed.
1982 The Politics of Informal Justice. New York: Academic Press.

Abercrombie, Thomas

1986 The Politics of Sacrifice: An Aymara Cosmology in Action. Ph.D. dissertation, University of Chicago.

1991 To Be Indian, to Be Bolivian: "Ethnic" and "National" Discourses of Identity. *In* Nation-States and Indians in Latin America. Greg Urban and Joel Sherzer, eds. Pp. 95–130. Austin: University of Texas Press.

1998a Pathways of Memory and Power: Ethnography and History Among an Andean People. Madison: University of Wisconsin Press.

1998b Tributes to Bad Conscience: Charity, Restitution, and Inheritance in Cacique and Encomendero Testaments of Sixteenth-Century Charcas. *In* Dead Giveaways: Indigenous Testaments of Colonial Mesoamerica and the Andes. S. Kellogg and Matthew Restall, eds. Pp. 249–89. Salt Lake City: University of Utah Press.

Alba, Victor

1968 Politics and the Labor Movement in Latin America. Stanford, CA: Stanford University Press.

Albó, Xavier

1975 La Paradoja Aymara: Solidaridad y Faccionalismo. Estudios Andinos 11: 67–109.

1979a The Future of Oppressed Languages in the Andes. *In* Language and Society. W. McCormack and S. A. Wurm, eds. Pp. 309–31. The Hague, The Netherlands: Mouton.

1979b Achacachi, Medio Siglo de Luchas Campesinas. La Paz, Bolivia: CIPCA.

1987a Algunas Pistas Antropológicas para un Orden Jurídico Andino. *In* Derechos Humanos y Servicios Legales en el Campo. D. Garcia-Sayan, ed. Lima, Perú: Comisión Andina de Juristas.

1987b From MNRistas to Kataristas to Katari. *In* Resistance, Rebellion, and Consciousness in the Andean Peasant World, 18th to 20th Centuries. S. Stern, ed. Pp. 379–419. Madison: University of Wisconsin Press.

2000 Andean People in the Twentieth Century. *In* Cambridge History of the Native Peoples of the Americas (South America). Frank Salomon and Stuart Schwartz, eds. Vol. 3. Pp. 765–871. Cambridge: Cambridge University Press.

2006 El Alto, La Vorágine de Una Ciudad Única. Journal of Latin American Anthropology 11(2): 329–50.

Albó, Xavier, and Raúl Barrios, eds.

1993 Violencias Encubiertas en Bolivia. La Paz, Bolivia: CIPCA-ARUWIYIRI.

Albro, Roberto

2001 Reciprocity and Realpolitik: Image, Career, and Factional Genealogies in Provincial Bolivia. American Ethnologist 28(1): 56–93.

2006 Bolivia's "Evo Phenomenon": From Identity to What? Journal of Latin American Anthropology 11(2): 408–28.

Alexander, Larry, ed.
1998 Constitutionalism. Cambridge: Cambridge University Press.

Álvarez Arenas, Armando
1996 Sacaca: Provincia Alonso de Ibáñez. Unpublished manuscript, Sacaca, Bolivia.

Angelis-Harmening, Kristina
2000 "Cada Uno Tiene en la Puna su Gente": Intercambio y Verticalidad en el Siglo XVI en los Yungas de La Paz. Markt Schwaben, Germany: A. Saurwein.

An-Na'im, Abdullahi Ahmed, ed.
1995 Human Rights in Cross-Cultural Perspective. Philadelphia: University of Pennsylvania Press.

Antezana, Luis E.
1999 Trampas y Mentiras de la Ley INRA. La Paz, Bolivia: Editorial Jurídica "Temis."

Appadurai, Arjun
1996 Modernity at Large: Cultural Dimensions of Globalization. Vol. 1, Public Worlds. Minneapolis: University of Minnesota Press.

Appelbaum, Nancy, Anne S. Macpherson, and Karin Alejandra Rosemblatt, eds.
2003 Race and Nation in Modern Latin America. Chapel Hill: University of North Carolina Press.

Arguedas, Alcídes
1909 Pueblo enfermo. Barcelona, Vda. de L. Tasso.
1919 Raza de bronce. La Paz, Bolivia: González y Medina.
1922 Historia General de Bolivia (el proceso de la nacionalidad) 1809–1921. La Paz, Bolivia: Arnó Hermanos.

Arnade, Charles W.
1957 The Emergence of the Republic of Bolivia. Gainesville: University of Florida Press.

Arnold, Denise
1988 Matrilineal Practice in a Patrilineal Setting: Rituals and Metaphors of Kinship in an Andean Ayllu. Ph.D. dissertation, University of London.

1997a Making Men in Her Own Image: Gender, Text, and Textile in Qaqachaka. *In* Creating Context in Andean Culture. R. Howard-Malverde, ed. Oxford: Oxford University Press.

————, ed.

1997b Más Allá del Silencio: Las Fronteras de Género en los Andes. La Paz, Bolivia: CIASE and Instituto de Lengua y Cultura Aymara.

Arnold, Denise, Domingo Jiménez, and Juan de Dios Yapita

1992 Hacia un Orden Andino de las Cosas: Tres Pistas de los Andes Meridionales. La Paz, Bolivia: Hisbol.

Arrieta, Mario, Fernando Mayorga, and Mario Galindo

1995 Participación Popular y Desarrollo Rural. La Paz, Bolivia: Club de Economía Agrícola y Sociología Rural.

Arze, José Roberto

1996 Figuras Centrales en la Historia de Bolivia: (Independencia y República). La Paz, Bolivia: Editorial Los Amigos del Libro.

Arze, Silvia, and Ximena Medinaceli

1991 Imágenes y Presagios: El Escudo de los Ayaviri, Mallkus de Charcas. La Paz, Bolivia: Hisbol.

Asad, Talal

1973 Anthropology and the Colonial Encounter. London: Ithaca Press.

Ballón Aguirre, Francisco

1990 Sistema Jurídico Aguaruna y Positivismo. *In* Entre la Ley y la Costumbre: El Derecho Consuetudinario Indígena en América Latina. R.a.D.I. Stavenhagen, ed. Mexico City: Instituto Indigenista Interamericano.

1993 Antropología Jurídica de Emergencias: Unir los Fragmentos. *In* Derecho, Pueblos Indígenas y Reforma del Estado. A. Wray, ed. Quito, Ecuador: Abya-Yala.

Barker, Paul

1999 Making a Difference for Afghan Women. Journal of Humanitarian Assistance. Online journal, http://jha.ac/1999/05/27/making-a-difference-for-afghan-women/, accessed on June 24, 2007.

Barnes, Trevor, and James Duncan, eds.
1992 Writing Worlds: Discourse, Texts, and Metaphors in the Representation of Landscape. New York: Routledge.

Barragán, Rossana
1999 Indios, Mujeres y Ciudadanos: Legislación y Ejercicio de la Ciudadanía en Bolivia (Siglo XIX). La Paz, Bolivia: Fundación Diálogo.

Barragán, Rossana, Dora Cajías, and Seemin Qayum, eds.
1997 El Siglo XIX. Bolivia y América Latina. La Paz, Bolivia: IFEA.

Barrett, Michele, and Mary McIntosh
1991 The Anti-Social Family. London: Verso.

Barrios de Chungara, Domitila
1978 Let Me Speak! Testimony of Domitila, a Woman of the Bolivian Mines. New York: Monthly Review Press.

Barstow, Jean
1979 An Aymara Class Structure: Town and Community in Carabuco. Ph.D. dissertation, University of Chicago.

Bastien, Joseph
1978 The Mountain of the Condor: Metaphor and Ritual in an Andean Ayllu. Prospect Heights, IL: Waveland Press.

Baxandall, Michael
1987 Patterns of Intention: On the Historical Explanation of Pictures. New Haven, CT: Yale University Press.

Beauvoir, Simone de
1972 [1949] The Second Sex. New York: Penguin.

Berlin, Isaiah
1958 Two Concepts of Liberty. Oxford: Clarendon Press.
1959 Historical Inevitability. Oxford: Oxford University Press.

Bernal, Irma
1984 Rebeliones Indígenas en la Puna: Aspectos de la Lucha por la Recuperación de la Tierra. Buenos Aires, Argentina: Búsqueda-Yuchan.

Bloch, Marc

1953 The Historian's Craft. New York: Vintage Books.

Blomley, Nicholas

1994 Law, Space, and the Geographies of Power. New York: Guilford Press.

Bobbit, Philip

1982 Constitutional Fate: Theory of the Constitution. New York: Oxford University Press.

Bohman, James

2005 Critical Theory. The Stanford Encyclopedia of Philosophy (Spring 2005 Edition). Edward N. Zalta, ed. http://plato.stanford.edu/archives/spr2005/entries/critical -theory.

Bolivia

1992 National Census. La Paz, Bolivia: INE.
2001 National Census. La Paz, Bolivia: INE.

Bouysse-Cassagne, Thérèse

1986 Urco and Uma: Aymara Concepts of Space. In Anthropological History of Andean Polities. J. Murra and Nathan Wachtel, eds. Cambridge: Cambridge University Press.
1987 La Identidad Aymara: Aproximación Histórica (Siglo XV, Siglo XVI). La Paz, Bolivia: Hisbol.
1988 Lluvias y Cenizas: Dos Pachacuti en la Historia. La Paz, Bolivia: Hisbol.

Brandt, H.-J.

1987 Justicia Popular: Nativos Campesinos. Lima, Perú: CDIJ.

Brown, Carlos Arce

1959 Diccionario de Jurisprudencia Boliviana: Con un Estudio Preliminar y una Historia de la Gaceta Judicial. La Paz, Bolivia: Empresa Industrial Gráfica E. Burillo.

Brown, Wendy

2006 Regulating Aversion: Tolerance in the Age of Identity and Empire. Princeton, NJ: Princeton University Press.

Brush, Stephen

1974 Conflictos Intercomunitarios en los Andes. Allpanchis 6: 29–41.

Burnett, Ben, and Moises P. Tronsoso

1960 The Rise of the Latin American Labor Movement. New Haven, CT: College and University Press.

Bustamante, P. Jose Antonio

1985 Apuntes para una Historia de la Iglesia en Sakaka (1560–1985). Karipuyo, Bolivia: Misión "Norte de Potosí."

Butler, Barbara

2006 Holy Intoxication to Drunken Dissipation: Alcohol Among Quichua Speakers in Otavalo, Ecuador. Albuquerque: University of New Mexico Press.

Buvinic, Maya, and Andrew Morrison

1999 Violence as an Obstacle to Development. 1–8. Washington, DC: Inter-American Development Bank.

Calhoun, Craig, ed.

1992 Habermas and the Public Sphere. Cambridge, MA: MIT Press.

Cardoso, Fernando Enrique, and Enzo Faletto

1979 Dependency and Development in Latin America. Berkeley: University of California Press.

Carty, Anthony

1991 English Constitutional Law from a Postmodernist Perspective. In Dangerous Supplements: Resistance and Renewal in Jurisprudence. P. Fitzpatrick, ed. Durham, NC: Duke University Press.

Castro, Jaime

1997 Reforma Constitucional y Crisis Política. Bogotá, Colombia: Ediciones Jurídicas Gustavo Ibañez.

Cepeda, Manuel Jose

1992 Democracy, State and Society in the 1991 Constitution: The Role of the Constitutional Court. In Colombia: The Politics of Reforming the State. E. Posada-Carbo, ed. New York: St. Martin's Press.

Chardon, Roland

1980 The Elusive Spanish League: A Problem of Measurement in Sixteenth-Century New Spain. Hispanic American Historical Review 60(2): 294–302.

Cheah, Pheng, and Bruce Robbins, eds.

1998 Cosmopolitics: Thinking and Feeling Beyond the Nation. Minneapolis: University of Minnesota Press.

Claretian Order

2006 Who We Are. www.claret.org.

Clifford, James

1986 Introduction: Partial Truths. *In* Writing Culture: The Poetics and Politics of Ethnography. J. Clifford and George Marcus, eds. Berkeley: University of California Press.

1988 The Predicament of Culture: Twentieth-Century Ethnography, Literature, and Art. Cambridge, MA: Harvard University Press.

1997 Routes: Travel and Translation in the Late Twentieth Century. Cambridge, MA: Harvard University Press.

Clifford, James, and George Marcus, eds.

1986 Writing Culture: The Poetics and Politics of Ethnography. Berkeley: University of California Press.

Cole, Jeffrey

1985 The Potosi Mita, 1573–1700: Compulsory Indian Labor in the Andes. Stanford, CA: Stanford University Press.

Condarco Morales, Ramiro

1982 Zarate, el "Temible" Willka: Historia de la Rebelión Indígena de 1889 en la República de Bolivia. La Paz, Bolivia: "Renovación" Ltda.

Corte Nacional Electoral-Bolivia

2007 Results of 2006 Referendum. www.cne.org.bo/, accessed on May 3, 2007.

Coutin, Susan

1993 The Culture of Protest: Religious Activism and the U.S. Sanctuary Movement. Boulder, CO: Westview Press.

Cowan, Jane

2001 Ambiguities of an Emancipatory Discourse: The Making of a Macedonian Minority in Greece. *In* Culture and Rights: Anthropological Perspectives. J. Cowan, Marie-Benedicte Dembour, and Richard Wilson, eds. Cambridge: Cambridge University Press.

Cowan, Jane, Marie-Benedicte Dembour, and Richard Wilson, eds.

2001 Culture and Rights: Anthropological Perspectives. Cambridge: Cambridge University Press.

Crespo, Alberto, José Crespo Fernández, and María Luisa Kent Solares

1995 Los Bolivianos en el Tiempo: Cuadernos de Historia. 2nd ed. La Paz, Bolivia: Instituto de Estudios Andinos y Amazónicos.

Cueto, Marcus, ed.

1994 Missionaries of Science: The Rockefeller Foundation and Latin America. Bloomington: Indiana University Press.

1995 Saberes Andinos: Ciencia y Tecnología en Bolivia, Ecuador y Perú. Lima, Perú: Instituto de Estudios Peruanos.

Da Matta, Roberto

1987 The Quest for Citizenship in a Relational Universe. In State and Society in Brazil. John D. Wirth, Edson de Oliveira Nunes, and Thomas E. Bogenschild, eds. Boulder, CO: Westview Press.

Darian-Smith, Eve

1998 Power in Paradise: The Political Implications of Santos's Utopia (review essay). Law and Social Inquiry 23: 81–120.

1999 Bridging Divides: The Channel Tunnel and English Legal Identity in the New Europe. Berkeley: University of California Press.

Darian-Smith, Eve, and Peter Fitzpatrick, eds.

1999 Laws of the Postcolonial. Ann Arbor: University of Michigan Press.

Davos, Filip

2003 Semantic Vagueness and Lexical Polyvalence. Studia Linguistica 57(3): 121–41.

de Certeau, Michel

1988 The Practice of Everyday Life. Berkeley: University of California Press.

de la Cruz, Rodrigo

1993 Aportes de Derecho Consuetudinario a la Reforma Jurídica del Estado. In Derecho, Pueblos Indígenas y Reforma del Estado. A. Wray, ed. Quito, Ecuador: Abya-Yala.

de Mesa, José, Teresa Gisbert, and Carlos Mesa Gisbert

2003 Historia de Bolivia. 5th ed. La Paz, Bolivia: Editorial Gisbert.

Drzewieniecki, J.

1995 Indigenous People, Law, and Politics in Peru. Paper presented at the Latin American Studies Association, Washington, DC.

Duncan, James, and David Ley, eds.

1993 Place/Culture/Representation. New York: Routledge.

Dunkerley, James

1981 Reassessing Caudillismo in Bolivia, 1825–79. Bulletin of Latin American Research 1(1): 13–25.

1984 Rebellion in the Veins: Political Struggle in Bolivia, 1952–1982. London: Verso.

2006 Crisis and Change in Bolivia: The Morales Government in Historical Perspective. Paper presented to the Institute for the Study of the Americas, University of London.

Einstein, Albert

1945 Mozart: His Character, His Work. New York: Oxford University Press.

ENDSA-Sacaca

1998 Anuario 1998. Ministerio de Salud y Previsión Social, Servicio Departamental de Salud Potosi.

Englund, Harri

2006 Prisoners of Freedom: Human Rights and the African Poor. Berkeley: University of California Press.

Escobar, Arturo

1995 Encountering Development: The Making and Unmaking of the Third World. Princeton, NJ: Princeton University Press.

Espinoza Soriano, Waldemar

1969 El "memorial" de Charcas, "Crónica" Inédita de 1582. Cantuta: Revista de la Universidad Nacional de Educación: 117–52.

Ewick, Patricia, and Susan Silbey

1998 The Common Place of Law: Stories from Everyday Life. Chicago: University of Chicago Press.

Fabian, Johannes

1983 Time and the Other: How Anthropology Makes Its Object. New York: Columbia University Press.

1991 Time and the Work of Anthropology: Critical Essays 1971–1991. Philadelphia: Harwood Academic Publishers.

Feierman, Steven

1990 Peasant Intellectuals: Anthropology and History in Tanzania. Madison: University of Wisconsin Press.

Ferguson, James

1999 Expectations of Modernity: Myths and Meanings of Urban Life on the Zambian Copperbelt. Berkeley: University of California Press.

2006 Global Shadows: Africa in the Neoliberal World Order. Durham, NC: Duke University Press.

Fernández Osco, Marcelo

2000 La Ley del Ayllu: Práctica de Jach'a Justicia y Jisk'a Justicia (Justicia Mayor y Justicia Menor) en la Comunidades Aymaras. La Paz, Bolivia: Programa de Investigación Estratégica en Bolivia.

Fisher, Melissa, and Greg Downey, eds.

2006 Frontiers of Capital: Ethnographic Reflections on the New Economy. Durham, NC: Duke University Press.

Fitzpatrick, Peter

1984 Law and Societies. Osgoode Hall Law Journal 22: 115.

2001 Modernism and the Grounds of Law. Cambridge: Cambridge University Press.

Flores Galindo, Alberto

1987 Buscando un Inca: Identidad y Utopía en los Andes. Lima, Perú: Instituto de Apoyo Agrario.

Flores Ochoa, Jorge A.

1977 Pastores de Puna = Uywamichiq Punarunakuna. Lima, Perú: Instituto de Estudios Peruanos.

Forman, Sylvia

1972 Law and Conflict in Rural Highland Ecuador. Ph.D. dissertation, University of California, Berkeley.

Foucault, Michel

1973 The Birth of the Clinic: An Archaeology of Medical Perception. London: Routledge.

Frank, Andres Gunder

1967 Capitalism and Underdevelopment in Latin America. New York: Monthly Review Press.

1972 The Development of Underdevelopment. *In* Dependence and Underdevelopment. J. D. Cockcroft, A. G. Frank, and D. Johnson, eds. Garden City, NY: Anchor Books.

Friedland, Roger, and Deidre Boden, eds.

1994 NowHere: Space, Time, and Modernity. Berkeley: University of California Press.

Frontaura Argandoña, Manuel

1974 La Revolución Nacional. La Paz, Bolivia: Editorial "Los Amigos del Libro."

Fulford, Tim, and Peter Kitson, eds.

1998 Romanticism and Colonialism: Writing and Empire, 1789–1830. New York: Cambridge University Press.

Galeano, Eduardo

1971 Las Venas Abiertas de América Latina. La Habana: Casa de las Américas.

Gamboa, Franco

2001 Itinerario de la Esperanza y el Desconcierto: Ensayos Sobre Política, Sociedad y Democracia en Bolivia. La Paz, Bolivia: Muela del Diablo Editores.

García Canclini, Néstor

1995 Hybrid Cultures: Strategies for Entering and Leaving Modernity. Minneapolis: University of Minnesota Press.

García Márquez, Gabriel

1967 Cien Años de Soledad. Buenos Aires, Argentina: Editorial Sudamericana.

Garcia-Villegas, Mauricio

1993 La Eficacia Simbólica del Derecho: Examen de Situaciones Colombianas. Bogotá, Colombia: Ediciones Uniandes.

2000 Legal Construction of Social Problems in a Context of Institutional Crisis: The Case of Colombia. Paper presented at the Law and Society Annual Meetings, Miami, FL.

Garth, Bryant, and Austin Sarat, eds.

1998 How Does Law Matter? Evanston, IL: Northwestern University Press.

Gelles, Paul

1990 Channels of Power, Fields of Contention: The Politics and Ideology of Irrigation in an Andean Peasant Community. Ph.D. dissertation, Harvard University.

Giddens, Anthony

1984 The Constitution of Society: Outline of the Theory of Structuration. Cambridge: Polity Press.

1991 Modernity and Self-Identity: Self and Society in the Late Modern Age. Cambridge: Polity Press.

Godio, Julio

1983 Sindicalismo y Política en América Latina. Caracas, Venezuela: Instituto Latinoamericano de Investigaciones Sociales.

Godoy, Ricardo

1983 From Indian to Miner and Back Again: Small-Scale Mining in the Jukumani Ayllu. Ph.D. dissertation, Columbia University.

1990 Mining and Agriculture in Highland Bolivia: Ecology, History, and Commerce Among the Jukumanis. Tucson: University of Arizona Press.

Goldstein, Daniel

2004 The Spectacular City: Violence and Performance in Urban Bolivia. Durham, NC: Duke University Press.

2007 The Violence of Rights: Human Rights as Culprit, Human Rights as Victim. *In* The Practice of Human Rights: Tracking Law Between the Global and the Local. Mark Goodale and Sally Engle Merry, eds. Cambridge: Cambridge University Press.

Gómez de Aranda, Blanca

1978 Casimiro Olañeta, Diplomático, 1824–1839. La Paz, Bolivia: Instituto Boliviano de Cultura.

Gonzalez Echevarria, Roberto

1990 Myth and Archive: A Theory of Latin American Narrative. Cambridge: Cambridge University Press.

Goodale, Mark

2001 A Complex Universe in Motion: Rights, Obligations, and Rural-Legal Intellectuality in the Bolivian Andes. Ph.D. dissertation, University of Wisconsin–Madison.

2002a Legal Ethnohistory in Rural Bolivia: Social History and Documentary Culture. Ethnohistory (49)3: 583–609.

2002b The Globalization of Sympathetic Law and its Consequences. Law and Social Inquiry 27(3): 401–15.

2005 Empires of Law: Discipline and Resistance Within the Transnational System. Social and Legal Studies 14(5): 553–83.

2006a Ethical Theory as Social Practice. American Anthropologist 108(1): 25–37.

2006b Reclaiming Modernity: Indigenous Cosmopolitanism and the Coming of the Second Bolivian Revolution. American Ethnologist 33(4): 634–49.

2007a Legalities and Illegalities. *In* The Blackwell Companion to Latin American Anthropology. D. Poole, ed. Oxford: Blackwell.

2007b The Power of Right(s): Tracking Empires of Law and New Modes of Social Resistance in Bolivia (and elsewhere). *In* The Practice of Human Rights: Tracking Law Between the Global and the Local. Mark Goodale and Sally Engle Merry, eds. Cambridge: Cambridge University Press.

2009 Surrendering to Utopia: An Anthropology of Human Rights. Stanford, CA: Stanford University Press.

Goodale, Mark, and Sally Engle Merry, eds.

2007 The Practice of Human Rights: Tracking Law Between the Global and the Local. Cambridge: Cambridge University Press.

Gordillo, Gastón

2004 Landscapes of Devils: Tensions of Place and Memory in the Argentinean Chaco Durham, NC: Duke University Press.

Gordillo, José

2000 Campesinos Revolucionarios en Bolivia. La Paz, Bolivia: Editorial Plural.

Gordillo, José Miguel

1999 Modernity, Politics, and Identity: Post-Revolutionary Peasant Struggles in the Upper Valley of Cochabamba (Bolivia), 1952–1964. Ph.D. dissertation, State University of New York at Stony Brook.

Gose, Peter

1994 Embodied Violence: Racial Identity and the Semiotics of Property in Huaquirca, Antabamba (Apurímac). *In* Unruly Order: Violence, Power and Cultural Identity in the High Provinces of Southern Peru. D. Poole, ed. Boulder, CO: Westview Press.

Gotkowitz, Laura

1997 Within the Boundaries of Equality: Race, Gender, and Citizenship in Bolivia (Cochabamba, 1880–1953). Ph.D. dissertation, University of Chicago.

Gramsci, Antonio

1971 Selections from the Prison Notebooks. New York: International Publishers.

Grieshaber, Erwin

1977 Survival of Indian Communities in Nineteenth-Century Bolivia. Ph.D. dissertation, University of North Carolina–Chapel Hill.

1980 Survival of Indian Communities in Nineteenth-Century Bolivia: A Regional Comparison. Journal of Latin American Studies 12(2): 223–69.

Grillo, R. D., and R. L. Stirrat, eds.

1997 Discourses of Development: Anthropological Perspectives. New York: Berg.

Grindle, Merilee S., and Pilar Domingo, eds.

2003 Proclaiming Revolution: Bolivia in Comparative Perspective. Cambridge, MA: David Rockefeller Center for Latin American Studies.

Grondin, Marcelo N.

1990 Método de Quechua: Runa Simi. La Paz, Bolivia: Los Amigos del Libro.

Gudeman, Stephen, and Alberto Rivera

1990 Conversations in Colombia: The Domestic Economy in Life and Text. Cambridge: Cambridge University Press.

Guevara Gil, Armando, and Joseph Thome

1992 Notes on Legal Pluralism. Beyond Law 5: 75–102.

Guillet, David

1992 Covering Ground: Communal Water Management and the State in the Peruvian Highlands. Ann Arbor: University of Michigan Press.

1998 Rethinking Legal Pluralism: Local Law and State Law in the Evolution of Water Property Rights in Northwestern Spain. Comparative Studies in Society and History 40(1): 42–70.

Gupta, Akhil, and James Ferguson, eds.

1997a Anthropological Locations: Boundaries and Grounds of a Field Science. Berkeley: University of California Press.

1997b Culture, Power, Place: Explorations in Critical Anthropology. Durham, NC: Duke University Press.

Gutmann, Matthew

1996 The Meanings of Macho: Being a Man in Mexico City. Berkeley: University of California Press.

————, ed.

2003 Changing Men and Masculinities in Latin America. Durham, NC: Duke University Press.

Guzmán Santiesteban, Jorge, and Alberto Muñoz Crespo

2002 Diccionario Moderno de Jurisprudencia Boliviana. Bogotá, Colombia: Fundación Académica Cultural.

Habermas, Jürgen

1996 Modernity: An Unfinished Project. *In* Habermas and the Unfinished Project of Modernity: Critical Essays on the Philosophical Discourse of Modernity Maurizio Passerin d'Entrèves and Seyla Benhabib, eds. Pp. 39–55. Cambridge, MA: MIT Press.

Hacking, Ian

2005 A New Way to See a Leaf. *In* The New York Review of Books. Vol. 52, No. 5, www.nybooks.com/articles/17908.

Harb, Benjamín Miguel, and Edgar M. Moreno

1999 Constitución Política del Estado: Reformada, Comentada, Concordada. La Paz/Cochabamba, Bolivia: Los Amigos del Libro.

Hardt, Michael, and Antonio Negri

2000 Empire. Cambridge, MA: Harvard University Press.

2004 Multitude: War and Democracy in the Age of Empire. New York: Penguin Press.

Harmen, I. M.

1987 Collective Labor and Rituals of Reciprocity in the Southern Bolivian Andes. Ph.D. dissertation, Cornell University.

Harrington, Christine, and Barbara Yngvesson

1990 Interpretive Sociolegal Research. Law and Social Inquiry 15(1): 135–48.

Harris, Olivia

1978a Complementarity and Conflict: An Andean View of Women and Men. *In* Sex and Age as Principles of Social Differentiation. S. LaFontaine, ed. Pp. 21–40. London: Academic Press.

1978b El Parentesco y la Economía Vertical en el Ayllu Laymi (Norte de Potosí). Avances 1: 51–64.

2000 To Make the Earth Bear Fruit: Ethnographic Essays on Fertility, Work and Gender in Highland Bolivia. London: Institute of Latin American Studies.

————, ed.

1980 The Power of Signs: Gender, Culture and the Wild in the Bolivian Andes. *In* Nature, Culture, Gender. C.M.a.M. Strathern, ed. Cambridge: Cambridge University Press.

1982 Labour and Produce in an Ethnic Economy, Northern Potosi, Bolivia. *In* Ecology and Exchange in the Andes. D. Lehman, ed. Pp. 70–96. Cambridge: Cambridge University Press.

1996 Inside and Outside the Law: Anthropological Studies of Authority and Ambiguity. London: Routledge.

Harris, Olivia, and Xavier Albó

1986 Monteras y Guardatojos: Campesinos y Mineros en el Norte de Potosí en 1974. La Paz, Bolivia: CIPCA.

Hart, Gillian

2001 Development Critiques in the 1990s: Culs de Sac and Promising Paths. Progress in Human Geography 25(4): 649–58.

Hart, H.L.A.

1961 The Concept of Law. Oxford: Oxford University Press.

Healy, Kevin

2001 Llamas, Weavings, and Organic Chocolate: Multicultural Grassroots Development in the Andes and Amazon of Bolivia. South Bend, IN: University of Notre Dame Press.

2006 Morales: A Historic Opening for Indigenous Peoples. *In* Indian Country Today. February 2, 2006. www.indiancountry.com/content.cfm?id=1096412385, accessed on May 10, 2007.

Hernández-Truyol, Berta Esperanza, ed.

2002 Moral Imperialism. New York: New York University Press.

Hollander, D.

2005 Traditional Gender Roles and Intimate Partner Violence Linked in China. International Family Planning Perspectives 31(1), online journal, www.guttmacher.org/pubs/journals/3104605.html.

Horkheimer, Max

1982 Critical Theory. New York: Seabury Press.

Hurtado, Jorge

1986 El Katarismo. La Paz, Bolivia: Hisbol.

Ignatieff, Michael

2001 Human Rights as Politics and Idolatry. Princeton, NJ: Princeton University Press.

Instituto Nacional de Estadísticas (INE), Bolivia

1992 National Census. La Paz, Bolivia.

International Labor Organization

2007 Status of Ratifications. www.ilo.ch/ilolex/english/convdisp1.htm, accessed on July 1, 2007.

Isbell, Billie Jean

1978 To Defend Ourselves: Ecology and Ritual in an Andean Village. Austin: University of Texas Press.

Iturralde, Diego

1990 Movimiento Indio, Costumbre Jurídica y Usos de la Ley. *In* Entre la Ley y la Costumbre: El Derecho Consuetudinario Indígena en América Latina. Rodolfo. Stavenhagen, ed. Mexico City: Instituto Indigenista Interamericano.

1993 Usos de la Ley y Usos de la Costumbre: La Reivindicación del Derecho Indígena y la Modernización del Estado. *In* Derecho, Pueblos Indígenas y Reforma del Estado. A. Wray, ed. Quito, Ecuador: Abya-Yala.

Izko, Xavier

1992 La Doble Frontera: Ecología, Política y Ritual en el Altiplano Central. La Paz, Bolivia: Hisbol.

1993 Etnopolítica y Costumbre en los Andes Bolivianos. *In* Derecho, Pueblos Indígenas y Reforma del Estado. A. Wray, ed. Quito, Ecuador: Abya-Yala.

Jackson, Jean

1995 Culture, Genuine and Spurious: The Politics of Indianness in the Vaupes, Colombia. American Ethnologist 22(1): 3–17.

Jameson, Fredric

1998 The Cultural Turn: Selected Writings on the Postmodern, 1983–1998. London: Verso.

Juristas, Comisión Andina de

1993 Bolivia: Administración de Justicia y Derechos Humanos. La Paz, Bolivia: CAJ.

Kairys, David, ed.

1996 The Politics of Law: A Progressive Critique. New York: Basic Books.

Kelley, Jonathan, and Herbert S. Klein

1981 Revolution and the Rebirth of Inequality: A Theory Applied to the National Revolution in Bolivia. Berkeley: University of California Press.

Kelly, John D.

2002 Alternative Modernities or an Alternative to "Modernity": Getting Out of the Modernist Sublime. In Critically Modern: Alternatives, Alterities, Anthropologies. B. Knauft, ed. Pp. 258–86. Bloomington: Indiana University Press.

King, Anthony D., ed.

1997 Culture, Globalization and the World-System: Contemporary Conditions for the Representation of Identity. Minneapolis: University of Minnesota Press.

Klein, Herbert S.

1982 Bolivia: The Evolution of a Multi-Ethnic Society. Oxford: Oxford University Press.

1993 Haciendas and Ayllus: Rural Society in the Bolivian Andes in the Eighteenth and Nineteenth Centuries. Stanford, CA: Stanford University Press.

2003 A Concise History of Bolivia. Cambridge: Cambridge University Press.

Klemola, Antero

1997 The Reproduction of Community Through Communal Practices in Kila Kila, Bolivia. Ph.D. dissertation, University of Liverpool.

Knauft, Bruce, ed.

2002 Critically Modern: Alternatives, Alterities, Anthropologies. Bloomington: Indiana University Press.

Kohen, Ari

2007 In Defense of Human Rights: A Non-Religious Grounding in a Pluralistic World. New York: Routledge.

Kohl, Ben, and Linda Farthing

2006 Impasse in Bolivia: Neoliberal Hegemony and Social Resistance. London: Zed Books.

Koskenniemi, Martti

2006 From Apology to Utopia: The Structure of International Legal Argument. Cambridge: Cambridge University Press.

Kymlicka, Will

1995 Multicultural Citizenship: A Liberal Theory of Minority Rights. Oxford: Oxford University Press.

Lagos, Maria

1988 Pathways to Autonomy, Roads to Power: Peasant-Elite Relations in Cochabamba Bolivia, 1900–1985. Ph.D. dissertation, Columbia University.

1991 The Politics of Representation: Class and Ethnic Identity in Cochabamba. Boletín de Antropología Americana 24: 143–50.

1994 Autonomy and Power: The Dynamics of Class and Culture in Rural Bolivia. Philadelphia: University of Pennsylvania Press.

Langer, Erick

1988 Liberalismo y la Abolición de la Comunidad Indígena en el Siglo XIX. Historia y Cultura 14: 59–95.

1989 Economic Change and Rural Resistance in Southern Bolivia, 1880–1930. Stanford, CA: Stanford University Press.

1990 Andean Rituals of Revolt: The Chayanta Rebellion of 1927. Ethnohistory 37(3): 227–53.

Lara, Jesús

1991 Diccionario, Qheshwa-Castellano, Castellano-Qheshwa. 3rd ed. La Paz, Bolivia: Los Amigos del Libro.

Larson, Brooke

1978 Hacendados y Campesinos en Cochabamba en el Siglo XVIII. Avances 2: 37–50.

1983 Explotación Agraria y Resistencia Campesina. Cochabamba, Bolivia: CERES.

1998 Cochabamba, 1550–1990: Colonialism and Agrarian Transformation in Bolivia. 2nd ed. Durham, NC: Duke University Press.
2000 Andean Highland Peasants and the Trials of Nation Making During the Nineteenth Century. *In* Cambridge History of the Native Peoples of the Americas (South America). Frank Salomon and Stuart Schwartz, eds. Vol. 3. Pp. 558–703. Cambridge: Cambridge University Press.
2004 Trials of Nation Making: Liberalism, Race, and Ethnicity in the Andes, 1810–1910. Cambridge: Cambridge University Press.

Larson, Brooke, Olivia Harris, and Enrique Tandeter, eds.
1995 Ethnicity, Markets, and Migration in the Andes: At the Crossroads of History and Anthropology. Durham, NC: Duke University Press.

Lasalle, Ferdinand.
1964 ¿Qué Es Una Constitución? Buenos Aires, Argentina: Siglo XXI.

Lazar, Sian
2006 El Alto, Ciudad Rebelde: Organizational Bases for Revolt. Bulletin of Latin American Research 25(2): 183–99.

Lazarus-Black, Mindie, and Susan Hirsch, eds.
1994 Contested States: Law, Hegemony and Resistance. New York: Routledge.

Lefebvre, Henri
1991 The Production of Space. Oxford: Blackwell Publishers.

León-Portilla, Miguel
1959 Visión de los Vencidos. Mexico City: Universidad Nacional Autónoma de México.

Léons, Madeline Barbara, and Harry Sanabria eds.
1997 Coca, Cocaine, and the Bolivian Reality. Albany: State University of New York Press.

Lerner, Gerda
1987 The Creation of Patriarchy. Oxford: Oxford University Press.

Lipovetsky, Gilles
2005 Hypermodern Times. Oxford: Polity Press.

Llewelyn, Karl, and E. Adamson Hoebel

1941 The Cheyenne Way: Conflict and Case Law in Primitive Jurisprudence. Norman: University of Oklahoma Press.

Lund, Sarah

1994 Lives Together—Worlds Apart: Quechua Colonization in Jungle and City. Oslo, Norway: Scandinavian University Press.

Macas, Luis

1993 An Interview with Luis Macas. Multinational Monitor 15(4): 21–23.

Maccormack, Sabine

2000 Ethnography in South America: The First Two Hundred Years. In Cambridge History of the Native Peoples of the Americas (South America). Frank Salomon and Stuart Schwartz, eds. Vol. 3. Pp. 96–187. Cambridge: Cambridge University Press.

Macdonald, Roderick

1998 Metaphors of Multiplicity: Civil Society, Regimes, and Legal Pluralism. Arizona Journal of International and Comparative Law 15: 69–91.

Malagón Barceló, Javier

1961 The Role of the Letrado in the Colonization of America. The Americas 18(1): 1–17.

Mallon, Florencia

1983 The Defense of Community in Peru's Central Highlands: Peasant Struggle and Capitalist Transition, 1860–1940. Princeton, NJ: Princeton University Press.

1994 The Promise and Dilemma of Subaltern Studies: Perspectives from Latin American History. American Historical Review 99(5): 1491–525.

1995 Peasant and Nation: The Making of Postcolonial Mexico and Peru. Berkeley: University of California Press.

Malloy, James M.

1970 Bolivia: The Uncompleted Revolution. Pittsburgh, PA: University of Pittsburgh Press.

Mannheim, Bruce

1991 The Language of the Inka Since the European Invasion. Austin: University of Texas Press.

Marcus, George

1995 Ethnography in/of the World System: The Emergence of Multi-Sited Ethnography. Annual Review of Anthropology 24: 95–117.

1998 Ethnography Through Thick and Thin. Princeton, NJ: Princeton University Press.

Marquéz S. J., Ignacio

1987 ¿Cómo Nació Fe y Alegría? Caracas, Venezuela: Fe y Alegría.

Marshall, Geoffrey

1984 Constitutional Conventions: The Rules and Forms of Political Accountability Oxford: Oxford University Press.

Martínez García, J. I.

1992 La Imaginación Jurídica. Madrid, Spain: Debate.

McIlwain, Charles

1947 Constitutionalism: Ancient and Modern. Ithaca, NY: Cornell University Press.

Medeiros, Carmen

2001 Civilizing the Popular: The Law of Popular Participation and the Design of a New Society. Critique of Anthropology 21: 401–25.

Meja, Volker, and Nico Stehr, eds.

1990 Knowledge and Politics: The Sociology of Knowledge Dispute. New York: Routledge.

Mendieta Parada, Pilar

2006 Caminantes Entre Dos Mundos: Los Apoderados Indígenas en Bolivia (Siglo XIX). Revista de Indias 66: 761–82.

Mendoza, Fernando T., and Felix Patzi G.

1997 Atlas de los Ayllus de Norte de Potosí, Territorio de los Antiguos Charka. Potosi, Bolivia: PAC-C.

Merry, Sally Engle

1988 Legal Pluralism. Law and Society 22(5): 869–96.

1990 Getting Justice and Getting Even: Legal Consciousness Among Working Class Americans. Chicago: University of Chicago Press.

2001 Changing Rights, Changing Culture. In Culture and Rights: Anthropological Perspectives. J. Cowan, Marie-Benedicte Dembour, and Richard Wilson, eds. Cambridge: Cambridge University Press.

2002 Ethnography in the Archives. *In* Practicing Ethnography in Law: New Methods, Enduring Practices. June Starr and Mark Goodale, eds. New York: Palgrave/St. Martin's Press.

2006a Human Rights and Gender Violence: Translating International Law into Local Justice. Chicago: University of Chicago Press.

2006b Transnational Human Rights and Local Activism: Mapping the Middle. American Anthropologist (108)1: 38–51.

Merryman, John

2007 The Civil Law Tradition, 3rd Edition: An Introduction to the Legal Systems of Europe and Latin America. Stanford, CA: Stanford University Press.

Meyer, Michael C., William L. Sherman, and Susan M. Deeds

2006 The Course of Mexican History. New York: Oxford University Press.

Mignolo, Walter

2005 The Idea of Latin America. Oxford: Blackwell.

Mill, John Stuart

1982 [1859] On Liberty. New York: Penguin Classics.

Ministerio de Comunicación Social

1994 Participación Popular: Proyecto de Ley y Comentarios. Pp. 8. La Paz, Bolivia: Ministerio de Comunicación Social.

Moore, Sally Falk

1973 Law and Social Change: The Semi-Autonomous Field as an Appropriate Subject of Study. Law and Society Review 7: 719.

1978 Law as Process: An Anthropological Approach. New York: Routledge.

1986 Social Facts and Fabrications: Customary Law on Kilimanjaro, 1880–1980. Cambridge: Cambridge University Press.

Morley, David, and Kevin Robbins

1995 Spaces of Identity: Global Media, Electronic Landscapes, and Cultural Boundaries. New York: Routledge.

Movimiento al Socialismo-Bolivia

2007 Statement of Ideological Principles. www.masbolivia.org, accessed on May 1, 2007.

Munger, Frank

1998 Mapping Law and Society. *In* Crossing Boundaries: Traditions and Transformations in Law and Society Research. Austin Sarat, et. al., eds. Evanston, IL: Northwestern University Press.

Murra, John

1972 El "Control Vertical" de un Máximo de Pisos Ecológicos en la Economía de las Sociedades Andinas. *In* Visita de la Provincia de León Huanuco en 1562. Inigo Ortiz de Zuniga, Visitador. J. Murra, ed. Pp. 427–68. Huanuco, Perú: Universidad Nacional Hermillo Valdizán.

1978 Los Límites y las Limitaciones de "Archipelago Vertical" en los Andes. Avances 1: 75–80.

Murra, John V.

1975 Formaciones Económicas y Políticas del Mundo Andino. Lima, Perú, Instituto de Estudios Peruanos.

Nader, Laura

1990 Harmony Ideology: Justice and Control in a Zapotec Mountain Village. Stanford, CA: Stanford University Press.

———, ed.

1996 Naked Science: Anthropological Inquiry into Boundaries, Power, and Knowledge. New York: Routledge.

Nash, June

1993 We Eat the Mines and the Mines Eat Us: Dependency and Exploitation in Bolivian Tin Mines. Berkeley: University of California Press.

Nugent, David

1997 Modernity at the Edge of Empire: State, Individual, and Nation in the Northern Peruvian Andes, 1885–1935. Stanford, CA: Stanford University Press.

Olivera, Oscar

2004 ¡Cochabamba! Water War in Bolivia. Boston: South End Press.

Ong, Aihwa, and Stephen Collier, eds.

2005 Global Assemblages: Technology, Politics, and Ethics as Anthropological Problems. Oxford: Blackwell.

Ortner, Sherry
1973 On Key Symbols. American Anthropologist 75: 1338–46.

Osorio, Oscar
2003 Alcídes Arguedas: El Dolor de ser Boliviano. Poligramas 20: 169–86.

Osorio y Gallardo, Ángel
1997 [1919] El Alma de la Toga. Buenos Aires, Argentina: Valleta Ediciones.

Pasara, Luis
1988 Derecho y Sociedad en el Perú. Lima, Perú: Instituto de Estudios Peruanos.

Paz, Octavio
1950 El Laberinto de la Soledad. México City: Cuadernos Americanos.

Peralta Ruiz, Víctor Manuel, and Marta Irurozqui Victoriano
2000 Por la Concordia, la Fusión y el Unitarismo. Estado y Caudillismo en Bolivia, 1825–1880. Madrid, Spain: CSIC.

Percy, Walker
1961 The Moviegoer. New York: Farrar, Straus and Giroux.

Petersen, Hanne, and Henrick Zahle
1995 Legal Polycentricity: Consequences of Pluralism in Law. Brookfield, VT: Dartmouth Publishing Company.

Piquet Carneiro, Leandro
2000 Violent Crime in Latin America Cities: Rio de Janeiro and São Paulo. Research report, World Bank, Washington, DC.

Piot, Charles
1999 Remotely Global: Village Modernity in West Africa. Chicago: University of Chicago Press.

Platt, Tristan
1976 Espejos y Maíz: Temas de la Estructura Simbólica Andina. La Paz, Bolivia: CIPCA.
1982 Estado Boliviano y Ayllu Andino: Tierra y Tributo en el Norte de Potosi. Lima, Perú: Instituto de Estudios Peruanos.
1984 Liberalism and Ethnocide in the Southern Andes. History Workshop 17: 3–18.

1986 Mirrors and Maize: The Concept of Yanantin Among the Macha of Bolivia. *In* Anthropological History of Andean Polities. J. Murra, N. Wachtel, and J. Revel, eds. Cambridge: Cambridge University Press.

1987a The Andean Experience of Bolivian Liberalism, 1825–1900: The Roots of Rebellion in Nineteenth-Century Chayanta (Potosí). *In* Resistance, Rebellion, and Consciousness in the Andean World: 18th to 20th Centuries. S. Stern, ed. Madison: University of Wisconsin Press.

1987b Entre Ch'axwa y Muxsa: Para una Historia del Pensamiento Político Andino. *In* Tres Reflexiones Sobre el Pensamiento Andino. J. Medina, ed. La Paz. Bolivia: Hisbol.

1993 Simón Bolívar, the Son of Justice and the Amerindian Virgin: Andean Conceptions of the Patria in Nineteenth Century Potosí. Journal of Latin American Studies 25: 159–85.

1996 Los Guerreros de Cristo: Cofradías, Misa Solar, y Guerra Regenerativa en una Doctrina Macha (Siglos XVIII–XX). Sucre and La Paz, Bolivia: ASUR/CID.

1997 "Sin Fraude ni Mentira": Variable Chinu Readings During a 16th Century Restitution Case, with some reflections on the study of regional khipu traditions. Unpublished manuscript.

1998 Historias Unidas, Memorias Escindidas: Las Empresas Mineras de los Hermanos Ortíz y la Construcción de las Elites Nacionales: Salta y Potosí, 1800–1880. Sucre, Bolivia: Universidad Andina Simón Bolívar.

Platt, Tristan, Thérèse Bouysse-Cassagne, and Olivia Harris (with Thierry Saignes)

2006 Qaraqara-Charka—Mallku, Inka y Rey en la Provincia de Charcas (Siglos XV–XVII): Historia Antropológica de una Confederación Aymara. La Paz, Bolivia: Institut Français d'Études Andines/Plural Editores.

Poole, Deborah, ed.

1994 Unruly Order: Violence, Power and Cultural Identity in the High Provinces of Southern Peru. Boulder, CO: Westview Press.

1997 Vision, Race, and Modernity: A Visual Economy of the Andean World. Princeton, NJ: Princeton University Press.

Postero, Nancy

2007a Now We Are Citizens: Indigenous Politics in Postmulticultural Bolivia. Stanford, CA: Stanford University Press.

2007b Andean Utopias in Evo Morales's Bolivia Latin American and Caribbean Ethnic Studies 2(1): 1–28.

Powers, Karen

1995 Andean Journeys: Migration, Ethnogenesis, and the State in Colonial Quito. Albuquerque: University of New Mexico Press.

1998 A Battle of Wills: Inventing Chiefly Legitimacy in the Colonial North Andes. *In* Dead Giveaways: Indigenous Testaments of Colonial Mesoamerica and the Andes. Susan Kellogg and Matthew Restall, eds. Pp. 183–213. Salt Lake City: University of Utah Press.

Preis, Ann-Belinda

1996 Human Rights as Cultural Practice: An Anthropological Critique. Human Rights Quarterly 18: 286–315.

Proctor, Robert

1991 Value-Free Science? Purity and Power in Modern Knowledge. Cambridge, MA: Harvard University Press.

Project Para

2006 Terminating a Lesson. University of Nebraska-Lincoln. http://para.unl.edu/para/Instruction/Closure.html, accessed on June 2, 2007.

Queensland, State of

2005 Factors Contributing to Personal Violence. Report by Queensland Police Service, http://www.police.qld.gov.au/programs/personalSafety/violence/factors.htm.

Querejazu Clavo, Roberto

1992 Andrés Santa Cruz: Su Vida y Su Obra. La Paz, Bolivia: Librería Editorial "Juventud."

Rajagopal, Balakrishnan

2003 International Law from Below: Development, Social Movements, and Third World Resistance. Cambridge: Cambridge University Press.

Ramírez, Susan

1998 Rich Man, Poor Man, Beggar Man, or Chief: Material Wealth as a Basis of Power in Sixteenth-Century Peru. *In* Dead Giveaways: Indigenous Testaments of Colonial Mesoamerica and the Andes. Susan Kellogg and Matthew Restall, eds. Salt Lake City: University of Utah Press.

Rappaport, Joanne

1987 Mythic Images, Historical Thought, and Printed Texts: The Páez and the Written Word. Journal of Anthropological Research 43: 43–61.
1990 The Politics of Memory: Native Historical Interpretations in the Colombian Andes. Cambridge: Cambridge University Press.
1994 Cumbe Reborn: An Andean Ethnography of History. Chicago: University of Chicago Press.

Rasnake, Roger

1988 Domination and Cultural Resistance: Authority and Power Among an Andean People. Durham, NC: Duke University Press.

Raz, Joseph

1980 The Concept of a Legal System. Oxford: Oxford University Press.
1990 Practical Reason and Norms. Princeton, NJ: Princeton University Press.

República de Bolivia

2007 Constituent Assembly. www.constituyente.bo, accessed on June 2, 2007.

Riles, Annelise

2000 The Network Inside Out. Ann Arbor: University of Michigan Press.

Rivera Cusicanqui, Silvia

1986 Oprimmidos Pero no Vencidos: Luchas del Campesinado Aymara y Qhechwa, 1900–1980. La Paz, Bolivia: Hisbol.
1991 Liberal Democracy and Ayllu Democracy in Bolivia: The Case of Northern Potosi. Journal of Development Studies 26(4): 97–121.

Roca, José Luis

1998 1809, la Revolución de la Audiencia de Charcas en Chuquisaca y en La Paz. La Paz, Bolivia: Plural Editores.

Rodríguez, Gustavo

1983 ¿Expansión de Latifundio o Supervivencia de las Comunidades Indígenas? Cambios en la Estructura Agraria Boliviana del Siglo XIX. Cochabamba, Bolivia: IESE/ UMSS.

Romero Sandoval, Raúl

1996 Derechos Reales. La Paz, Bolivia: Los Amigos del Libro.

Rose, Nikolas

1996 Governing "Advanced" Liberal Democracies. In Foucault and Political Reason: Liberalism, Neo-Liberalism, and Rationalities of Government. A. Barry, T. Osborne, and N. Rose, eds. Pp. 37–64. Chicago: University of Chicago Press.

Rosen, Lawrence

1989 The Anthropology of Justice. Cambridge: Cambridge University Press.

Rostworoski de Diez Canseco, Maria

1988 Conflicts over Coca Fields in Sixteenth Century Peru. Vol. 4, Studies in Latin American Ethnohistory and Archaeology. Ann Arbor: University of Michigan Press.

Sadofsky, David

1990 Knowledge as Power: Political and Legal Control of Information. New York: Praeger.

Saignes, Thierry

1984 Nota Sobre la Contribución Regional a la Mita de Potosí a Comienzos del Siglo XVII. Historiografía y Bibliografía Americanistas (Seville) 24: 3–21.

1985 Caciques, Tribute, and Migration in the Southern Andes: Indian Society and the 17th Century Colonial Order (Audiencia de Charcas). London: Institute of Latin American Studies Occasional Papers, No. 15.

1987 De la Borrachera al Retrato: Los Caciques Andinos Entre Dos Legitimidades (Charcas). Revista Andina 3(1): 425–50.

1993 Borracheras Andinas: ¿Por qué los Indios Ebrios Hablan en Español? *In* Borrachera y Memoria: La Experiencia de lo Sagrado en los Andes. T. Saignes, ed. Pp. 43–72. La Paz, Bolivia: Hisbol/IFEA.

2000 The Colonial Condition in the Quechua-Aymara Heartland. *In* Cambridge History of the Native Peoples of the Americas (South America). Frank Salomon and Stuart Schwartz, eds. Vol. 3. Pp. 59–137. Cambridge: Cambridge University Press.

Salomon, Frank

1982 Chronicles of the Impossible: Notes on Three Peruvian Indigenous Historians. *In* From Oral to Written Expression: Native Andean Chronicles of the Early Colonial Period. R. Adorna, ed. Pp. 9–39. Syracuse, NY: Latin American Series, Foreign and Comparative Studies Program, No. 4, Maxwell School of Citizenship and Public Affairs, Syracuse University.

1986 Native Lords of Quito in the Age of the Incas: The Political Economy of North Andean Kingdoms. Cambridge: Cambridge University Press.

1987 Ancestor Cults and Resistance to the State in Arequipa, ca. 1748–1754. *In* Resistance, Rebellion, and Consciousness in the Andean World: 18th to 20th Centuries. S. Stern, ed. Pp. 148–65. Madison: University of Wisconsin Press.

2000 Testimonies: The Making and Reading of Native South American Historical sources. *In* Cambridge History of the Native Peoples of the Americas (South America). F.a.S.S. Salomon, ed. Vol. 3. Cambridge: Cambridge University Press.

2001 Review of To Make the Earth Bear Fruit: Ethnographic Essays on Fertility, Work and Gender in Highland Bolivia. Journal of Latin American Studies 33(3): 654–56.

2004 The Cord Keepers: Khipus and Cultural Life in a Peruvian Village. Durham, NC: Duke University Press.

Salomon, Frank, and Stuart Schwartz, eds.
2000 Cambridge History of the Native Peoples of the Americas (South America). Vol. 3. Cambridge: Cambridge University Press.

Salomon, Frank, and George Urioste, trans.
1991 The Huarochiri Manuscript: A Testament of Ancient and Colonial Andean Religion. Austin: University of Texas Press.

Santamaría, Daniel
1988 Hacendados y Campesinos en el Alto Perú Colonial. Buenos Aires, Argentina: Biblios.

Santos, Boaventura de Sousa
1987 Law: A Map of Misreading; Toward a Postmodern Conception of Law. Journal of Law and Society 14: 279.
1995 Toward a New Common Sense: Law, Science and Politics in the Paradigmatic Transition. New York: Routledge.

Santos, Boaventura de Sousa, and César A. Rodríguez-Garavito, eds.
2003 Law and Globalization from Below: Towards a Cosmopolitan Legality. Cambridge: Cambridge University Press.

Sarat, Austin, Lawrence Douglas, and Martha Merrill Umphrey, eds.
2002 Lives in the Law. Ann Arbor: University of Michigan Press.

Schelling, Vivian, ed.
2000 Through the Kaleidoscope: The Experience of Modernity in Latin America. New York: Verso.

Schmidhauser, J.
1992 Legal Imperialism: Its Enduring Impact on Colonial and Post-Colonial Judicial Systems. International Political Science Review 13: 321–34.

Schwartz, Stuart, and Frank Salomon
2000 New Peoples and New Kinds of People: Adaptation, Readjustment, and Ethnogenesis in South American Indigenous Societies (Colonial Era). *In* Cambridge

History of the Native Peoples of the Americas (South America). F. Salomon and Stuart Schwartz, eds. Vol. 3. Pp. 443–501. Cambridge: Cambridge University Press.

Scott, David

2004 Conscripts of Modernity: The Tragedy of Colonial Enlightenment. Durham, NC: Duke University Press.

Scott, James

1987 Weapons of the Weak: Everyday Forms of Peasant Resistance. New Haven, CT: Yale University Press.

Sebill, Nadine

1989 Ayllus y Haciendas: Dos Estudios de Caso Sobre la Agricultura Colonial en los Andes. La Paz, Bolivia: Hisbol.

Seligmann, Linda

1993 The Burden of Vision Amidst Reform: Peasant Relations to Law in the Peruvian Andes. American Ethnologist 20(1): 25–51.
1995 Between Reform and Revolution: Political Struggles in the Peruvian Andes, 1969–1991. Stanford, CA: Stanford University Press.

Shapiro, Michael

1988 The Politics of Representation: Writing Practices in Biography, Photography, and Policy Analysis. Madison: University of Wisconsin Press.

Sheleff, Leon

2000 The Future of Tradition: Customary Law, Common Law, and Legal Pluralism. London: Frank Cass.

Silverblatt, Irene

1987 Moon, Sun, and Witches: Gender Ideologies and Class in Inca and Colonial Peru. Princeton, NJ: Princeton University Press.

Sinha, S. Prakash

1996 Legal Polycentricity and International Law. Durham, NC: Carolina Academic Press.

Smith, Lisa

1992 Indigenous Land Rights in Ecuador. Race and Class 33(3): 102–5.

Solón, Pablo

1997 ¿Horizontes sin Tierra? Análisis Crítico de la Ley Inra. La Paz, Bolivia: Cedoin.

Spalding, Karen

2000 The Crises and Transformations of Invaded Societies: Andean Area (1500–1580). *In* Cambridge History of the Native Peoples of the Americas (South America). F. Salomon and Stuart Schwartz, eds. Vol. 3. Pp. 904–72. Cambridge: Cambridge University Press.

Speed, Shannon

2006 At the Crossroads of Human Rights and Anthropology: Toward a Critically Engaged Activist Research. American Anthropologist 108(1): 66–76.

2008 Rights in Rebellion: Indigenous Struggle and Human Rights in Chiapas. Stanford, CA: Stanford University Press.

Spitulnik, Debra

2002 Accessing "Local" Modernities: Reflections on the Place of Linguistic Evidence in Ethnography. *In* Critically Modern: Alternatives, Alterities, Anthropologies. B. Knauft, ed. Bloomington: Indiana University Press.

Starn, Orin

1994 Rethinking the Politics of Anthropology: The Case of the Andes. Current Anthropology 35(1): 13–38.

Starr, June, and Mark Goodale, eds.

2002 Practicing Ethnography in Law: New Dialogues, Enduring Methods. New York: Palgrave/St. Martin's Press.

Stavenhagen, Rodolfo

1988 Derecho Indígena y Derechos Humanos en América Latina. Mexico City: Instituto Interamericano de Derechos Humanos, Colegio de Méjico.

1990 Derecho Consuetudinario Indígena en América Latina. *In* Entre la Ley y la Costumbre: El Derecho Consuetudinario Indígena en América Latina. R.a.D.I. Stavenhagen, ed. Mexico City: Instituto Indigenista Interamericano.

Stern, Steve

1982a The Indians and Spanish Justice. *In* Peru's Indian Peoples and the Challenge of Spanish Conquest: Huamanga to 1640. S. Stern, ed. Pp. 114–37. Madison: University of Wisconsin Press.

1982b Peru's Indian Peoples and the Challenge of Spanish Conquest: Huamanga to 1640. Madison: University of Wisconsin Press.

————, ed.

1987 Resistance, Rebellion, and Consciousness in the Andean World: 18th to 20th Centuries. Madison: University of Wisconsin Press.

Strathern, Marilyn

1987 The Persuasive Fictions of Anthropology. Current Anthropology 28(3): 251–81.

Tamayo Flores, Ana

1992 Derecho en los Andes: Un Estudio de Antropología Jurídica. Lima, Perú: CEPAR.

Tapia de Aguilar, Bertha E.

1999 La Historia de la Educación en el Pueblo de Sacaca. Unpublished manuscript.

Tate, Winifred

2007 Counting the Dead: The Culture and Politics of Human Rights Activism in Colombia. Berkeley: University of California Press.

Taylor, Gerald

1975 Le Parler Quechua d'Olto, Amazonas, Perou: Phonologie, Esquisse Grammaticale, Textes. Paris: Societe d'Etudes Linguistiques et Anthropologiques de France.

Thompson, E. P.

1975 Whigs and Hunters: The Origin of the Black Act. London: Penguin Books.

Thomson, Sinclair

2003 We Alone Will Rule: Native Andean Politics in the Age of Insurgency. Madison: University of Wisconsin Press.

Todorov, Tzvetan

1999 The Conquest of America: The Question of the Other. Norman: University of Oklahoma Press.

Toulmin, Stephen

1990 Cosmopolis: The Hidden Agenda of Modernity. Chicago: University of Chicago Press.

Trazegnies, F. de

1987 Law in a Multicultural Society: The Peruvian Experience, Institute of Legal Studies Working Papers. Madison: ILS, University of Wisconsin Law School.

Trigo, Ciro Félix

1958 Las Constituciones en Bolivia. Madrid, Spain: Instituto de Estudios Políticos.

Trigoso, Gonzalo

1998 Apuntes Sobre la Masacre de Navidad. La Paz, Bolivia: Última Hora.

Trouillot, Michel-Rolph

1991 Anthropology and the Savage Slot: The Poetics and Politics of Otherness. *In* Recapturing Anthropology: Working in the Present. R. Fox, ed. Santa Fe, NM: School of American Research Press.

Tsing, Anna

2004 Friction: An Ethnography of Global Connection. Princeton, NJ: Princeton University Press.

Unger, Roberto

1986 The Critical Legal Studies Movement. Cambridge, MA: Harvard University Press.

United Nations Development Program

2008 2007/2008 Human Development Index Rankings. 2007/2008. hdr.undp.org/en/statistics, accessed on June 16, 2008.

United Nations Population Division

2003. World Population Monitoring 2003: Population, Education, and Development. http://www.un.org/esa/population/publications/publications.htm.

United States Agency for International Development

2007 Selected Economic and Social Data. http://qesdb.cdie.org/lac/index.html.

Universidad Técnica de Oruro

2006 Plan de estudios. Carrera de Derecho. Unpublished document.

Urton, Gary

1981 At the Crossroads of the Earth and Sky: An Andean Cosmology. Austin: University of Texas Press.

1992 Communalism and Differentiation in an Andean Community. *In* Andean Cosmologies Through Time: Persistence and Emergence. K.S.R. Dover and J. McDowell, eds. Bloomington: Indiana University Press.

Vaca Díez, Hormando

1998 Pensamiento Constitucional Boliviano, 1826–1995. La Paz, Bolivia: Fondo Editorial de los Diputados.

Valderrama Fernández, Ricardo, and Carmen Escalante Gutiérrez

1996 Andean Lives: Gregorio Condori Mamani and Asunta Quispe Huamán. Austin: University of Texas Press.

Valencia Vega, Alipio

1984 Fundamentos del Derecho Político. La Paz, Bolivia: Juventud.

Van Cott, Donna Lee

1993 Indigenismo Shakes the Andes. North and South 3(3): 43–47.

1998 Constitution-Making and Democratic Transformation: The Bolivian and Colombian Constitutional Reforms (Political Participation, Multiculturalism). Ph.D. dissertation, Georgetown University.

2000 The Friendly Liquidation of the Past: The Politics of Diversity in Latin America. Pittsburgh, PA: University of Pittsburgh Press.

Veliz, Claudio

1980 The Centralist Tradition in Latin America. Princeton, NJ: Princeton University Press.

Vidal, Ana Maria

1990 Derecho Oficial y Derecho Campesino en el Mundo Andino. *In* Entre la Ley y la Costumbre: El Derecho Consuetudinario Indígena en América Latina. R. Stavenhagen, ed. Mexico City: Instituto Indigenista Interamericano.

Vila De Prado, Roberto

2003 Liberal Thought and Bolivian Political Culture (1899–1934). Revista de Humanidades y Ciencias Sociales 9(1–2): 79–118.

Wachtel, Nathan

1977 The Vision of the Vanquished. New York: Barnes & Noble.

1994 Gods and Vampires: Return to Chipaya. Chicago: University of Chicago Press.

Wade, Peter

1997 Race and Ethnicity in Latin America. London: Pluto Press.

Wallerstein, Immanuel

1974 The Modern World System, Vols. 1 and 2. New York: Academic Press.

Watson, Graham

1987 Make Me Reflexive—But Not Yet: Strategies for Managing Essential Reflexivity in Ethnographic Discourse. Journal of Anthropological Research 43(1): 29–41.

White, Hayden

1973 Metahistory: The Historical Imagination in Nineteenth-Century Europe. Baltimore, MD: The Johns Hopkins University Press.

Wilson, Richard A.

1997 Human Rights, Culture and Context: An Introduction. *In* Human Rights, Culture and Context: Anthropological Perspectives. R. Wilson, ed. London: Pluto Press.

2001 The Politics of Truth and Reconciliation in South Africa: Legitimizing the Post-Apartheid State. Cambridge: Cambridge University Press.

————, ed.

1997 Human Rights, Culture and Context: Anthropological Perspectives. London: Pluto Press.

Yashar, Deborah

2005 Contesting Citizenship in Latin America: The Rise of Indigenous Movements and the Postliberal Challenge. Cambridge: Cambridge University Press.

Yrigoyen, Rachel

1993 Las Rondas Campesinas de Cajamarca, Perú: Una Aproximación Desde la Antropología Jurídica. Lima, Perú: Universidad Católica del Perú.

1994 Estudios Socio-Legales en el Perú (1975–1993): Los Textos en Contexto. *In* Nuevas Tendencias de los Estudios Socio-Jurídicos en América y Europa. Oñati, ed. Oñati: Instituto Internacional de Sociología del Derecho.

Zimmerer, Karl

1996 Changing Fortunes: Biodiversity and Peasant Livelihood in the Peruvian Andes. Berkeley: University of California Press.

Zorn, Elayne

1997 Marketing Diversity: Global Transformations in Cloth and Identity in Highland Peru and Bolivia. Ph.D. dissertation, Cornell University.

INDEX

"f" denotes a figure reference

The authorized representative in the EU for product safety and compliance is:
Mare Nostrum Group
B.V Doelen 72
4831 GR Breda
The Netherlands

www.ingramcontent.com/pod-product-compliance
Lightning Source LLC
Chambersburg PA
CBHW020659270326
41928CB00005B/191